Alexander William Kinglake

The Invasion of the Crimea

Its Origin and an Account of its Progress down to the Death of Lord Raglan

Alexander William Kinglake

The Invasion of the Crimea
Its Origin and an Account of its Progress down to the Death of Lord Raglan

ISBN/EAN: 9783742822048

Manufactured in Europe, USA, Canada, Australia, Japa

Cover: Foto ©Thomas Meinert / pixelio.de

Manufactured and distributed by brebook publishing software
(www.brebook.com)

Alexander William Kinglake

The Invasion of the Crimea

COLLECTION

OF

BRITISH AUTHORS.

VOL. 650.

THE INVASION OF THE CRIMEA
BY
A. W. KINGLAKE.

VOL. III.

THE

INVASION OF THE CRIMEA:

ITS ORIGIN,

AND

AN ACCOUNT OF ITS PROGRESS

DOWN TO THE DEATH OF

LORD RAGLAN.

BY

ALEXANDER WILLIAM KINGLAKE

COPYRIGHT EDITION.

WITH ALL THE PLANS, MAPS AND EMENDATIONS
OF THE THIRD LONDON EDITION.

VOL. III.

LEIPZIG

BERNHARD TAUCHNITZ

1863.

CONTENTS

OF VOLUME III.

INVASION OF THE CRIMEA.

CHAPTER XXIX.

	Page
The commanders of the French and English armies, . . .	1
Marshal St Arnaud, ...	1
Lord Raglan, ...	18
Marshal St Arnaud and Lord Raglan brought together at the Tulleries, ...	23
Conference at the Tulleries, ...	28
Lord Raglan's departure for the East, ...	32
The French and English troops on the shores of the Dardanelles, ...	32
Cordial intercourse between the two armies, ...	32
St Arnaud's scheme for obtaining the command of the Turkish army, ...	33
St Arnaud in the presence of Lord Stratford and Lord Raglan,	35
His scheme defeated, ...	37
His scheme for obtaining the command of English troops, .	38
This also defeated, ...	39
Attempts of this kind checked by the French Emperor, . .	39
St Arnaud suddenly declines to move his army towards the seat of War, ...	39
Lord Raglan's disapproval of the proposed delay, . . .	41
St Arnaud's sudden determination to take up a defensive position in rear of the Balkan, ...	42
Lord Raglan's determined resistance to this plan, . . .	43
Lord Raglan refuses to place any part of his army behind the Balkan, ...	47
St Arnaud gives way and consents to move his army to Varna,	47

	Page
The armies move accordingly,	48
Bosquet's overland march,	48
The way in which St Arnaud's schemes escaped publicity,	49

CHAPTER XXX.

Tidings which kindled in England a zeal for the invasion of the Crimea,	51
Siege of Silistria,	51
The battle of Giurgevo,	59
Effect of the campaign of the Danube on the military ascendancy of Russia,	64
The agony of the Czar,	65
Lord Raglan's dislike of undisciplined combatants,	67
Importance to England of native auxiliaries,	67

CHAPTER XXXI.

The events in the Danube removed the grounds of the war,	70
Helplessness of the French people,	71
Course taken by the French Emperor,	71
Desire of the English for an offensive war,	72
Sebastopol,	72
The longing of the English to attack it,	73
The Duke of Newcastle,	74
His zeal for the destruction of Sebastopol,	77
Commanding power of the people when of one mind,	78
Means of forming and declaring the opinion of the nation,	79
Effect of political writings in saving men from the trouble of thinking,	80
Want of proportion between the skill of the public writer and the judicial competence of his readers,	80
The task of ascertaining and declaring the opinion of the country falls into the hands of a company,	82
That opinion demands the destruction of Sebastopol,	91
Qualms of some members of the Government,	91
The Government yields,	85
No good stand made in Parliament against the invasion,	96

	Page
Preparation of the instructions addressed to Lord Raglan,	97
Instructions sent to the French commander,	100

CHAPTER XXXII.

The Allies at Varna,	102
Their state of preparation in the middle of July,	102
Their command of the sea,	103
Information obtained by the Foreign Office as to the defences of the Crimea,	104
No information obtained in the Levant,	104
Lord Raglan conceives that he is without trustworthy information,	105

CHAPTER XXXIII.

The instructions for the invasion reach the Allied camp,	106
The men who had to determine upon the effect to be given to the instructions,	107
Marshal St Arnaud,	107
Admiral Hamelin, Omar Pasha, and Admiral Dundas,	109
Lord Raglan,	111
The instructions addressed to him by the Home Government,	111
Their extreme stringency,	117
Considerations tending to justify this stringency,	117
The power of deciding practically invested in Lord Raglan,	119
His deliberations,	120
He requests the opinion of Sir George Brown,	121
His determination, and the grounds on which it rested,	122
His decision governs the counsels of the Allies,	127
He announces it to the Home Government,	128
The Duke of Newcastle's reply,	128
The Queen's expression of feeling,	129

CHAPTER XXXIV.

Conference at the French Headquarters,	130
Lord Raglan's way of eluding objections,	131

Page

Reconnaissance of the coast, ... 132
Sir Edmund Lyons, ... 133
Rumoured change in the plans of the Czar, ... 135
Second conference, ... 135
The French urge the abandonment of the expedition, . . 136
Lord Raglan's way of bending the French to the plans of the
        English Government, ... 136
Preparations, ... 137
Ineffectual attempts of the Allies to deceive the enemy, . . 139
Fire at Varna, ... 140
Cholera, ... 140
Weakly condition of the English soldiery, ... 143

CHAPTER XXXV.

Arrangements first made for the starting of the expedition, . 145
The embarkations, ... 145
Failure of the French calculations as to their steam-power, . 148

CHAPTER XXXVI.

Excitement and impatience of St Arnaud, ... 151
He is induced to set sail without the English, . . . 150
The naval forces of the Allies, ... 151
Duty devolving on the English fleet, ... 151
Arrangements in regard to the English convoy, . . . 152
The forces and supplies now on board, ... 152
Troops and supplies left at Varna, ... 153
Departure of the English Armada and of the French steam-
        vessels, ... 154

CHAPTER XXXVII.

The Black Sea, ... 157
Marshal St Arnaud at sea without the English, . . . 158
His anxiety, ... 158
He sails back, ... 158

Page

Lord Raglan's reproof, ... 158
Its good effect, ... 159
Lord Raglan's increasing ascendancy, ... 159
The whole Allied Armada together at sea, ... 159
The fleets again parted, ... 160
Step taken by French officers to stop the expedition, . . 160
Conference on board the Ville de Paris, ... 161
St Arnaud disabled by illness, ... 162
Unsigned papers read to the Conference, ... 162
St Arnaud leaves all to Lord Raglan, ... 163
Conference adjourned to the Caradoc, ... 164
Lord Raglan's way of dealing with the French remonstrants, . 166
His now complete ascendant, ... 166
The use he makes of his power, ... 167
The English fleet at the point of rendezvous, . . . 167
Lord Raglan's reconnaissance of the coast, . . . 167
He chooses the landing-place, ... 168
The whole Armada converges on the coast of the Crimea, . 169
St Arnaud's sudden recovery, ... 171
The progress made by Lord Raglan during the Marshal's illness, 171

CHAPTER XXXVIII.

Our ignorance of the country and of the enemy's strength, . 172
Gives to the expedition the character of an adventure, . . 173
Occupation of Eupatoria, ... 174
The whole Armada gathers towards the chosen landing-place, . 177

CHAPTER XXXIX.

The landing-place, ... 178
Step taken by the French in the night, ... 179
Destroys the whole plan of the landing, ... 179
Sir Edmund Lyons, ... 180
His way of dealing with the emergency, ... 180
New landing-place found for the English at Kamishlu, . 181
Position of the English flotilla adapted to the change, . . 182
The cause and nature of the change kept secret, . . . 182

	Page
Position of the in-shore squadrons,	183
Of the main English fleet,	183
Plan of the landing,	183
General Airey,	184
The first day's landing,	190
Zeal and energy of the sailors,	192
Wet night's bivouac,	193
Continuance of the landing,	193
Its completion,	194
By the English, French, and Turks,	194, 195

CHAPTER XL.

	Page
Deputations from the Tartar villages to the English Head-quarters,	197
Result of exploring expeditions,	198
The English army — Its absolute freedom from crime,	199
Kindly intercourse between our soldiery and the villagers,	199
Outrages perpetrated by the Zouaves,	200
The duty of sweeping the country for supplies,	200
Airey's quick perception of the need to get means of land-transport,	201
His seizure of a convoy,	202
His continued exertions, and their result,	202, 203
The Tartar drivers,	203

CHAPTER XLI.

	Page
The forces now on shore,	205
The nature of the operations for the advance to Sebastopol,	205
Comparison between regular operations and the system of the "movable column,"	206
The Allies to operate as a "movable column,"	212
Perilous character of the march from Old Fort,	213
The fate of the Allied armies dependent upon the firmness of the left,	215
The French take the right,	216
Their trustfulness and good sense,	217

Page

The advance begun, ...   217
The order of march, ...   217
The march, ...   220
Sickness and failing strength of many of the soldiers, . .   222
The stream of the Bulganak, ...   223

CHAPTER XLII.

The affair of the Bulganak, ...   225

CHAPTER XLIII.

Apparently dangerous situation of the English army, . .   231
Lord Raglan causes it to bivouac in order of battle, . .   231

CHAPTER XLIV.

I.

Position on the Alma, ...   234

II.

Mentschikoff's plan for availing himself of the position, . .   242
His forces, ...   243
His personal position, ...   243
His plan of campaign, ...   244
His reliance on the natural strength of the position, . .   245
The means he took for strengthening it, ...   245
Disposition of his troops, ...   246
Forces originally posted in the part of the position assailed by
    the French, ...   247
In the part of the position assailed by the English, . .   248
The numbers actually opposed to the French and English re-
    spectively, ...   252
Forces of the Allies, ...   253
The tasks undertaken by the French and the English respect-
    ively, ...   255

III.

Conference between St Arnaud and Lord Raglan, . . .   256
The French plan, ...   256

	Page
The part taken by Lord Raglan at the conference, . .	257
French plan for the operations of the English army, . .	258
St Arnaud's demeanour, ...	259
Result of the conference, ...	260

IV.

March of the Allies, ...	261
Causes delaying the march of the English army, . . .	262

V.

The last halt of the Allies before the battle, ...	265

VI.

Meeting between St Arnaud and Lord Raglan, . . .	267

VII.

Bosquet's advance, ...	268
He divides his force, ...	269
Disposition of the main body of the French army, . . .	270
Of the English army, ...	270
The leading Divisions of the English army deploy into line, .	271
The Light Division not on its right ground, . . .	272
The march continued, ...	273

VIII.

Spectacle presented to the Russians by the advance of the Allies, ...	274
Notion entertained by the Russian soldiers of the English army, ...	275
Surprise at the sight of the English array, ...	276
Fire from the shipping, ...	276
Movement made without orders by the Taroutine and the "Militia" battalions, ...	277

IX.

Half-past one o'clock. Cannonade against the English line, .	277
Men of our leading Divisions ordered to lie down, . . .	278
The 1st Division deployed into line, ...	278

	Page
Sir Richard England ordered to support the Guards, . . .	279
Fire undergone by our men whilst lying down, . . .	280

X.

Cannonade directed against Lord Raglan and his staff, . .	282

XI.

The Allies could now measure their front with that of the enemy, ...	285
The bearing of this admeasurement upon the French plan, .	285
The ground which each of the leading Divisions had to assail, .	286
Village of Bourliouk set on fire by the enemy, . . .	287
Effect of this in cramping the English line, ...	287

XII.

General Bosquet, ...	288
His plan of operations, ...	290
Advance of Autemarre under Bosquet in person, . . .	290
Advance of the detached force under Bouat, . . .	291
Further advance of Autemarre's brigade, ...	292
Guns brought out against him from Ulukul Akles, . . .	293
Bosquet establishes himself on the cliff, ...	293
Measures taken by Kiriakoff, ...	294
Horsemen on the cliff, ...	295

XIII.

The effect of Bosquet's turning movement upon the mind of Prince Mentschikoff, ...	295
His measures for dealing with it and his flank march, . . .	297
Mentschikoff on the cliff, ...	297
Cannonade between his and Bosquet's artillery, . . .	298
Bosquet maintains himself, ...	298
Mentschikoff counter-marching, ...	299
Position of Bosquet on the cliff, ...	300

PLANS AND ILLUSTRATIONS TO VOL. III.

Plate II.	.	.	.	.	.	.	.	.	.	*to face* page 179
„ III.	.	.	.	.	.	.	.	.	.	„ 230
„ IV.	.	.	.	.	.	.	.,	.	.	„ 257
„ V.	.	.	.	.	.	.	.	.	.	„ 250

INVASION OF THE CRIMEA.

CHAPTER XXIX.

WHEN it had been resolved that the French and the English forces already despatched to the East should be raised to a strength which might enable them to be more than auxiliary to the defence of the Turkish dominions, the French Emperor named an officer to the command of his army in the field, and the General who was to have charge of the Queen's land-forces had already been chosen. It seems right for me now to say something of these two commanders; and, the better to make each of them known, I am willing to speak of some of the transactions which brought them together between the time of their meeting in Paris and the day when they received their instructions for the invasion of the Crimea.

The commanders of the French and the English armies.

The officer intrusted with the command of the French army in the East was a Marshal of France, and was the person before spoken of who had changed his name from Le Roy to "St Arnaud," and from James to "Achilles." He impersonated with singular

Marshal St Arnaud.

exactness the idea which our forefathers had in their
minds when they spoke of what they called "a Frenchman;" for although (by cowing the rich, and by filling
the poor with envy) the great French Revolution had
thrown a lasting gloom on the national character, it
left this one man untouched. He was bold, gay, reckless, and vain; but beneath the mere glitter of the
surface there was a great capacity for administrative
business, and a more than common willingness to
take away human life. In Algerine warfare he had
proved himself from the first an active, enterprising
officer, and in later years a brisk commander. He
was skilled in the duties of a military governor,
knowing how to hold tight under martial law a conquered or a half-conquered province. The empire of
his mind over his actions was so often interrupted
by bodily pain and weakness, that it is hard to say
whether, if he had been gifted with health, he would
have been a firm, steadfast man; but he had violent
energies, and a spirit so elastic that, when for any
interval the pressure of misery or of bodily pain was
lifted off, he seemed as strong and as joyous as
though he had never been crushed. He chose to
subordinate the lives and the rights of other men to
his own advancement; therefore he was ruthless, but
not in any other sense cruel. No one, as he himself
said, could be more good-natured. In the intervals
between the grave deeds that he did, he danced and
sung. To men in authority, no less than to women,
he paid court with flattering stanzas and songs. He

had extraordinary activity of body, and was highly skilled in the performance of gymnastic feats; he CHAP.
XLIX.

had extraordinary activity of body, and was highly
skilled in the performance of gymnastic feats; he
played the violin; and, as though he were resolved
in all things to be the Frenchman of the old time,
there was once at least in his life, a time of depres-
sion, when (to the astonishment of the good priest,
who fell on his knees and thanked God as for a
miracle wrought) he knelt down and confessed himself, seeking comfort and absolution from his Church.

He thrice went through a career in the army.
First he entered it in 1816 as a sub-lieutenant of the
Royal Guard. He soon plunged into a course of life
which was of such a kind as to cause him to cease
from being an officer. He kept away from France
for many years, and became acquainted with several
languages. For a long time he was in England, and
he spoke our language very well; but in later years
he was accustomed to be silent in regard to the time
of his exile, and there is no need to lift the veil
which he threw over this part of his life.

When the Revolution of 1830 broke out he returned to France, and being then thirty-three years
of age, he again entered the French army as a sub-
lieutenant. He wrote some stanzas to Meunier, and
gained a step by it. "Tell me, after that," said he,
"that songs are good for nothing!" His next enterprise was in prose. It chanced that Bugeaud, then
the General in command of the district, had printed
a small military work on the camping of troops.
St Arnaud or Le Roy (for the time of the change of

1*

name is not certain) translated the book into several
languages, and presented the fruit of his labour, with,
no doubt, an appropriate letter of dedication, to the
General. Bugeaud was pleased; and from that time
until his death he never lost sight of the judicious
translator. St Arnaud was immediately put upon the
General's staff, and soon became one of his aides-de-
camp. When the Duchess of Berri fell a prisoner
into the hands of the Government, M. St Arnaud,
whose regiment was on duty at the place of her de-
tention, found means to make himself useful to the
Government without incurring the dislike of his captive; and he seemed to be in a fair road to promo-
tion. But again the clouds passed over him.

In 1836, for the third and last time, being then
near forty years of age, he entered the military profession. He began this his third career as a lieutenant
in the "Foreign Legion," and joined the corps in
Algeria. Every man of the corps, St Arnaud said,
had passed through a wild youth;* but with comrades of that quality a man might entertain better
hopes of gaining renown than with a mere French
regiment of the line; and St Arnaud at this time
made a strong resolve. He said, "I will be remark-
able, or die." And he remained so faithful to this
his covenant with himself, that even by acute illness

* "Jeunesse orageuse." I translate this by the words, "wild
youth;" but I believe the phrase, in the mouths of Frenchmen,
generally implies that the things done by the person spoken of are
closely bordering upon crime.

he could not be kept out of action. When he lay CHAP.
upon the sick-bed, if it chanced that the Arabs or XXIX
the Kabyles were offering any prospect of a fight
upon ground within reach of the hospital, he almost
always managed to drag his helpless, tortured body
towards the scene of the conflict; and this he would
do, not with an idea of being able to take an active
part, but simply in order that the list of officers present might not fail to comprise his name. At the
storming of Constantine, however, he really helped
to govern the event; for when a great explosion took
place, and many were blown into the air, the French
soldiers ran back with a cry that all was ruined; but
Bedeau and Combes, withstanding the madness of
the common terror, strove hard to rally the crowd;
and St Arnaud having with him in his company of
the legion some bold reckless outcasts of the North,
he bethought him of the shout, very strange to the
ears of Frenchmen, which he had heard in other
climes. Skilled in the art of imitation, he uttered
the warlike cry. Instantly from the Northmen around
him, whether Germans or Swedes, or English, Scots,
Irish, or Danes, there sprang their native "Hurrah!"
and with it came the thronging of men who must
and would go forward. It was mainly the torrent of
this new onslaught by St Arnaud and his men of the
"stormy youth" which carried the breach, and brought
about the fall of the city.

Even if, for the recruiting of his health, he were
passing a few weeks of holiday in France, he would

still seek personal distinction with a singular strength
of will. If, for instance, there chanced to be a fire
at night, he would fly to the spot, would scale the
ladders, mount the roof, and contrive to appear aloft
in seeming peril, displayed to a wondering crowd by
the lurid glare of the flames. Then he would disap-
pear, and then suddenly he would be seen again
suspended in the air, and passing athwart the sky
that divided one roof from another by the help of a
rope or a pole. In the early part of his service in
Algeria, his old patron, General Bugeaud, was in
command there, and was still a warm friend to him.
Of course this circumstance helped to open a path
for him; and the result was that, first by acts of
bravery and vigour, and then by a display of administrative ability, the all but desperate lieutenant
of the foreign legion rose in eight years to be intrusted with a General's command.* In 1845 he
commanded in the valley of the Chelif; and he was
so dire a scourge to the neighbouring tribes, that the
force which obeyed his orders was called the "Infernal Column."

When first I saw him in that year he was moving
with his force to wreak vengeance on a revolted
tribe, and he was to march five weeks deep into the
desert. He spoke with luminous force, and with a
charming animation; and it seemed to me, as we
rode along by the side of the heavy-laden soldiery,

* But up to that time with the rank of Colonel only.

that the clear incisive words in which he described to me the mechanism of the "movable column," were a model of military diction; but his keen, handsome, eager features so kindled with the mere stir and pomp of war — he seemed so to love the swift going and coming of his aides-de-camp, and the rolling drums, and the joyful appeal of the bugles — he was so content with the gleam of his epaulettes, half-hidden and half-revealed by the graceful white cabaan — so happy in the bounding pride of his Arab charger — that he did not seem like a man destined to be chosen from out of all others as the instrument of a scheme requiring grave care and secrecy. Yet of secrecy he was most capable; and at that very time he had upon his mind,* and was concealing, not from me only (for that would be only natural), but from every officer and man around him, a deed of such a kind that few men perhaps have ever done the like of it in secret.

We saw that, before the December of 1851, the enterprising and resolute Fleury was in Algeria, seeking out a fit African officer, who would take the post of Minister of War, with a view of joining the President in his plans for the overthrow of the Republic. Monsieur St Arnaud formerly Le Roy had not so lived as to occasion any difficulty in approaching him with dishonouring proposals; and

---

* The act here alluded to is spoken of further on. It took place about six weeks before the time when I first saw Colonel St Arnaud.

there was ground for inferring that he might prove equal to the task which was to be set before him. The able administrator of a great district in Algeria might be competent to head a department. The commander of the "Infernal Column" was not likely to be wanting in the ruthlessness which was needed; and if his vanity made it seem doubtful whether he was a man who could keep a secret, there was a confidential paper in existence which might tend to allay the fear.

St Arnaud had warmly approved the destruction of life which had been effected in 1844 by filling with smoke the crowded caves of the Dahra; but he had sagaciously observed that the popularity of the measure in Europe was not co-extensive with the approbation which seems to have been bestowed upon its author by the military authorities. These counterviews guided M. St Arnaud. In the summer of 1845 he received private information that a body of Arabs had taken refuge in the cave of Shelas. Thither he marched a body of troops. Eleven of the fugitives came out and surrendered; but it was known to St Arnaud, though not to any other Frenchman, that five hundred men remained in the cave. All these people Colonel St Arnaud determined to kill, and so far he perhaps felt that he was only an imitator of Pelissier;* but the resolve which ac-

---

* It is believed, however, that Pelissier left open some of the entrances to the cave, and that he only resorted to the smoke as a means of compelling the fugitives to come out and surrender.

companied the formation of this scheme was original.
He determined to keep the deed secret even from
the troops engaged in the operation. Except his
brother, and Marshal Bugeaud, whose approval was
the prize he sought for, no one was to know what
he did. He contrived to execute both his purposes.
"Then," he writes to his brother, "I had all the
"apertures hermetically stopped up. I made one
"vast sepulchre. No one went into the caverns; no
"one but myself knew that under there, there are five
"hundred brigands who will never again slaughter
"Frenchmen. A confidential report has told all to
"the Marshal, without terrible poetry or imagery.
"Brother, no one is so good as I am by taste and
"by nature. From the 8th to the 12th I have been
"ill, but my conscience does not reproach me. I have
"done my duty as a commander, and to-morrow I
"would do the same over again; but I have taken a
"disgust to Africa."*

The officer who could cause French soldiery to be
the unconscious instruments for putting to death five
hundred fugitive men, and who could afterwards keep
concealed from the whole force all knowledge of what
it had done, was likely to be the very person for
whom Fleury was seeking. He was brought back to
Paris, and made Minister of War, with a view to the
great plot of the 2d of December. France knows
how well, sooner or later, he answered to Fleury's

* St Arnaud's letters, published by his relatives after his death.

best hopes. He kept his counsel close until the appointed night, and then (whatever faltering there may have been between midnight and three in the morning) he was out in time for the deed; and before the daylight came he had stabbed France through in her sleep.

Amongst men who make a great capture, there will often spring up questions concerning the division of the spoil. When he helped to make prize of France, St Arnaud of course got much; but his wants were vast, and he had earned a clear right to extort from his chief accomplice, and to go back again, and again, and yet again, with the terrible demand for "more!" He was in such a condition of health as to be unfit to command an army in the field; for although, during intervals, he was free from pain and glowing with energy, he was from time to time utterly cast down by his recurring malady. It is possible that notwithstanding his bodily state, he may have sincerely longed to have the command of an army in a European campaign; but whether he thus longed or not, he unquestionably said that he did; and the French Emperor took him at his word, consenting, as was very natural, that his dangerous, insatiate friend should have a command which would take him into the country of the Lower Danube. Apparently it was not believed that, in point of warlike skill, M. St Arnaud was well fitted to the command; for the French Emperor, as will be seen, resorted to the plan of surrounding him with men who were virtually empowered to guide him with their overruling counsels.

To try to understand the relations between the allied Generals of France and England, without knowing something of the repute in which Marshal St Arnaud was held by his fellow-countrymen, would be to go blindfold; and a narrator keeping silence on this subject would be hiding a fact which belongs to history, and a fact, too, which is one of deep moment, and fruitful of lessons. Paris stripped of the weapons which kill the body, and robbed of her appeal to honest print, was more than ever pitiless with the tongue; and M. St Arnaud being laid open by the tenor of the life that he had led, his reputation fell a prey to cruel speech. The people of the capital knew of no crime too vile to be imputed to the new Marshal of France now intrusted with the command of her army in the field. Yet, so far as I know, they failed to make out that he had ever been convicted, or even arrested, on a criminal charge; and when I look at the affectionate correspondence which almost through his life M. St Arnaud seems to have maintained with his near relatives, I am led to imagine that they at least — and they would have been likely to know something of the truth — could have hardly believed his worst errors to be errors of the more dishonouring sort. Therefore there is ground for surmising that the Marshal was a man slandered. But in these times the chief defence against slanders upon public men is to be found in the award that

results from free printing; and the right of free printing in France, Marshal St Arnaud, with his own
midnight hand, had stealthily helped to destroy.
Whether he was a man bitterly wronged by his
fellow-countrymen, or whether what he suffered was
mere justice, the state of his repute in the spring of
1854 is a thing lying within the reach of historical
certainty.   He had an ill name.

But State policy is a shameless leveller — is a leveller of even that difficult steep which seems to divide the man of high honour from those of mean repute.
The plotters of the 2d of December had overturned
the social structure of France. They had stifled men's
minds, and had made their eloquence mute. They
had forced those who were of high estate by character,
or by intellect, or by birth, or by honourable wealth,
to endure to see France handled at will by persons of
no account, and to submit to be governed by them,
and to pay taxes into their hands, and to maintain
them in luxury, and in all so much of pomp as can
be copied from the splendour of kings.   The new
Emperor could not but know that he was breaking
down yet another of the world's barriers, and was
carrying subversion across the Channel, when he contrived that all Europe should see him presenting his
fellow-venturer of the December night to the appointed commander of an English army.

But when he knew who the English General was
to be, he might well give the rein to his cynic joy.
He could have been sure that the General placed in

command of our army would be an officer of unsullied
name; but he who had been chosen was one whose
life was mixed with history — the friend, the com-
panion of Wellington. It is true this Englishman was
known to be very simple, very careless of self — a
man hardly capable of imagining that he could be
humbled by obeying the orders of his sovereign;
and it is true also that the mass of the English people,
being eager in the war, and little used to lay stress,
as the French do, on the impersonation of a principle,
were blind to the moral import of what their Government was doing.   But the French Emperor
understood England; and he remembered that his
coming guest was one of a great and powerful body
of nobles, who were proud on behalf of this favourite
member of their class, and fenced him round with
honour.   For the levelling of these heights, and for
the bringing down of those in Europe who were tall
with the pride which sustains man's old strife between good and evil, no dreamer could dream of a
solemnisation more signal than the coming together
of Marshal Le Roy St Arnaud, and him whom old
friends still called Lord Fitzroy Somerset. The
French Emperor knew that the mind of Germany
and France would be swift to interpret this public
contact, and would see in it the terms of a great
surrender.

I conceive that in these latter times the scale upon Lord
which we measure warlike prowess has been brought Raglan.
down too low by the custom of awarding wild vio-

lent praise to the common performance of duty, and
even now and then to actual misfeasance; so, if I
keep from this path, it is not because I think coldly
of our army or our navy; but because I desire — as
I am very sure our best officers do — that we should
return to our ancient and more severe standard of
excellence. There is another reason which moves
me in the same direction. Not only is the utterance
of mere praise a lazy and futile method of attempting to do justice to worthy deeds, but it even inter-
cepts the honest growth of a man's renown by serving as a contrivance for avoiding that labour of
narration upon which, for the most part, all lasting
fame must rest.

Too often the repute of a soldier who has done
some heroic act is dealt with by a formal report
declaring that he has been "brave," or "gallant," or
"has conducted himself to the perfect satisfaction of
"his commanding officer." The cheap sugared words
are quickly forgotten, and nothing remains; whereas,
if his countrymen were told, not of the mere conclusion that the man had done bravely, but of the
very deed from which the inference was drawn, the
story, however simple, might dwell perhaps in their
minds, and they might tell it to their children, and
the soldier would have his fame. Now, this history
will virtually embrace the whole of the short period
in which Lord Raglan's quality as a General was
tried: and it seems to me, therefore, that if in nar-
rating what happened I can reach to near the truth;

if I give honest samples of what our General said, and of what he wrote — of his manner of commanding men, and his way of maintaining an alliance; if I show how he dealt with armies in the hour of battle, and how he comported himself in times of heavy trial, — his true nature, with its strength and with its human failings, will be so far brought to light that I may be dispensed from the need of striving to portray it; and, contenting myself with speaking of some of the mere outward and visible signs which showed upon the surface, may leave it to his countrymen to ascend, by the knowledge of what he did, to the knowledge of what he was. Where I think Lord Raglan's measures were right, I suppose I shall allow my belief to appear; and where I think they were wrong, I shall be likely to speak with an equal freedom: but it is not for me, who am no soldier, to undertake to compute the great account between the English people and a General who commanded their Queen's army in the field. Still, it must be remembered that the less I take upon myself in this regard, the graver will be the task of those who read. When the countrymen of Lord Raglan shall believe that they have in their hands sufficing means of knowledge, they will pass judgment, — not, as I should, with the slender authority of a single bystander, but with the weight of an honest nation, in time of calm, judging firmly, yet not ungenerously, the career of a public servant.

Lord Fitzroy Somerset, afterwards Lord Raglan,

was a younger son of the fifth Duke of Beaufort, and of a daughter of Admiral Boscawen. He was born in 1788. He entered the army in 1804. In 1808, Sir Arthur Wellesley, being about to depart for his first campaign in Portugal attached the young Lord Fitzroy Somerset to his staff;* and during his career in the Peninsula he kept him close to his side, first as his aide-de-camp, and then as military secretary. Between the time of the first restoration of the Bourbons in 1814, and the flight of Louis XVIII. in the spring of the following year, Lord Fitzroy Somerset was secretary of the Embassy at Paris. It was during this interval of peace that he married Emily Wellesley, a daughter of the third Earl of Mornington, and a niece of the Duke of Wellington. When the war was renewed, he again became military secretary and aide-de-camp to the Duke of Wellington, and served with him in his last campaign. At Waterloo — he was riding at the time near the farm of La Haie Sainte — he lost his right arm from a shot. But he quickly gained a great facility of writing with his left hand; and, the war being ended, he resumed his function as secretary of embassy at Paris. There he remained until 1819. He then returned to England, and became secretary to the Master-General of the Ordnance. In

* Sir Arthur Wellesley and Lord Fitzroy Somerset sailed in the same ship, and during the voyage they worked together at the Spanish language.

1825 he went with the Duke of Wellington to St Petersburg as secretary of embassy. In 1827 he was appointed military secretary to the Commander-in-Chief at the Horse Guards, and there he remained until the death of the Duke of Wellington in 1852. After that event he was made Master-General of the Ordnance, was appointed a Privy Councillor, and raised to the peerage. In February 1854 he became a full General.

Thus, from his very boyhood until the autumn of 1852, Lord Fitzroy Somerset had passed his life under the immediate guidance of the Duke of Wellington. The gain was not without its drawback; for in proportion as the great Duke's comprehensive grasp and prodigious power of work made him independent and self-sufficing, his subordinates were of course relieved from the necessity, and even shut out from the opportunity, of thinking for themselves; but still, to have been in the close presence and intimacy of Wellington from the very rising of his fame in Europe — to have toiled at the desk where the immortal despatches were penned — to have ridden at his side and carried his orders in all the great campaigns — and then, when peace returned, to have engaged in the labours of diplomacy and military administration under the auspices of the same commanding mind, — all this was to have a wealth of experience which common times cannot give.

But for more than thirty years of his life Lord

Raglan had been administering the current business
of military offices in peace-time, and this is a kind
of experience which, if it be very long protracted, is
far from being a good preparative for the command
of an army in the field; because a military office in
time of peace is impelled by its very constitution to
aim at uniformity; and, on the other hand, the genius
of war abhors uniformity, and tramples upon forms
and regulations.

An armed force is a means to an end — the end
is victory over enemies; and this is to be achieved,
partly indeed by a due use of discipline and method,
but partly also by keeping alive, in those who may
come to have command, a knowledge and love of
war, and by cherishing that unlabelled, undocketed
state of mind which shall enable a man to encounter
the unknown. In England, however, and in all the
great States of Europe except France, the end had
been so much forgotten in pursuit of the means, and
the industry exerted in the regulation of troops in
peacetime had become so foreign to the business of
war, that the more a man was military in the nar-
rowed sense of the term, the less he was likely to be
fitted for the perturbing exigencies of a campaign.
In one country this singular perversity of busy, "cold,
"formal man," had been carried so far, that an army
and a war had been actually treated as things an-
tagonistic the one to the other; for the late Grand
Duke Constantine of Russia once declared that he
dreaded a war, because he was sure it would spoil

the troops, which, with ceaseless care and labour, he CHAP.
had striven to bring to perfection. XXIX.

It is to be observed also, that partly from the
way in which our military system was framed, and
partly from political causes, the sympathy which
England ought ever to have with her troops had been
materially lessened after the first few years of the
peace. The Duke of Wellington, dreading lest our
forces should be dangerously reduced by the House
of Commons, made it his policy to withdraw the army
as much as possible from public observation. This
method had tended still further to dissociate the
country from its armed defenders: but naturally the
Duke of Wellington's view was law; and it became
the duty of those who were employed in the military
administration, not to cause the country to practise
itself heartily for the eventuality of another war, but
simply to maintain, as far as they could, a monoton-
ous quiet in the army. For half a lifetime Lord
Fitzroy Somerset was engaged in preventing and
allaying discussion, and making the wheels of office
run smooth. Against the baneful effect of this sort
of experience, and against the habit of mind which
it tended to generate, Lord Raglan had to combat
with all the fire and strength of his nature.

When Lord Raglan was appointed to the command
he was sixty-six years old. But although there were
intervals when a sudden relaxation of the muscles
of the face used to show the impress of time, those
moments were few; and in general, his well-braced

2*

features, his wakeful attention, his uncommon swift-
ness of thought, his upright, manly carriage, and his
easy seat on horseback, made him look the same as
a man in the strong mid-season of life.

He had one peculiarity which, although it went
near to being a foible, was likely to give smoothness
to his relations with the French. Beyond and apart
from a just contempt for mere display, he had a
strange hatred of the outward signs and tokens of
military energy. Versed of old in real war, he knew
that the clatter of a General briskly galloping hither
and thither with staff and orderlies did not of necessity imply any momentous resolve, — that the aides-
de-camp, swiftly shot off by a word like arrows from
a bow, were no sure signs of despatch or decisive
action; and because such outward signs might mean
little, he shrank from them more than was right. He
would have liked, if it had been possible, that he
and his army should have glided unnoticed from the
banks of the Thames to their position in the battle-
field. It was certain, therefore, that although a French
General would be sure to find himself checked in any
really hurtful attempt to encroach upon the just station
of the British army, yet that if, as was not unnatural,
he should evince a desire for personal prominence, he
would find no rival in Lord Raglan until he reached
the enemy's presence.

He was gifted with a diction very apt for public
business, and of a kind rarely found in Englishmen;
for though it was so easy as to be just what men

like in the intercourse of private friendship, it was still so constructed as to be fit for the ear of all the world; and whether he spoke or whether he wrote — whether he used the French tongue or his own clear, graceful English — it seemed that there had come from him the very words which were the best and no more. It was so natural to him to be prudent in speech, that he avoided dangerous utterance without seeming cautious or reserved.

He had the subtle power to draw men along with him. To say that he was persuasive might mean that he could adduce reasons which tended to bring men to his views. His was a power of another sort, for without pressure of argument, his mind by its mere impact broke down resistance for the moment; and although the easy graciousness of his manner quickly set people free from all awkward constraint, it did not so liberate men's minds that, whilst they were still in his presence, they at all liked the duty of trying to uphold their own opinions against him. This dominion, however, was in a great degree dependent upon his actual personal presence; for, with all the power and grace of his pen, he could not, at a distance, work effects proportioned to those which he wrought when he dealt with men face to face.

It is plain that, in one respect, his empire over those who were in his presence was of a kind likely to become dangerous to him in the command of an army, because it prevented men from differing from him, and even made them shrink from conveying to

him an unwelcome truth. Indeed, after the death
of the Duke of Wellington, the proudest Englishman,
if only he had intellect and a little knowledge of his
country's latter history, had generally the grace to
understand that, unless he too were a soldier who had
taken his orders from the lips of Sir Arthur Wellesley,
he could hardly be the equal of one whose mere presence was a record of England's great days. Thence
it followed that, without pretension on the one side
or servility on the other, men who were with him had
a tendency to become courtiers. It was in vain that,
so far as it had to do with their personal contentment,
his manner placed men at their ease; there was some
quality in him, or else some outward circumstance
— it was partly, perhaps, the historic appeal of his
maimed sword-arm — which was always enforcing
remembrance, and preventing his fusion with other
men.

In truth, Lord Raglan's manner was of such a
kind as to be, not simply ornament, but a real engine
of power. It swayed events. There was no mere
gloss in it. By some gift of imagination he divined
the feelings of all sorts and conditions of men; and
whether he talked to a statesman or a schoolboy,
his hearer went away captive. I knew a shy, thoughtful, sensitive youth, just gazetted to a regiment of
the Guards, who had to render his visit of thanks
to the military secretary at the Horse Guards. He
went in trepidation; he came back radiant with joy
and wholesome confidence. Lord Fitzroy, instead

of receiving him in solemn form and ceremony, had
walked forward to meet him, had put his hand kindly
on the boy's shoulder, and had said a few words so
cheering, so interesting, and so free from the vice
of being commonplace, that the impression clung to
the lad, shaping his career for years, and helped to
make him the man he was when he was out with
his battalion in the winter of the first campaign.
From the same presence the foremost statesman of
the time once came away saying, that the man in
England most fitted by nature to be at the head of
the Government was Lord Fitzroy Somerset; and he
who so judged was himself a Prime Minister.

The enemies of the Imperial Government in
France had long made it a reproach against the
English that they were joining in close alliance with
the midnight destroyers of law and freedom; but
when Lord Raglan came to Paris — when he went
to the Tuileries — when he was presented by the
Emperor to Marshal St Arnaud, — the notion that
such things could be was a very torment to those
of the Parisian malcontents who chanced to know
something of the English General: — "You English
"are a robust, stirring people, and perhaps every
"man of you imagines that he covers himself with
"dignity and grandeur by trampling upon the feelings
"of the rest of mankind; but surely those men wrong
"you who call you a proud people. Pride causes
"men to stand aloof, as we do, from that which
"is base; and if ever again we call you haughty

Marshal
St Arnaud
and Lord
Raglan
brought
together
at the
Tuileries.

"islanders, you may silence the calumny by remind-
"ing us of this 13th day of April in the year of
"grace 1854. It was not enough that, for the sake
"of this silly war, you should ally yourselves body
"and soul to 'Monsieur de Morny's Lawgiver,' and
"that you should suffer him to drag you down into
"close intercourse with persons whom the humblest
"of us here decline to know; but now, as though
"you really wished that your dishonour should be
"made signal in Europe, you send hither your Ge-
"neral to be presented by this 'French Emperor,'
"as you call him, to his henchman, Mr Le Roy St
"Arnaud, and the man whom you choose out for this
"great public sacrifice is Fitzroy Somerset, the friend
"and the companion-in-arms of your Wellington.
"You say that Lord Raglan cares not with whom
"he associates, so that he is under the orders of the
"Queen whom he serves, and in the performance of
"a public duty; but because he, in the loyalty, in
"the high-bred simplicity of his nature, is careless
"and forgetful of self — is that a reason why you
"should fail to be proud for him — why you should
"forget to be careful on his behalf? If the modesty
"of his nature hindered him from seeing the mo-
"mentous significance of his contact with the people
"who have got into our palaces, ought you not to
"have interposed to prevent him from incurring the
"scene of to-day? We imagined that you knew
"how to honour the memory of your Wellington,
"and that, after his death, when you looked towards

"Fitzroy Somerset, or spoke to him, or listened to
"his words, you looked and spoke and listened like
"men who remembered. Him, nevertheless, you now
"offer up. To have brought you down to this is a
"great achievement — the realisation of what they
"call here a 'Napoleonic idea!' The prisoner of
"St Helena is avenged at last. We are classic here,
"and we strike commemorative medals. You will
"soon see the honoured image of your Fitzroy
"Somerset undergoing presentation at the Tuileries.
"Already our artists have caught some glimpses of
"him, and they declare it is the colouring, the glow
"of the complexion, which makes him look so English,
"and that in bronze he will be grandly Roman.
"Those noble lineaments of his, that upright manly
"form — nay, even the empty sleeve which speaks
"to you of your day of glory—will worthily signify
"what England was; and then the effigy of our
"counterfeit Cæsar receiving the homage of a stain-
"less Englishman, and joining him hand to hand
"with Mr Le Roy St Arnaud, this will show what
"England is. We hear that you are well pleased
"with the prospect of all this, and that, far from
"shrinking, your 'virtuous middle class,' as you call
"it, is going into a state of coarse rapture. For
"shame!"

Lord Raglan, all unconscious of exciting this
kind of sympathy in the heart of the angry Faubourg,
had left England on the 10th of April 1854; and
on the following day both he and His Royal High-

26 INVASION OF THE CRIMEA.

CHAP.
XXIX.

ness the Duke of Cambridge were received in state at the Tuileries. The presence of a member of our Royal Family was welcome to the new Emperor: he understood its significance. The Parisians love to see a momentous idea so impersonated as to be visible to the eyes of the body; and when their monarch attained to be seen riding between the near kinsman of the English Queen and the appointed commander of her army in the field — when, on a bright spring day, he showed his guests some thirty thousand of his best troops in the Champ de Mars, and the scarlet of the ancient enemy sparkled gaily by the side of the blue and the gold — the people seemed to accept the scene as a fitting picture of the great alliance of the West. Almost for the first time in the history of France, the accustomed cheers given to the Head of the State were mingled with cheers for England.

But now the time for concerted action had come; and though France and England were already allied by such bonds as are made with parchment and wax, it remained to be seen whether the great rivals could act together in arms. The conjuncture, indeed, drew them towards each other; but it was certain that the coherence of the union would greatly depend on one man. It might seem that he who had first sworn to maintain the French Republic, and had afterwards destroyed it by stealth in the night-time, would not be much trusted again by his fellow-creatures; but the alliance rested upon ground more firm than the

trust which one Prince puts in another. It rested
— not, indeed, upon the common interests of France
and England, for France, as we have seen, was suppressed — but upon the prospect of personal advantage which was offered to the new French Emperor
by an armed and warlike alliance with England.
It being clear that the alliance was for his good,
and that, for the time, he had really the control of
France, the only remaining question was, whether
he would pursue what was plainly for his own advantage with steadiness and good sense. Upon the
whole, it seemed likely that he would; for though
he was not a man to be stopped by scruples, he did
not discard the use of loyalty and faithfulness, where
loyalty and faithfulness seemed likely to answer his
purpose; and there was a persistency in his nature
which gave ground for hoping that, unless he should
be induced to change by some really cogent reason,
his steadfastness would endure. Moreover, as we have
seen, he had the faculty — very easy to apply to
geometry, but harder to use in politics — the faculty
of keeping himself awake to the distinction between
the Greater and the Less; and he did not forget that
for the time, the alliance with England was the
greater thing, and that most other objects belonged
to the category of the Less. These qualities, supported by good-humour, and often by generous im-
pulses, went far to make him an ally with whom (so
long as he might find it advantageous to remain in

CHAP.
XXIX.
accord with us) it would be possible, nay easy, and not unpleasant to act.

Confer-
ence at the
Tuileries.
Lord Raglan submitted to the publicity and ceremonial visits forced upon him during the days of the 11th and 12th of April, and at one o'clock on the 13th he had a private interview with the French Emperor at the Tuileries. The Emperor and the English General were not strangers to one another. They had been frequently brought together in London; and, indeed, it was by Lord Fitzroy Somerset that the heir of the First Napoleon, deeply moved by the historic significance of the incident, had been brought to Apsley House and presented to the Duke of Wellington. The Emperor showed Lord Raglan the draft of the instructions which he proposed to address to Marshal St Arnaud.

It may be said that at this hour Lord Raglan began to have upon him the weight of that anxious charge which was never again to be thrown off so long as life and consciousness should endure. He had charge on behalf of England of the great alliance of the West; and since it happened that, in this the outset of his undertaking, he followed a method which characterised his relations with the French from first to last, there is a reason for now pointing it out. It seemed to him that in the intercourse of two proud and sensitive nations undertaking to act in concert, one of the chief dangers lay in that kind of mental activity which is generated by the process of arguing.

He made it a rule to avoid and avert all needless discussion; and he regarded as needless not only those discussions which spring out of abstract questions, but many also of those which are generated by men's anxiety to provide for hypothetical conjunctures. He was very English in this respect, and he was no less English in the simple contrivance by which he sought to ward off the evil. Whenever there seemed to be impending a question which he regarded as avoidable, he prevented or obstructed its discussion by interposing for consideration some practical matter which was more or less important in its way, but not unsafe. And now, when there was perhaps some fear that questions of an embarrassing and delicate kind might be raised by the pondering Emperor, Lord Raglan kept them aloof by engaging attention to the choice of the camping-ground best suited for the two armies. He seems to have succeeded in confining all discussion to this one safe and practical subject.

When the Emperor at length brought his guest back into the outer room, there were there assembled Prince Jerome, the Duke of Cambridge, Marshal Vaillant the Minister of War, Marshal St Arnaud, and Lord De Ros. The vital business of making arrangements best fitted to prevent collision between the armies was anxiously weighed. Marshal Vaillant, laborious, well instructed, precise, and rather, perhaps, fatiguing in his tendency to probe deep every question, strove hard to anticipate the eventualities likely to occasion difficulty in the relations of the two

CHAP.
XXIX.

armies, and to force a clear understanding beforehand as to the way in which each question should be dealt with. This he endeavoured to do by putting it to St Arnaud in a categorical way* to say what solution he proposed for each of the imagined problems; but St Arnaud, it then appeared, was hardly more fond than Lord Raglan was of hypothetical questions, for after a little while his endurance of Vaillant's interrogatories came to an end; and he answered impatiently, and in a general way, that when the conjunctures arose they would be met, as best they might, by the concerted action of the Generals.

The period of the great French Revolution has gathered so much of the mellowness of age from later events, that it seems like a disturbance of chronology to be bringing into the joint council of France and England, in the year 1854, a brother of the First Napoleon. Yet Prince Jerome was one of the speakers, and he spoke with sound judgment upon the great problem of how France and England should act together in arms. He spoke, as might be expected, with less sagacity when the subject of "The Turks" floated up into notice. The whole French people, and many even of the people of this country, imagine that the wisdom and power of man are tested by his proximity to the newest stage of civilisation: and from those whose minds are in that state, the true

* The French verb "poser" would describe Marshal Vaillant's labours; the English verb active "to pose" would describe the effect upon the patient.

worth of the Osmanli, whether in policy or in arms, must always be hidden. If he sustains reverses, their minds are satisfied, because in that case the sum of their knowledge seems to have come right; but his success disturbs their most deep-set notions of logical sequence; and now, after all Omar Pasha's achievements on the Danube, it seemed to be the impression of Prince Jerome and the French Marshals that the Turkish General would be a source of trouble and anxiety to the alliance. They looked upon the events which had been occurring as accidental and anomalous, and tending to produce a wrong conclusion. The Russians, as they well knew, had carried the industry of military preparation to the utmost verge of human endurance. The Turks had provided themselves with a powerful field-artillery, had kept their old yatagans bright, and had cherished their ancient love of war; but, for the rest, they had trusted much in Heaven. Yet during some six or seven months these pious, improvident, warlike men had been getting the better of drilled masses. Their success seemed to carry a dangerous lesson; and the French Councillors thought it so important for the Turks to be broken in to the yoke of a newer civilisation, that they even said it might be advantageous for Omar Pasha to undergo the discipline of a few wholesome reverses.*

---

* Some might imagine that this hope must have been expressed in jest, but that is not the case. Incredible as it may seem, it is nevertheless certain that this view was gravely put forward.

From all he observed in the course of these inter-
views, Lord Raglan was led to believe in the stability
of the Emperor's character, and the value he set upon
the alliance.

After a few days, the arrangements detaining Lord
Raglan in Paris were complete, and he took his departure for the East.

The
French
and the
English
troops on
the shores
of the
Dardan-
elles.

The joint occupation by French and English
troops of the ground on the shores of the Dardanelles,
had yielded the first experience of the relations likely
to subsist between the armies of the two nations when
quartered near to each other. It quickly appeared
that the troops of each force could be cordially good-

humoured in their intercourse with those of the other.
Canrobert, Bosquet, and Sir George Brown, all destined to take prominent share in the coming events,
made a kindly beginning of acquaintanceship amid
the early difficulties and discomforts of Gallipoli; and
upon the departure of Sir George Brown from the
Dardanelles, there occurred one of those opportunities
for the display of good feeling on which the French
are accustomed to seize with a quickness, tact, and
grace belonging to no other nation. Sir George
Brown was to bring up with him to headquarters
two of the English regiments; and the French —
spontaneously, as it appeared, and from a simple
impulse of goodwill — came down to aid in the
embarkation. They set themselves to the work with
all that briskness and gay energy by which the
French soldiery convert an operation of mere labour

and industry into a cheerful and animating scene.
The incident in itself was a small one; but, viewed
as a sign of things to come, it had greater proportions. It was accepted at the time by Lord Raglan
as a happy omen — an omen which seemed to promise
that the alliance of the West would hold good.

But whilst the soldier was giving the best of St Arnaud's
sanctions to the great Alliance, the Marshal of France scheme for
obtaining
was putting it in jeopardy. M. St Arnaud had not the command of
been long on the shores of the Bosphorus when he the Turkish army.
entered upon a tempting scheme of ambition. General
Bosquet, despatched to the headquarters at Shumla,
had brought back accounts, which the Marshal at
first could hardly credit, of the good state and apparent effectiveness of the Turkish troops; and it was
then, perhaps, that St Arnaud first thought of the
step which he afterwards took. He conceived the
idea of obtaining the command of the whole Turkish
army. The effect which this united command would
have upon the relations between the French and the
English General was obvious. The English General,
with his force of some twenty-five thousand men, had
always foreseen that he was likely to be somewhat
embarrassed in having to claim due consideration for
a force which was less by one-half than the army sent
out by the French; but if Marshal St Arnaud should
be at the head, not only of his fifty thousand French,
but of the whole force of Turkey, it would obviously
become very hard, nay, even unfitting, for the Eng-

lish General to maintain an equality in council with
one who, in this case, would command altogether
nearly two hundred thousand men. Marshal St Arnaud
pressed his demand with the Ministers of the Porte
at Constantinople, and he seems to have imagined
that he had obtained their assent to his demand. If,
indeed, they did really give a seeming assent to the
proposed encroachment, they could hardly have meant
it to take effect. They perhaps put their trust then
where they had put their trust before. They knew
that Lord Stratford was at Therapia, and they might
well believe that he would make the elaborate world
go back into chaos before he would suffer the armies
of the Caliph to pass, like the contingent of some
mere petty Christian State, under the orders of a
French Commander.

On the 11th of May, Marshal St Arnaud called
upon Lord Raglan, and stated, in the course of conversation, that the Turkish Government had determined to place Omar Pasha's army under his (the
Marshal's) command; and that he was then going to
Reshid Pasha in order to have the matter finally
settled. Lord Raglan merely said he believed the
British Ambassador was not aware of the arrangement.
On the 13th, Marshal St Arnaud sent to propose that
Lord Raglan would meet him at Lord Stratford's, and
intimated that he had an important communication
to make. It was arranged that the English Ambassador should receive the Marshal alone, "in order,"
as Lord Stratford almost cruelly expressed it — "in

"order to make his acquaintance," and that afterwards Lord Raglan should join them.

It jars upon one's love of fair strife to see Marshal St Arnaud brought in cold blood into the presence of the two men whom he ventured to encounter;
into the presence of Lord Stratford, prepared and
calmed by his foreknowledge of the intrigue — and
of Lord Raglan, roused by his sense of the danger
which threatened the alliance. But the interview
took place. The Marshal went to the English Embassy, and the operation of "making his acquaintance"
was carried into full effect. Imagination may see the
process — may see the light, agile Frenchman coming
gaily into the room, content with himself, content with
all the world, and charmed at first with the sea-blue
depth of the eyes that lightened upon him from under
the shadow of the Canning brow, but presently beginning to understand the thin, tight, merciless lips of
his host, and then finding himself cowed and pressed
down by the majesty and the graciousness of the welcome; for the welcome was such as the great Eltchi
would be sure to give to one who (for imperative
reasons of State) was to be treated as his honoured
guest, but who was also a vain mortal, pretending
to the command of the Ottoman army, and daring to
come with his plot avowed into the very presence of
an English Ambassador. Afterwards Lord Raglan
came into the room, and then the Marshal began upon
the business in hand. He said he had required, and
the Turkish Government had consented, that Omar

3*

Pasha should be placed under his orders; that a brigade of Turkish infantry and a battery of artillery
should be incorporated into each of the French divisions; that fifteen hundred of the Bashi-Bazouks
should be dismounted, that their horses should be
turned over to the French troopers, and that the
Bashi-Bazouks should be paid (it was not said by
whom), and then be sent back to their homes.

If this proposal had been then for the first time
made known to Lord Stratford, his fiery nature would
scarcely perhaps have suffered him to hear with temper; but he had been prepared by Lord Raglan for
what was coming, and he seemed all calm and gen-
tleness. After hearing the proposal with benign attention, he quietly asked the Marshal whether he had
cognisance of the tripartite treaty; and then, turning
to a copy of the treaty which happened — not at all
by chance — to be lying within his reach, he read
aloud the fourth article: an article which proceeds
upon the assumption that the three armies would be
under the orders of distinct commanders. The Marshal — ready perhaps to encounter the more obvious
arguments against the expediency of the plan — was
scarcely prepared for this quiet reference to the terms
of the treaty. Lord Raglan then said he thought a
good deal of inconvenience might result from the
adoption of the Marshal's plan; that Omar Pasha was
the ablest of the Turkish generals; that his services
had been recognised by the grant of the rank of
Generalissimo and the title of Highness; and that to

deprive him of the superior command, and to dis-
member his army, at a moment when it was in presence of the enemy, would not only lower him in the
estimation of those who looked up to him with confidence, but would probably induce him to throw up
his charge in disgust, and declare that he would not
suffer himself to be degraded.

But both Lord Raglan and the English Ambassador were gifted with the power which is one of the
most keen and graceful of all the accomplishments
of the diplomatist — the power of affecting the hearer
with an apprehension of what remains unsaid. It is
a power which exerts great sway over human actions;
for men are more cogently governed by what they
are forced to imagine than by what they are allowed
to know. "The Marshal," Lord Raglan wrote, "saw
"that our opinions were stronger than our expression
"of them." He gave way. He immediately declared
that, far from wishing to diminish the consequence of
Omar Pasha, he was anxious to add to it, to uphold
him to the utmost, and to increase his importance;
and he added that he saw the propriety of deciding
nothing until after a conference with Omar Pasha.
By the time that St Arnaud passed out of the Embassy
gate his enterprise was virtually abandoned.

Some good perhaps resulted from the attempt to His
bring the Ottoman army under French command. scheme
defeated.
Of all the faults tending to impair the value of Lord
Raglan's advice to the Home Government, there was
none more grave than his want of power to appre-

ciate warlike people belonging to an earlier state
of civilisation than that to which he had been accustomed in his latter years; and although nothing
could ever soften his antipathy towards Turkish
Irregulars of all kinds, and especially to the Bashi-
Bazouks, he was by this incident drawn more than
ever towards the Turkish Generalissimo, and he
always thenceforth did his best to defeat any plan
which tended to narrow the sphere of the Pasha's
authority.

His
scheme
for obtain-
ing the
command
of English
troops.
So great was the elasticity of Marshal St Arnaud's
mind, that, far from remaining cast down under the
discomfiture which he had undergone, he very soon
entered upon a scheme yet more ambitious than the
first. It seems he had become possessed with the
idea that great achievements were within his reach,
if only he could add to the powers which he already
wielded the occasional command of English troops.
He proposed that when French and English troops
were acting together, the senior officer, whether he
chanced to be French or English, should take the
command of the joint force; and although this proposal was so expressed that it might be regarded as
applying only to the command of detachments, it
was surmised that (M. St Arnaud's military rank
being higher than that of Lord Raglan) the control
of the whole British force was the object really in
view.

The experience of the conference at the British
Embassy had proved the good sedative effect of a

dry document; and as the instructions addressed to the English General chanced to contain some words directing him to take no orders except from the Secretary of State,* the clause was happily put forward by Lord Raglan as an impediment to the proposed plan. Marshal St Arnaud gave way, and thenceforth desisted from all further prosecution of his scheme.

This also defeated.

So skilful was the resistance opposed to these enterprises of M. St Arnaud, and the character of the Marshal was so free from all admixture of spite and bitterness, that their frustration did not create ill-feeling. It was plain, however, that recurrence to projects of this sort would be dangerous to the alliance; and when the French Emperor knew that these schemes had been tried and defeated, he forbade all attempts to revive them.

Attempts of this kind checked by the French Emperor.

Hitherto the cause which had been threatening the cohesion of the alliance was M. St Arnaud's ambition. The next obstruction which Lord Raglan had to deal with was one of a very different kind. Checked, as is supposed, by the authoritative counsels sent out to him from Paris, Marshal St Arnaud suddenly announced that, for some time to come, the French army could not be suffered to move towards the seat of the war.

St Arnaud suddenly declines to move his army towards the seat of war.

The measures for sending up the British forces

* The clause, I imagine, had been introduced in order to negative the supposition that the Ambassador at Constantinople was to have the control of the military operations.

to Varna were in progress, and the Light Division
had been already despatched, when, at eleven o'clock
at night, Colonel Trochu presented himself at the
British headquarters, and requested an immediate
interview with Lord Raglan.   The name of Colonel
Trochu will recur in this narrative, for he was an
officer of great weight in the councils of the French
army.   He had come from France so lately as the
10th of May, and although his nominal office was
simply that of first aide-de-camp to Marshal St Arnaud, it was known that he came out fully charged
with the notions and the wishes of the French Emperor.   Colonel Trochu was a cautious, thinking
man, well versed in strategic science and it was
surmised that it was part of his mission to check
anything like wildness in the movements of the
French Marshal.*   He stated that he had been sent
by Marshal St Arnaud to request that Lord Raglan
would postpone any further movement towards
Varna, until the Marshal should have an opportunity of satisfying himself that any considerable
portion of the French army was in a condition to
take the field.

Up to this moment no doubt had been entertained
of the forwardness of the French preparations; and
Lord Raglan, much astonished, expressed strong objection to the proposed delay.

Colonel Trochu replied that, upon his arrival in

* Modérer la fougue de M. le Maréchal.

the Levant, he had gone to Gallipoli in order to see CHAP.
what degree of forwardness the preparations of the XXIX.
French army had really attained; and he had come,
he said, to the conclusion that the French army was
not as yet so equipped and provided as to render
it practicable, with anything like common prudence,
to attempt operations against the enemy. He went
on to justify his conclusion by details, showing the
deficiencies under which the French army laboured:
he said that he had communicated the result of his
inspection and the opinion which he had formed to
Marshal St Arnaud, and that Marshal St Arnaud,
entirely adopting that opinion, had sent him to
the English headquarters in order that he might
prevail upon Lord Raglan to suspend the intended
movement.

Lord Raglan observed that great inconvenience Lord Rag-
would result from the proposed suspension of the approval
movement; that the movement was one actually proposed
proposed by the French and English commanders to delay.
Omar Pasha, and by him, as well as by the Turkish
Ministers, entirely approved; and that thus the French
and the English commanders stood pledged to Omar
Pasha, and to the Porte, at a moment, too, when
much anxiety existed for the fate of Silistria. Colonel
Trochu admitted all this; but he again urged the
necessity for delay.

The interview lasted till an hour after midnight,
and Colonel Trochu's request was followed up on
the ensuing day by written communications from

the French Marshal. But the importance of these
discussions was superseded by a further and more
perilous change in the French counsels.

St Ar-
naud's
sudden de-
termina-
tion to
take up a
defensive
position in
rear of the
Balkan.
At seven o'clock in the morning of Sunday the
4th of June, Marshal St Arnaud called upon Lord
Raglan, and announced that he had determined
upon an entirely new plan of operations for his
army. Instead of moving his force to Varna, as
had been agreed, he had resolved, he said, to send
there only one division, and to place all the rest
of his army in position — not in advance, but in
rear of the Balkan range. He was to have his right
resting on the sea at Bourgas; his headquarters were
to be at Aidos; and he hoped, he said, to be able
to establish himself there by the third week of June.
He invited Lord Raglan to conform to this plan,
and to take up a position at Bournabat, a part of
the proposed position which was the most remote
from the sea.

Thus, at a time when the eyes of all Europe
were upon Silistria and the campaign on the Danube,
it was proposed that the armies of the Western
Powers should take up a mere defensive — a timidly
defensive — position, placing all Bulgaria, a part
of Roumelia, and the whole range of the Balkan,
between them and the scene of conflict! What
made the matter still more grave was this, that
Marshal St Arnaud did not come to consult. He
had already adopted this almost incredible plan,

and his troops were then actually in march for the new position.

It might now, indeed, seem that those were right who had deemed the great alliance of the West to be impracticable. For all the purposes of the campaign the proposed plan would have caused the armies of the two Western Powers to become simply null. Lord Raglan at once declared his entire disapproval of it.

Lord Raglan's determined resistance to this plan.

Tied, perhaps, to this singular plan by the counsels which Trochu had brought him, Marshal St Arnaud, for the time, did not yield. But the English General, as I have already said, had a quality which made it difficult and painful for men to maintain a difference with him whilst they were in his presence. St Arnaud was under this stress; and as though he shrank from the ascendancy of Lord Raglan, and sought a respite from the effort of having to oppose him in oral discussion, he imagined the idea of bending over a table and writing down what he had to say. This he did; and when the writing was finished, he left it with Lord Raglan. But the Marshal seems to have inwardly determined that Colonel Trochu, who had probably suggested this new plan of campaign, should himself be made to bear the pain of further sustaining it; for he took his leave, saying that the Colonel should be sent to Lord Raglan on the following day.

In this curious paper, written by St Arnaud in Lord Raglan's presence, the Marshal said the great advantage of the French and English having only one division each at Varna would be, that they would not get entangled prematurely in hostile operations; for with such a small force, no one could taunt the Western Powers for not marching to relieve Silistria, or for not giving battle to the Russians; whereas, argued the Marshal, if the Allies were present in greater strength, it was to be feared that they might suffer themselves to be carried away by the Turks. "It is important," said the Marshal, "not to give battle "to the Russians, except with all possible chances of "success, and the certainty of obtaining great results." Then, after describing the supposed advantages of his intended position in rear of the Balkan, the Marshal reverted to his dread of being carried forward by the warlike Turks. "We must not," said he, "lose sight "of this; that we are here to aid the Turks — to "succour them, to save them — but not by following "their plans and their ideas. It is evident that Omar "Pasha has no other idea but that of drawing on the "allied army to give battle to the Russians, and to "relieve Silistria. The safety of Turkey is not in "Silistria; and it is necessary to aid and succour the "Turks in our own way."

No one perhaps will now defend a plan of campaign which was to place the allied armies of the Western Powers in a position some hundreds of miles from the scene of any conflict, and to withdraw them from the very proximity of the Turk because of his warlike counsels. Still, such justice as is due must be rendered to the French strategists. France and England had sent to the East that portion of the two armies which consists of combatants; but neither of the Western Powers had hitherto constituted on the Dardanelles or the Bosphorus that vast accumulation of stores, of munitions of war, and means of transport which would enable it to live, to move freely, and to fight. Both of the two armies had the most of what for the moment they needed, but neither of them had hitherto any sufficing base of operations to rest upon. Both of the armies had means of subsistence for the next few days, and were so equipped as to be able to fight a battle on the beach; but neither army had, nor could have for many months, those vast warehouses of stores and those immense means of land-transport which could alone sustain regular and extended operations in the field. Therefore, if purely military views were to govern, and if Russia were really the formidable invader of Turkey which the world had believed her to be, there would have been some rashness in pushing forward the combatants of the two armies towards the scene of conflict, with a knowledge that for some time to come they would be unable to move freely in the field.

The true ground for overruling the hesitation of the French strategists lay in the now obvious fact that (to say nothing of the armies of France and England assembled on the Bosphorus, with vast means of sea-transport at their command) Russia, ill-prepared for a great war in the South, driven out of the Euxine, threatened by Austria, and fiercely encountered and

hitherto repulsed by the Ottoman forces, was not so
formidable an invader of European Turkey as to de-
serve that her despairing struggles in the country of
the Lower Danube should be encountered with all the
resources of strategic prudence. Besides, the question
was not purely a military one. It was certain that
the mere presence of the French and the English
forces in the neighbourhood of the conflict would have
a moral weight more than proportioned to their actual
readiness for offensive operations. Finally, the question had been settled. The allied Generals, in their
conference with Omar Pasha, had engaged to move
their troops to Varna; and the honour of France and
England stood pledged.

But if there was a semblance of military wisdom
in the hesitation of the French to move up to Varna,
there was none in their plan for the defensive line
behind the Balkan at Aidos; for if the want of
means of land-transport threatened to hamper the
activity of the force even in the advanced position
of Varna, it is obvious that the same cause would
have reduced the French and English forces to sheer
uselessness if they had taken up a position at so
vast a distance as Aidos is from the scene of the conflict. If the plan had been followed, no French nor
English troops in that year would have seen the shape
of a Russian battalion. Yet Marshal St Arnaud,
so far as concerned France, had determined thus to
forfeit all military significance in the pending campaign, and had done so, and had begun to carry the

plan into execution, without consulting his English
colleague.

How France was saved from this humiliation, and
how the great alliance was preserved, will now be
seen.

On the day following the interview with Marshal
St Arnaud, Colonel Trochu came, as had been agreed,
to Lord Raglan's quarters. After repeating what Marshal St Arnaud had stated the day before — namely,
that Bosquet's Division was already in march for
Adrianople — the Colonel pressed the advantages of
the position which Marshal St Arnaud had proposed
to take up in rear of the Balkan.

Lord Raglan heard all, and then simply requested
Colonel Trochu to inform Marshal St Arnaud that
he, Lord Raglan, objected to place any portion of
Her Majesty's army in Roumelia. Lord Raglan refuses
to place
any part
of his army
behind the
Balkan.

Lord Raglan added, that the movement which
seemed to him the best was an advance to the front
with a view to join Omar Pasha in an effort to relieve
Silistria; and he said that if the Marshal were not
prepared for such a movement, he (Lord Raglan)
would keep his divisions on the Asiatic side of the
Bosphorus, and hold them ready to embark at any
moment for Varna.

Firmness conquered. On the morning of the 10th
of June, Colonel Rose came to the English headquarters and announced that Marshal St Arnaud
now consented to abandon his plan of taking up a
defensive position behind the Balkan, and that, re- St Arnaud
gives way,
abandons
his plan of
a position
behind the
Balkan,
and con-

sents to
move his
army to
Varna.

verting to the original determination of the Allies,
he would assemble his army at Varna.

Thus the danger passed. Secrecy, it would appear,
had been well maintained; and the world did not
know that, for all purposes of concerted military operations, the alliance of the Western Powers had lain
in abeyance for five days.

The
armies
moved ac-
cordingly.

Leaving small detachments at Gallipoli, the French
and the English armies were now moved up to
Varna.   General Bosquet's Division, however, was
made to feel the consequences of the resolution adopted
by the French strategists; for this division having
actually commenced its march towards Adrianople,
in furtherance of the then intended plan of taking
up a position behind the Balkan, Marshal St Arnaud
it seems, did not like to issue a countermand which
would have disclosed to a sagacious soldiery his
double change of counsels — nay, perhaps might
have given them a glimpse of the almost ridiculous
destiny from which they had been saved by Lord

Bosquet's
overland
march.

Raglan.   So, whilst all the rest of the allied forces
were gliding up to Varna by water, Bosquet's Division continued to follow the direction first given it,
and was brought into Bulgaria by long, painful
marches.   If the warlike Zouaves composing part of
the division had known that their long, toilsome
movement in the midst of the great summer-heats
was the result of a plan for placing the French army
in position at a distance of several hundreds of miles
from the enemy, they would have solaced the labours

of the march by tearing the repute of the schemer who contrived it, and making him the butt for their wit.

It is obvious that the premature disclosure either of Marshal St Arnaud's ambitious schemes or of his faltering counsels would have been fraught with danger to the alliance; and since it used to happen in those days that tidings freshly intrusted to the English Cabinet were often disclosed to the world, it seems useful to show how it was that Lord Raglan was able to screen these transactions of Marshal St Arnaud from the inquiring eye of the public. Apparently he did this by being careful in the choice of the time for making disclosures to the authorities at home. Except when there was a good reason for taking a contrary course, he liked to delay the communication of affairs involving danger until the danger was past. Thus, for instance, he would describe the beginning of an intrigue and also its final defeat at the same time; and the result was, that the end of the despatch not only made the disclosure of the earlier part of it comparatively harmless, but even destroyed its value as an article of "news;" for in proportion as people were greedy for fresh tidings, they were careless of things which ranged with the past, and the time was so stirring that the tale of an abandoned plan of campaign, or an intrigue already baffled and extinct, was hardly a rich enough gift for a Minister to carry to a newsman.

The way in which St Arnaud's schemes escaped publicity.

Thus were averted the early dangers which threatened the alliance; and thus, after resolving to take
up a position some hundreds of miles distant from
the nearest Russian outpost, the French Marshal gave
way at last to Lord Raglan's ascendant, and was
soon pushed forward to a camping-ground within
hearing of the enemy's guns.

CHAPTER XXX.

THE closing events of the summer campaign in
Bulgaria did so much to kindle that zeal which
forced on the invasion of the Crimea, that it seems
right to speak of them here, not with any notion of
putting into the set form of "History" things which
all Europe knew at the time in the most authentic
way, but rather for the purpose of showing how the
armies at Varna, and the statesmen and the people
in England, were touched, were stirred, nay, were
governed, by the tidings which came from the
Danube. Prince Paskievitch stood charged to execute
with his own hand the plan of campaign which his
Sovereign had persuaded him to design;* and accordingly, in the summer of the year 1854, he found
himself marching on the Danube at the head of the
Russian army then engaged in attempting an invasion of the Ottoman Empire. He had insisted,
as we have seen, that, as the needful condition of a
prosperous campaign, Silistria must fall by the 1st
of May.** It was not before the middle of the month

CHAP.
XXX.
Tidings
which
kindled in
England a
zeal for
the inva-
sion of the
Crimea.

Siege of
Silistria.

* See vol. II. p. 140.
** Ibid. p. 142.

4*

that he was able to appear before the place; but
thenceforth he lost no time, and on the 19th he
opened his first parallel.

The new defences of the fortress had been planned
by Colonel Grach, a Prussian officer in the service
of the Porte. He had brought to the work a great
deal of knowledge and judgment. He was still in
the place, and he continued to lend the aid of his
science to the garrison whenever he could do so
without going out of his dwelling-house; but, ad-
hering, it seems, to the bare terms on which he had
engaged his services, he stiffly abstained from taking
any other than a scientific part in the struggle.

Prince Paskievitch pressed the siege with a vehe-
mence which seemed to disdain all economy of the
lives of his soldiery; and the place being weakly
garrisoned, and seemingly abandoned to its fate, its
fall was supposed to be nigh. To uphold the Sultan's cause three armies were at hand, but no one
of them was moved forward with a view to relieve
the place. Omar Pasha, shrewd and wary, was
gathering the strength of the Ottoman Empire at
Shumla, and it did not enter into his plan of campaign to smooth the path of the Russian General
by going forward in strength to give him a meeting
under the guns of the beleaguered fortress. On the
other hand, France and England were rapidly as-
sembling their forces in the neighbourhood of Varna,
but, for want of sufficing means of land-transport,
they were not yet in a condition to take the field.

Day by day the two armies at Varna were moved
by fitful tidings of a conflict in which, though it
raged within earshot, they were suffered to take
no part. At first, few men harboured the thought
that, without deliverance brought by a relieving
force, a humble Turkish fortress would be able to
hold out against the collected strength of Russia and
the most renowned of her Generals. Soon it was
known that, of their own free-will and humours, two
young Englishmen — Captain Butler of the Ceylon
Rifles, and Lieutenant Nasmyth of the East India
Company's Service — had thrown themselves into
the place, and were exercising a strange mastery
over the garrison. On one of the hills overlooking
the town there was a seam of earth which, as though
it were a kind of low fence designed and thrown up
by a peasant, passed along three sides of the slope
in a doubtful meandering course. This was the
earthwork which soon became famous in Europe.
It was called the Arab Tabia. The work was one of
a slight and rude sort; but the ground it stood on
was judged to be needful to the besiegers, and, at
almost any cost of life to his people, Prince Paskievitch resolved to seize it. By diligent fighting on
the hill-side — by sapping close up to the ditch —
by springing mines which more than once blew in the
counterscarp and levelled the parapet — by storming
it in the day-time — by storming it at night — the
Russians strove hard to carry the work; but when
they sprang a mine, they ever found that behind the

ruins the Turks stood retrenched; and whether they
stormed it by day or by night, their masses of columns
were always met fiercely — were always driven back
with a cruel slaughter.   Prince Paskievitch, the
General commanding in chief, and General Schilder,
who commanded the siege-works, were both struck
down by shot and disabled.   On the side of the
Turks, Mussa Pasha, who commanded the garrison,
was killed; but Butler and Nasmyth, now obeyed
with a touching affection and trustfulness by the
Ottoman soldiery, were equal to the historic occasion
which they had had the fortune and the spirit to
seize.   At one time they were laying down some new
work of defence; at another, the two firm lads were
governing the judgment of the Turkish commanders
in a council of war.   Sometimes, with ear pressed to
the earth, they were listening for the dull blows of
the enemy's underground pickaxes.   Now and then
they were engaged in dragging to his place under
fire some unworthy Turkish commander; and once,
in their sportive and English way, they were busy
in getting together a sweepstakes, to be won by him
who should name the day when Silistria would be
relieved; but always when danger gathered in the
Arab Tabia, the grateful Turks looked and saw that
their young English guests were amongst them, ever
ready with counsel for the new emergency, forbidding
all thought of surrender, and even, it seems, determined to lay rough hands on the General who sought
to withdraw with his troops from the famous earth-

work.* It seemed that the presence of these youths
was all that was needed for making of the Moslem
hordes a faithful, heroic, and devoted soldiery. Upon
ground known to be mined they stood as tranquilly
as upon any other hill-side. "It was impossible,"
said Nasmyth's successor in the Arab Tabia — "it
"was impossible not to admire the cool indifference
"of the Turks to danger. Three men were shot in
"the space of five minutes while throwing up earth
"for the new parapet, at which only two men could
"work at a time so as to be at all protected; and
"they were succeeded by the nearest bystander, who
"took the spade from the dying man's hands and
"set to work as calmly as if he were going to cut a
"ditch by the road-side." Indeed, the childlike
trust which these men were able to put in their
young English leaders, so freed them from all doubt
and question concerning the wisdom of the orders
given, that they joyfully abandoned themselves to
the rapture of fighting for religion, and grew so
enamoured of death — so enamoured 'of the very
blackness of the grave — that sometimes in the
pauses of the fight a pious Mussulman, intent on
close fighting and blissful thoughts of Paradise,
would come up with a pickaxe in hand, would speak
some touching words of devotion and gratitude to

* I take it that this is what was meant by Nasmyth's expression,
"peculiar inducement." The man upon whom the "peculiar inducement" was brought to bear was one whom Butler had dragged out
bodily from his hiding-place.

Butler and Nasmyth, and then proudly fall to work
and dig for himself the last home, where he charged
his comrades to lay him as soon as he attained
to die.

Omar Pasha not choosing to march to the relief
of Silistria, but being unwilling to leave its defenders to sheer despair, sent General Cannon* (Behram
Pasha he was called in the Turkish army) with a
brigade of irregular light infantry, and instructed
him to occupy some of the wooded ground in the
neighbourhood of the place, with a view to trouble
the enemy and to encourage the garrison. General
Cannon, however, learnt, on reaching the neighbourhood of Silistria, that the hopes of the garrison had
already ebbed very low; and therefore, though without the warrant of orders, he resolved to throw himself into the place with his whole brigade. This,
by means of a stratagem and a long circuitous night-
march, he was able to do. His achievement, as was
natural, gave joy to the garrison; and, turning to
account the enthusiasm of the moment, he adminis-
tered, as is said, a direful oath to the Pasha in
command — an oath whereby the Turk swore that,
happen what might, he would never surrender the
place.

It was whilst General Cannon was in Silistria
that Captain Butler received the wound of which he

---

* General Cannon was an officer of our Indian army who had
served with distinction in India, and in the force (the British Legion)
which operated in Spain under the orders of General Evans.

afterwards died. The Russians had sapped up so close to the ditch that, if a man behind the parapet spoke much above a whisper, the sound of his voice used to draw the enemy's fire towards the nearest loophole or embrasure. Captain Butler, it seems, with a view to throw up a new work of defence, was reconnoitring the enemy's approaches through an aperture made in the parapet, and in consulting about his plan with General Cannon, he spoke loud enough to be heard by a Russian marksman, for the sound of his voice brought a rifle-ball in through the loophole and struck him the blow from which (being weakened by toil and privation) he died before the end of the siege.

For some reason which he deemed to be imperative — stringent orders, perhaps, from Shumla — General Cannon marched out of the place with his brigade on the 17th of June, and at his request Nasmyth also went away for a time in order to confer with Omar Pasha at the Turkish head-quarters; but meanwhile Lieutenant Ballard of the Indian army, coming thither of his own free-will, had thrown himself into the besieged town; and whenever the enemy stirred, there was always, at the least, one English lad in the Arab Tabia, directing the counsels of the garrison, repressing the thought of surrender, and keeping the men in good heart.*

* The narratives of the siege of Silistria which appeared in the "Times" were given, as is well known, by Nasmyth himself, and by

There was a part of the allied camp where the French and the English soldiery could hear in a quiet hour the distant guns of Silistria. Day after day they listened for the continuing of the sound; and they listened keenly, for they were expecting the end, and there was nothing but the booming of the cannon to assure them that the fortress held out. On the 22d of June, and during a great part of the night which followed it, they heard the low thunder of the siege more continuously than ever before; but on the dawn of the following day they listened, and listened in vain. The cannonade had ceased, and it was believed in camp that the place had been taken. The opposite of this was the truth. The siege had been raised. The event was one upon which the course of history was destined to hinge; for this miscarriage at Silistria put an end at once to all schemes for the invasion of the Sultan's dominions in Europe.

Whilst Europe was still in wonder at the deliverance of Silistria, the French and the English armies

---

the officer who succeeded to him and to Butler in governing the counsels of the garrison and helping to defend the Arab Tabia. Therefore any other account of the siege which I might have founded upon the official materials in my possession would have been obviously inferior to the newspaper in point of authenticity. Accordingly, with the exception of two or three minor facts drawn from the correspondence which is in my possession, all I have said of the siege is taken from those journals of Nasmyth and his successor which were printed in the "Times" during the summer of 1854.

at Varna were greeted with tidings of yet another
victory won by the Turks.

Hassan Pasha was at Rustchuk with a large
body of Turkish troops; and at Giurgevo, on the
opposite bank of the river, General Soimonoff commanded twelve battalions of Russian infantry, with
several squadrons of horse and some guns. Both
the Russian and the Turkish commanders desired
that at this time there should be no conflict; and it
might be thought that in this respect they would
have their way; for although the forces at Rustchuk
and at Giurgevo were near to each other, the broad
Danube rolled between them. But the Ottoman
soldiery are of so warlike a nature that, when their
enemy is at hand, they are oftentimes seized with a
raging desire for the fight; and the one check which
tends to keep down this passion is a sense of the
incoherency which results from the want of good
officers. But so ready and so deep is their trust in
any of our countrymen who will take the trouble to
lead them, that, if Turkish soldiers be camped within
reach of the enemy, the coming amongst them of a
few English youths supplies the one thing needed,
completes the electric circle, and in general brings
on a fight. Now it happened that, besides General
Cannon, who was on duty, and in command of a
Turkish brigade, seven young English officers had
found their way to the camp of Hassan Pasha.
Two of these, Captain Bent and Lieutenant Burke,
were officers of the Royal Engineers; Meynell was

a Lieutenant in the 75th Regiment; Hinde, Arnold,
and Ballard (the last of them fresh come from
Silistria), were officers of our Indian army: Colonel
Ogilvy was General Cannon's aide-de-camp, but he
gave his services freely; and, indeed, it may be said
that, so far as concerns the part they took in the
battle, every one of these seven young Englishmen
was there of his own mere will.*

On the morning of the 7th of July it was observed that the Russians had struck their tents; and
they were so posted that their numbers could not be
descried from the right bank of the river. It was
believed in the Turkish camp that Soimonoff had
withdrawn the main part of his force; and it seems
that what Hassan Pasha really meant to do was to
execute a reconnaissance, and assure himself of the
enemy's retreat. Be this as it may, he ordered, or
consented, that the river should be crossed at two
points; and General Cannon, embarking in boats
with 300 riflemen, and speedily followed by a battalion of infantry under Ferik Bekir Pasha, succeeded
in reaching the left bank of the river without encountering resistance. As soon as they had landed, the
Turks tried to gain a lodgment upon a strip of
ground where their front was covered by a long

* The two Engineer officers, Captain Bent and Lieutenant Burke,
had been sent to the Turkish camp with instructions to advise and aid
in the construction of military works; but of course they had not been
ordered to lead the Turks into battle; and therefore I include them
with the rest of the seven as men taking part in the battle without professional sanction.

narrow mere or pool of water. Soon, however, they
were attacked on their left flank by a body of Russian infantry, which issued from an earthwork placed
above the western extremity of the mere. Cannon
and Bent, with their riflemen, not only withstood
this attack, but drove their assailants back into the
fosso from which they had issued, and there, it seems,
a good deal of slaughter took place. Afterwards
the riflemen were forced to give way, and fall back
upon the main body of the troops, which had effected
their landing; but young Ballard led forward another
body of skirmishers, and kept the enemy back.
What was needed was, that the troops which had
landed should intrench themselves; but they had
come without gabions or sand-bags, and nothing as
yet could be done towards gaining a firm lodgment.
There was a good deal of confusion amongst the
troops, and the enterprise seemed likely to fail, when
Ali Pasha, who was a brave and an able officer,
came over with fresh troops. He soon restored
order, and the men began to throw up intrenchments.

Meanwhile two battalions, led on by Ogilvy,
Hinde, Arnold, Meynell, and Burke, had crossed the
river higher up, in detached bodies; and although
these small bands were left from first to last without
reinforcements — although they had to move flank-
wise close under the guns of a Russian battery, which
killed very many — and although they were sharply
attacked and at one time hard pressed by the enemy's

infantry, as well as by four squadrons of cavalry—the
remnant of these venturesome men fought their way
down along the river's bank, and at last made good
their junction with the main body, then intrenching
itself behind the mere.   But before they attained to
this they had lost a great proportion of their comrades, and of their five youthful leaders they had
lost three, for Burke, Arnold, and Meynell were
killed.

Meanwhile fresh troops had been crossing the
river at the point opposite to the landing-place first
seized; and at length there was established on the
ground behind the mere a force of some five thousand
men.

Upon either flank of this body the Russian infantry came down in strong columns.   Four times
the attack was made, and four times the Turks,
commanded or led on by Ali Pasha and General
Cannon, by Bent, Hinde, Ogilvy, and Ballard, drove
back their assailants with great slaughter.   With
pious and warlike cries, the Turks sallied over their
newmade parapets, brought their bayonets down to
the charge, forced mass after mass to give way, and
fiercely pressed the retreat.

At sunset the action ceased. All night the Turks
were intrenching themselves on the ground which
they had gained; but when the morning dawned
there was no sign that the enemy would hasten to
renew the battle.

To keep a safe hold of the ground which had

been won, it was necessary for the Turks to advance in the direction of their left front, and occupy a ridge which went by the name of the Slobenzie Heights; but Hassan Pasha dreaded the blame which might fall upon him if the movement should prove to be a wrong one. General Cannon pressed him hard—for some time in vain; but at length the Pasha yielded, upon condition that the English General would give him a written warranty certifying the wisdom of the step.

On the third day after the battle, Prince Gortschakoff came up with a force which was said to number some sixty or seventy thousand men. He had been set free by the raising of the siege of Silistria, and he now appeared upon one of the ranges of hills looking down upon Giurgevo from the north-west. It seemed that he meant to cover over the stain of the defeat sustained at Giurgevo by driving the Turks back into the river; but before he camped for the night the British flag was already in the waters beneath him.

Lieutenant Glyn and the young Prince Leiningen, both serving on board the Britannia, had come up from the sea, with some gunboats and thirty seamen, together with a like number of sappers. Glyn quickly carried his gunboats into the narrow loop-stream which escapes from the main of the river above Giurgevo and meets it again lower down. By this movement Glyn thrust his gunboats into the interval which divided the Russian army from the

Turks. Gortschakoff perbaps overrated the force which had come with the British flag. At all events, he did not instantly move down to the attack; and whilst he seemed to hesitate, the Turks and the English worked hard. Captain Bent and his sappers, with the aid of our seamen and the Turks, threw a bridge of boats across the main stream of the Danube. This done, it was plain that, if Gortschakoff were to attack, he would have to do, not merely with the five thousand Turks already established on the left bank, but with the whole of the force which lay at Rustchuk. He resolved to avoid the encounter. Retreating upon Bucharest, he no longer disputed with the Turks for the mastery of the Lower Danube.

In this campaign on the Danube, those who fought for the cause of the Sultan were helped, it is true, by Fortune, by the anger and unskilfulness of the Czar, by the assured support of Austria, and by the impending power of England and France; but still there is one point of view in which their achieve-

Effect
of the
campaign
of the
Danube
on the
military
ascend-
ancy of
Russia.

ment was a great one. Military ascendancy is so closely connected with military reputation, that to be the first to bring down the warlike fame of a great empire is to do a mighty work, and a work, too, which hardly can fail to change the career of nations. By the time that Prince Gortschakoff retreated upon Bucharest, people no longer thought of the Czar as they thought of him eight months before; and the glory of thus breaking down the military reputation of Russia is due of right, not to the Governments nor the armies of France or England, but to the warlike prowess of the Ottoman soldiery, and the ten or twelve resolute Englishmen who cheered and helped and led them.

The failure of the attempted invasion was almost instantly followed by the relinquishment of Moldavia and Wallachia. The Emperor Nicholas, as we saw, had been placed by Austria under the stress of a peremptory summons requiring him to withdraw from the Principalities; and the demand being supported by powerful bodies of troops, which threatened the flank of the intruding army, the Czar was schooled at last, and compelled to see that he must surrender his hold of the provinces which he had chosen to call his "material guarantee."

Thus, by the course of the events which followed it, the Czar's last defeat on the Danube was made to appear more signal than it really was. Of course, men versed in war and in politics knew that causes of a larger kind than a few hours' fight at Giurgevo were bringing about the abandonment of the Principalities; but people who drew their conclusions from the mere advance or retreat of armies, and from the issue of battles, were left to infer that the once-dreaded Emperor of the Russias was chased from the country of the Danube by the sheer prowess of the victorious Turks.

It is therefore very easy to believe that this dis- The agony comfiture at Giurgevo was more bitter to the Czar of the Czar. than any of the disasters which had hitherto tried

CHAP.
III.
his fortitude. People knew, or affected to know,
what the troubled man uttered in torment, and the
words they put in his mouth ran somewhat to this
effect: —

"I can understand Oltenitza — I can even under-
"stand that Omar Pasha should have been able to
"hold against me his lines at Kalafat — I can partly
"account for the result of those fights at Citate — I
"can understand Silistria — the strongest may fail in
"a siege — and it chanced that both Paskievitch and
"Schilder were struck down and disabled by shot —
"but — but — but — that Turks — mere Turks — led
"on by a General of Sepoys and six or seven English
"boys — that they should dare to cross the Danube
"in the face of my troops — that, daring to attempt
"this, they should do it, and hold fast their ground
"— that my troops should give way before them;
"and that this — that this should be the last act
"of the campaign which is ending in the retreat
"of my whole army, and the abandonment of the
"Principalities. Heaven lays upon me more than I
"can bear!"

Many men in the Anglo-French camp were fretted
by the tidings of this last Turkish victory; for, besides that, with their natural and healthy impatience
of delay, they were stung by the example of their
Moslem ally, there was in the staff of the French
and the English armies a pedantic dislike of wild
troops. In this respect Lord Raglan had no breadth

of view. Far from understanding that the hardy, the fierce, the devout, the temperate Moslems of the Ottoman provinces were the rough yet sound material with which superb troops could be made, he always looked upon these brave men, but especially upon the genus which people called "Bashi-Bazouks," with an almost superstitious horror. He was so constituted, or rather he was so schooled down by long years of flat office labour, that it shocked him to see a man bearing no uniform, yet warlike, and armed to the teeth. Indeed, from Bulgaria he once wrote and complained quite gravely that every Turk he saw had the appearance of being a "bandit;" and the prejudice clung to him; for long after the period now spoken of, and even in the very hour when the fatal storm of the 14th of November was roaring through his port and his camp, he found time to sit at a desk and write down the Bashi-Bazouks.

This hatred of undrilled warriors was the more perverse, since England above all other nations was rich in men (men like Hodson, for instance, or Jacob) who knew how to make themselves the adored chiefs of Asiatic soldiers.

Besides, it must be borne in mind, that when an English Government undertakes to wage war in a country beyond the seas without doing all it can to get soldiery aid from the natives, it does not merely neglect a slight or collateral advantage; on the contrary, it throws away its power of acting with efficient numbers, and is in danger of frittering away the

5*

nation's strength upon those (often ill-fated) schemes
which go by the name of "expeditions." Without our
Portuguese auxiliaries there would have been no great
Peninsular War, no successful invasion of France;
without the native soldiery of Hindostan there
would have been no British India; without the
German auxiliaries who served under Wellington in
his last campaign, he could not have given battle to
Napoleon in the Netherlands, and the course of
English history would not have run as it did.   The
truth is, that (especially at the beginning of a war)
any body of troops which England brings together
at one time and one place is in general so costly,
and of so high a quality, but also so scant in numbers, that to use it, and use it singly, for all the work
of the campaign, is to consume and squander the
precious essence of the nation's strength without
making it the means of attaining any worthy result.

Therefore, whenever it is possible, a British force
serving abroad and engaged in an arduous campaign,
ought to have on its side, not mere allies — for that
is but a doubtful, and often a poor support to have to
lean upon — but auxiliaries obeying the English commander, and capable of being trusted with a large
share of the duties required from an army in the
field. Nor is this an advantage which commonly lies
out of our reach; for in most of the countries of the
Old World the cost of labour is much lower than in
England; and it is one of the prerogatives of the
English, as indeed of all conquering nations, to be

able to lead other races of men, and to impart to them its warlike fire. By beginning its preparations at the right time, and by bringing under the orders of some of our Indian officers a fitting number of the brave men who came flocking to the war from every province of the Ottoman Empire, our Government might have enabled their General to take the field with an army of great strength — with an army more fit for warlike enterprises than two armies, French and English, instructed to work side by side, and baffled by divided command.[*]

CHAP.
XXX.

* The opinions which the Duke of Newcastle entertained on this subject were sound, and his efforts to give effect to them were vigorous; but he was thwarted by the curious antagonism which commonly shows itself at the beginning of a war — the antagonism between views really warlike and views which are only "military."

CHAPTER XXXI.

CHAP.
XXXI.

The
events
on the
Danube
removed
the
grounds
of the
war.

By their own prowess, with the aid only of a moral support from their great allies and the actual presence of a few young English officers, the Ottoman soldiery had repelled the invasion; and the defence of Turkey being accomplished in a way very glorious to the Sultan, and the deliverance of the Principalities being secured, it suddenly became apparent that the objects for which the Western Powers undertook the war had been already attained. And since (by the mere act of declaring war against the Czar) the Porte had freed itself from the obnoxious treaties which heretofore entangled its freedom, the condition of affairs was such that a prudent statesman of France or of England or of the Ottoman Empire might have well enough rested content. And in that condition of affairs the Emperor of Russia must have acquiesced; for having now learnt that he could not maintain an invasion of European Turkey, and being driven from the seas, he was cut off from all means of waging an offensive war against the Sultan except upon the desolate frontiers of Armenia; and the pressure of the naval blockade enforced against

him by the Allies, together with the torture of seeing
the Baltic and the Euxine placed under the dominion
of their fleets, would have more than sufficed to make
him sign a peace.

If France had been mistress of herself, or if England had been free from passion and craving for
adventure, the war would have been virtually at an
end on the day when the Russian army completed
its retreat from the country of the Danube and re-
entered the Czar's dominions.

How came it to happen that, rejecting the peace
which seemed to be thus prepared by the mere course
of events, the Western Powers determined to undertake the invasion of a Russian province?

France was still lying under the men who had Helpless-
got her down on the night of the 2d of December; French
and it was in vain that her people at that time people.
chanced to love peace better than war, for they
had no longer a voice in State affairs. The French
Emperor still wielded the whole strength of the
nation; and, labouring to turn away men's thoughts
from the origin of his power, he was very willing to
try to earn for the restored Empire that kind of Course
station and title which the newest of dynasties may the French
acquire by signal achievements in war. It was still Emperor.
of great moment to him to remain in close friendship
with England, and to use the alliance as an engine of
war; but he observed that there was a spirit on this
side of the Channel which, springing from motives
very unlike his own, was nevertheless tending in

the same direction; and therefore, to draw England in, he no longer needed to resort to those ingenious contrivances which he had employed against her in the foregoing year. All that he had to do was to encourage her desire to go on with the war, and, if necessary, to make his own plans yield to those of his ally. To do all this he was very able; for he had, as we have seen, at that time, the power of keeping his mind alive to the difference between the greater and the less; and after he had once resolved to engage in alliance with England, he did not allow his main purpose to be baffled by differences on minor questions. Therefore, now when it became known that the Russian army was in full retreat, he was so willing to defer to English counsels, that virtually, though not in terms, he left it to the Queen's Government to determine what next step the Western Powers should take in the conduct of the war.

Desire of the English for an offensive war.
England had become so eager for conflict that the idea of desisting from the war merely because the war had ceased to be necessary was not tolerable to the people. In the Baltic their hopes had been bitterly disappointed; and as soon as it became clear that the defence of Turkey was a thing already accomplished, men longed to try the prowess of our land and sea forces in some enterprise against the Russian dominions. Already they had cast their eyes upon Sebastopol.

Sebasto-
pol.
With a view to the conquest of empire on the Bosphorus, the ambition of Russia had taken advan-

tage of the spacious port on the south-west coast of
the Crimea — had made there a great arsenal, and
furnished it with an enormous supply of warlike
stores. And having been warned a quarter of a
century ago* that, if he thus gathered his strength
in Sebastopol, he might have to count some day
with the English, the Czar Nicholas had caused the
place to be defended towards the sea by forts of
great power. In the harbour, barred by these forts,
his Black Sea fleet lay at anchor. Plainly it would The long-
ing of the
English to
attack it.
be a natural and fitting consummation of a war in
defence of the Sultan to destroy those very resources
which the labours of years had gathered together
against him. Moreover, the English, who hate the
mechanic contrivances which prevent fair, open
fighting, could hardly now bear that the vast sea-
forts of Sebastopol should continue to shelter the
Russian fleet from the guns of our men-of-war.
Those who thought more warily than the multitude
foresaw that the enterprise might take time; but
they also perceived that even this result would not
be one of unmixed evil; for if Russia should commit
herself to a lengthened conflict in the neighbourhood
of Sebastopol, she would be put to a great trial, and
would see her wealth and strength ruinously con-

---

* Despatch from Count Pozzo di Borgo, dated the 28th of November
1828-9. "Although," writes the Count, "it may not be probable that
"we shall see an English fleet in the Black Sea, it will be prudent to
"make Sebastopol very secure against attacks from the sea. If ever
"England were to come to a rupture with us, this is the point to which
"she would direct her attacks, if only she believed them possible."

sumed by the mere stress of the distance between
the military centre of the Empire and the south-
westernmost angle of the Crimea.

The more the English people thought of the enterprise, the more eager they became to attempt it;
and it chanced that their feelings and opinions were
shared and represented with great exactness by the
Minister of War.

The Duke
of New-
castle.
The Duke of Newcastle was a man of sanguine,
eager nature, very prone to action.* He had a good
clear intellect, with more of strength than keenness,
unwearied industry, and an astonishing facility of
writing. In the assumption of responsibility he was
generous and bold even to rashness. Indeed, he was
so eager to see his views carried into effect, and
so willing to take all the risk upon his own head,
that there was danger of his withdrawing from other
men their wholesome share of discretion. He threw
his whole heart into the project of the invasion; and
if the Prime Minister and Mr Gladstone were men
driven forward by the feeling of the country, in spite
of their opinions and their scruples, it was not so
with the Duke of Newcastle. The character of his
mind was such as to make him essentially one with
the public. Far from being propelled by others
against his will, he himself was one of the very fore-

* I, of course, know that this view will not be assented to by those
who found their opinion upon observation made in later years; but I
am speaking of the summer of 1854, and I am very sure that the sentence to which this note has been appended is true.

most members of the warlike throng which was pressing upon the Cabinet and craving for adventure and glory. He easily received new impressions, and had nevertheless a quick good sense, which generally enabled him to distinguish what was useful from what was worthless. He seemed to understand the great truth that, without being military, the English are a warlike people, and that it is one of the great prerogatives of a nation gifted with this higher quality to be able to command other races of men, and to impart to them the fire of martial virtue. He also knew that when England undertakes war against a great European Power, she must engage the energies of the people at large, and must not presume to rely altogether upon the merely professional exertions of her small Peace Establishment. It was not from his default, but in spite of his endeavours, that for several months people lingered in the notion that our military system was an apparatus sufficing for war.

But the Duke had not an authority proportioned to the merits which a reader of his despatches and letters would be inclined to attribute to him. Perhaps the very zeal with which he seized and adopted the ideas of the outer public was one of the causes which tended to lessen his weight; for he who comes into council with common and popular views, however likely it may be that he will get them assented to, can scarcely hope to kindle men's minds with the fire that springs from a man's own thought and

from his own strong will. Moreover, it was by a
kind of chance rather than by intentional selection
that the Duke of Newcastle had become intrusted
with the momentous business of the war; and seemingly it was only from this circumstance that the
propriety of his continuing to hold the office was
afterwards brought into question by one of his
principal colleagues.* But whatever may have been
the cause, it seems clear that there was a languor,
not to say hollowness, in the support which the
Duke got from his colleagues. They did not perversely thwart him in the business of the war;**

* So Lord John Russell himself declared. What I have above called
"a kind of chance" was brought about in this way: — According to the
practice which was in force up to the summer of 1854, the Secretary of
State for the Colonies was also the "Secretary of War." Before the
war, however, the public hardly observed, and in fact hardly knew
this, because in peace-time (thanks to the labours of the "Horse
Guards," the office of the Secretary at War, the Ordnance, and several
other offices) the duties of the Colonial Secretary, in his character as
Secretary of War, were very slight; and there being no prospect of war
when Lord Aberdeen's Ministry was formed, the Duke of Newcastle
was of course selected with a view to his qualifications for the administration of the Colonies, and not with any consideration, either one
way or the other, as to his aptitude for the business of the War Department. When the rupture with Russia occurred, it became apparent
that, unless a change were made, the minister who happened to be the
Colonial Secretary would stand charged with the business of the war.

** The rejection by the Cabinet of the Duke's proposal to ask for
a vote adding 15,000 men to the army, does not in reality displace the
above statement; because the addition to which the Cabinet agreed,
though falling far short of the Duke's demand, was large enough to
warrant the reception of all the recruits who could be obtained in the
course of the year, and therefore the proposed vote for a number
larger than what could be really obtained was a measure of general
policy not tending in any direct way to increase the strength of the army.

but, on the other hand, they did not at all fasten
themselves to his measures like men who would
stand or fall with him. The Duke of Newcastle
had not the gift of knowing how to surround himself with able assistants; and it was his misfortune
to be without that precious aid which a Minister
commonly finds in the permanent staff of his office.
At the outbreak of hostilities, the little bevy of distinct public offices on which the military administration depended was in a condition unfit to meet the
exigencies of war. The first Army Surgeon who
applied for certain of the medical stores required
on foreign service was met with no less than five
official theories as to the functionary upon whom
the demand should be made; and when, in the
month of June, the scattered departments connected
with the land service were gathered at last into
one, the office thus newly formed was, after all,
so ill constituted as to be wanting in some of the
simplest appliances required for the transaction of
business.

From the first, the Duke of Newcastle, resisting His zeal
all proposals for operating against Russia on the side destruc-
of Poland, had warmly shared the popular desire to bastopol.
invade the Crimea and lay siege to Sebastopol. The
Emperor of the French, steadily following his main
policy, had long ago consented to look to this enterprise as next in importance to the defence of the
Sultan's territory; and in the early part of April

instructions to this effect had been given to the French and the English Generals.

It would seem, however, that at first the Duke of Newcastle was the only member of the Government who was fired with a great eagerness for the destruction of Sebastopol; and of himself he had not the ascendancy which sometimes enables a Minister to bend other men to his purpose. Unless by the help of a mighty force pressing from without, he could not have brought the Cabinet of Lord Aberdeen to partake his zeal for the enterprise.

But — impending over the counsels of all the ostensible rulers — there was an authority, not deriving from the Queen or the Parliament, which was destined to have a great sway over events. It would be possible to elude the task; but it seems to me that a history would be wanting in fulness of truth if it failed to impart some conception of this other power.

Commanding power of the people when of one mind. England was free; and although, whilst there was indifference or divided opinion in the country, the Government had very full latitude of action, yet, whenever it chanced that the feelings of the people were roused, and that they were known to be nearly of one mind, they spoke with a voice so commanding that no Administration could safely try to withstand it.

But the will of the nation being thus puissant, who was charged to declare it?

In former times almost everybody who could was accustomed to contribute in an active way to the formation of opinion. Men evolved their own political ideas and drew forth the ideas of their friends by keen oral discussion, and in later times by long elaborate letters. But gradually, and following somewhat slowly upon the invention of printing, there came to be introduced a new division of labour. It was found that if a small number of competent men would make it their calling to transact the business of thinking upon political questions, the work might be more handily performed by them than by the casual efforts of people who were commonly busied in other sorts of toil; and as soon as this change took effect, the weighing of State questions and the judging of public men lapsed away from the direct cognisance of the nation at large, and passed into the hands of those who knew how to utter in print. What had been an intellectual exercise, practised in a random way by thousands, was turned into a branch of industry and pursued with great skill by a few. People soon found out that an essay in print — an essay strong and terse, but, above all, opportune — seemed to clear their minds more effectually than the sayings which they heard in conversation, or the letters they received from their friends; and at length the principle of divided labour became so complete in its application to the forming of political opinions, that by glancing at a newspaper, and giving swift assent to its assertions and arguments, many

CHAP. XXXI.

Means of forming and declaring the opinion of the nation.

CHAP.
XXXI.
an Englishman was saved the labour of further examining his political conscience, and dispensed from
the necessity of having to work his own way to a
conclusion.

Effect of
political
writings
in saving
men from
the trouble
of think-
ing.
But to spare a man from a healthy toil is not
always an unmixed good. To save a free-born
citizen from the trouble of thinking upon questions
of State is to take from him his share of dominion;
and although it be true that he who follows printed
advice is under a guidance more skilful and dexterous
than any he could have got from his own untutored
mind, he is less of a man — and, upon the whole,
is less fair, less righteous — than one who in a ruder
fashion contrives to think for himself. Just as a
man's quality may in some respects be lowered by
his habitual reliance on the policeman and the soldier
who relieve him from the trouble and the anxiety
of self-defence, so his intellectual strength, and his
means of knowing how to be just, may easily become impaired if he suffers himself to walk too obe-
diently under the leading of a political writer.

Want of
proportion
between
the skill
of the
public
writer
and the
judicial
compe-
tence of
his read-
ers.
But the ability of men engaged in political
writing grow even more rapidly than the power to
which they were attaining, and after a while they so
gained upon the ostensible statesmen that Parliament
no longer stood alone as the exponent of opinion, and
was obliged to share its privilege with a number
of gifted men whose names it could hardly ever find
out. Still, Parliament had valour and strength of
its own, and, except in the matter of mere celebrity,

it was a gainer rather than a loser from the wholesome rivalry forced upon it by its new and mysterious associate. It was the public which lagged.
Men commonly take a long time to adapt themselves
to the successive advances of civilisation; and the
people were backward in fitting themselves to deal
with the increasing ability and the increasing knowledge of the public writer. They indeed hardly
knew the true scope of the change which had been
taking place; for whilst the writer was a personage
chosen for his skill, and acting with the force which
belongs to discipline and organisation, the readers
were men straying loose; and for their means of
acting in anything like concert with one another,
they were dependent in a great degree upon that
very engine of publicity which was fast usurping
their power. Moreover, these readers of public
prints were slow to understand the new kind of duty
which had come upon them. They were slow to see
that it became them to look in a very critical spirit
upon the writings of a stranger, unseen and unknown,
who was not only proposing to guide them, but even
to speak in their name; and they did not yet understand that they ought to read print, not, perhaps, in
a captious spirit, but, to say the least, with something of the measured confidence which their forefathers had been accustomed to place in the words
of princes and statesmen. The blessing conferred
by print will perhaps be complete when the diligence,
the weariness, and, above all, the courageous justice

of those who read, shall be brought into fair proportion with the skill and the power of those who address them in print. Already a wholesome change
has been wrought; and if in these days a man goes
chanting and chanting in servile response to a newspaper, he misses the voices of the tens of thousands
of fellow-choristers who sang with him five years ago.
But certainly, at the time of the Russian war, the
common discourse of an Englishman was too often a
mere "Amen" to something he had seen in print.

For a long time there had remained to the general
public a vestige of their old custom of thinking for
themselves, because in last resort they were privileged
to determine between the rival counsels pressed upon
them by contending journalists; but several years
before the outbreak of the war there had come yet
another change. The apparatus provided by the
constitution for collecting the opinions of the people
was far from being complete; and notwithstanding
the indications afforded by Parliament and by public
writings, the direction which the nation's opinion had
taken was a matter which could often be called in
question. Some could say that the people desired
one thing, and some, with equal boldness, that the
people desire the contrary. Thence it came that the
task of finding out the will of the nation, and giving
to it a full voice and expression, was undertaken by
private citizens.

Long before the outbreak of the war, there were
living in some of the English counties certain widows

and gentlemen who were the depositories of a power
destined to exercise a great sway over the conduct
of the war. Their ways were peaceful, and they
were not perhaps more turned towards politics than
other widows and country gentlemen; but by force
of deeds and testaments, by force of births, deaths,
and marriages, they had become the members of an
ancient firm or Company which made it its business
to collect and disseminate news. They had so much
good sense of the worldly sort, that, instead of strug-
gling with one another for the control of their powerful engine, they remained quietly at their homes,
and engaged some active and gifted men to manage
the concern for them in London. The practice of
the Company was to issue a paper daily, containing
an account of what was going on in the world, together with letters from men of all sorts and conditions who were seeking to bring their favourite
subjects under the eye of the public, and also a few
short essays upon the topics of the day. Likewise,
upon paying the sum required by the Company, any
person could cause whatever he chose to be inserted
in the paper as an "advertisement," and the sheet
containing these four descriptions of matter was sold
to the public at a low rate.

Extraordinary enterprise was shown by the Company in the gathering of intelligence; and during the
wars following the French Revolution they caused
their despatches from the Continent to reach them
so early that they were able to forestall the Govern-

CHAP.
XXXI.

and de-
claring
the opin-
ion of the
country
falls into
the hands
of a com-
pany.

6*

CHAP.
XXXI.
ment of the day. In other countries the spectacle
of a Government outdone in this way by private
enterprise would have seemed a scandal; but the
Englishman liked the thought that he could buy and
bring to his own home as much knowledge as was
in the hands of a Minister of State, and he enjoyed
the success of his fellow-countrymen in their rivalry
with the Government. From this time the paper
gathered strength. It became the foremost journal
of the world; and this was no sooner the case, than
the mere fact of its being thus foremost gave a great
acceleration to its rise; for, simply because it was
recognised as the most public of prints, it became
the clue with which anxious man went seeking in
the maze of the busy world for the lost and the
unknown, and all that was beyond his own reach.
The prince who was claiming a kingdom, the servant
who wanted a place, the mother who had lost her
boy, they all went thither; thither Folly ran hurrying,
and was brought to a wholesome parley with Wisdom;
thither went righteous anger; thither also went hatred
and malice. And not in vain was all this concourse;
for either the troubled and angry men got the discipline of finding that the world would not listen to
their cries, or else they gained a vent for their passions, and brought all their theories to a test by
calling a whole nation — nay, by calling the civilised
world — to hearken and be their witness. Over all
this throng of appellants men unknown sat in judgment, and — violently, perhaps, but never corruptly

— a rough sort of justice was done. The style which
Oriental hyperbole used to give to the Sultan might
be claimed with more colour of truth by the journal.
In a sense it was the 'asylum of the world.'

Still up to this point the Company occupied ground
in common with many other speculators; and if they
had gone no further, it would not have been my
province to notice the result of their labours; but
many years ago it had occurred to the managers of
this Company that there was one important article
of news which had not been effectually supplied.
It seemed likely that, without moving from his fire-
side, an Englishman would be glad to know what
the bulk of his fellow-countrymen thought upon the
uppermost questions of the day. The letters received
from correspondents furnished some means of acquiring
this knowledge; and it seemed to the managers of
the Company, that at some pains, and at a moderate
cost, it would be possible to ascertain the opinions
which were coming into vogue, and see the direction
in which the current would flow. It is said that,
with this intent, they many years ago employed a
shrewd, idle clergyman, who made it his duty to
loiter about in places of common resort, and find out
what people thought upon the principal subjects of
the time. He was not to listen very much to extreme
foolishness, and still less was he to hearken to clever
people. His duty was to wait and wait until he observed that some common and obvious thought was
repeated in many places, and by numbers of men

who had probably never seen one another. That one
common thought was the prize he sought for, and he
carried it home to his employers. He became so
skilled in his peculiar calling that, as long as he
served them, the Company was rarely misled; and
although in later times they were frequently baffled
in their pursuit of this kind of knowledge, they never
neglected to do what they could to search the heart
of the nation.

When the managers had armed themselves with
the knowledge thus gathered, they prepared to disseminate it, but they did not state baldly what they
had ascertained to be the opinion of the country.
Their method was as follows: they employed able
writers to argue in support of the opinion which, as
they believed, the country was already adopting; and,
supposing that they had been well informed, their
arguments of course fell upon willing ears. Those
who had already formed a judgment saw their own
notions stated and pressed with an ability greater
than they could themselves command; and those who
had not yet come to an opinion were strongly moved
to do so when they saw the path taken by a Company
which notoriously strove to follow the changes of the
public mind. The report which the paper gave of
the opinion formed by the public was so closely
blended with arguments in support of that same
opinion, that he who looked at the paper merely to
know what other people thought, was seized, as he
read, by the cogency of the reasoning; and, on the

other hand, he who imagined that he was being governed by the force of sheer logic, was merely obeying
a guide who, by telling him that the world was already
agreed, made him go and flock along with his fellows:
for as the utterance of a prophecy is sometimes a
main step towards its fulfilment, so a rumour asserting
that multitudes have already adopted a given opinion
will often generate that very concurrence of thought
which was prematurely declared to exist. From the
operation of this double process it resulted, of course,
that the opinion of the English public was generally
in accord with the writings of the Company; and
the more the paper came to be regarded as a true
exponent of the national mind, the more vast was the
publicity which it obtained.

Plainly, then, this printing Company wielded a
great power; and if I have written with sufficient
clearness, I have made it apparent that this was a
power of more vast dimensions than that which men
describe when they speak of "the power of the Press."
It is one thing, for instance, to denounce a public
man by printed arguments and invectives which are
believed to utter nothing more than the opinion of
the writers, and it is another and a graver thing to
denounce him in writings which, though having the
form of arguments, are (rightly or wrongly) regarded
as manifestoes — as manifestoes declaring the judgment of the English people. In the one case the
man is only accused; in the other he seems to stand
already condemned.

But though the Company held all this power,
their tenure of it was of such a kind that they could
not exercise it perversely or whimsically without
doing a great harm to their singular trade; for the
whole scheme of their existence went to make them,
not autocratic, but representative, in their character;
and they were obliged, by the law of their being, to
keep themselves as closely as they could in accord
with the nation at large.

This, then, was the great English journal; and
whether men spoke of the mere printed sheet which
lay upon their table, or of the mysterious organisation which produced it, they habitually called either
one or the other "The Times." Moreover, they often
prefixed to the word such adjectives and participles
as showed that they regarded the subject of their
comments in the light of a sentient, active being,
having a life beyond the span of mortal men, gifted
with reason, armed with a cruel strength, endued
with some of the darkest of the human passions,
but clearly liable hereafter to the direst penalty of
sin. *

---

* The form of speech which thus impersonates a manufactory and
its wares has now so obtained in our language that, discarding the
forcible epithets, one may venture to adopt it in writing, and to give
"The Times" the same place in grammatical construction as though it
were the proper name of an angel or a hero, a devil or a saint, or a
sinner already condemned. Custom makes it good English to say:
"The 'Times' will protect him;" "The 'Times' is savage;" "The
'Times' is crushing him;" "The blessed 'Times' has put the thing
right;" "That d——d 'Times' has done all the mischief."

On the Sabbath England had rest; but in the early morning of all other days the irrevocable words were poured forth and scattered abroad to the corners of the earth, measuring out honour to some, and upon others bringing scorn and disgrace. Where and with whom the real power lay, and what was its true source, and how it was to be propitiated, — these were questions wrapped in more or less obscurity; for some had a theory that one man ruled, and some another, and some were sure that the Great Newspaper governed all England, and others that England governed the Newspaper. Philosophic politicians traced events to what they called "Public opinion." With almost the same meaning, women and practical men simply spoke of "The "Times." But whether the power of the great journal was a power all its own, or whether it was only the vast shadow of the public mind, it was almost equally to be dreaded and revered by worldly men; for plainly, in that summer of 1854, it was one with England. Its words might be wrong, but it was certain that to tens of thousands of men they would seem to be right. They might be the collected voice of all these isles, or the mere utterance of some one unknown man sitting pale by a midnight lamp, — but there they were. They were the handwriting on the wall.

Of the temper and spirit in which this strange power had been wielded, up to the time of the outbreak of the war, it is not very hard to speak. In

general "The Times" had been more willing to lead
the nation in its tendencies to improvement than to
follow it in its errors: what it mainly sought was —
not to be much better or wiser than the English
people, but to be the very same as they were — to
go along with them in all their adventures, whether
prudent or rash — to be one with them in their hopes
and their despair, in their joy and in their sorrow, in
their gratitude and in their anger.   So, although in
general it was willing enough to repress the growth
of any new popular error which seemed to be weakly
rooted, still the whole scheme and purpose of the
Company forbade it all thought of trying to make a
stand against any great and general delusion. Upon
the whole, the potentate dealt with England in a
bluff, kingly, Tudor-like way, but also with a Tudor-
like policy; for though he treated all adversaries as
"brute folk" until they became formidable, he had
always been careful to mark the growth of a public
sentiment or opinion; and as soon as he was able to
make out that a cause was waxing strong, he went
up and offered to lead it, and so reigned.

I have said that, partly by guiding, but more by
ascertaining and following, the current of men's
opinion, "The Times" always sought to be one with
the great body of the people; and since it happened
that there was at this period a rare concurrence of
feeling, and that the journal, after a good deal of
experiment, had now at length thoroughly seized and
embodied the soul of the nation, its utterance came

with increasing force; and in proportion as the growing concord of the people enabled it to speak with
more and more authority, power lapsed, and continued
to lapse, from out of the hands of the Government,
until at length public opinion, no longer content to
direct the general policy of the State, was preparing
to undertake the almost scientific, the almost tech-
nical duty of planning a campaign.

On the morning of the 15th of June, the great
newspaper declared and said that "The grand poli-
"tical and military objects of the war could not be
"attained as long as Sebastopol and the Russian fleet
"were in existence; but that, if that central position
"of the Russian power in the south of the empire
"were annihilated, the whole fabric, which it had
"cost the Czars of Russia centuries to raise, must
"fall to the ground:" and, moreover, it declared,
"that the taking of Sebastopol and the occupation
"of the Crimea were objects which would repay all
"the costs of the war, and would permanently settle
"in our favour the principal questions in dispute;
"and that it was equally clear that those objects
"were to be accomplished by no other means — be-
"cause a peace which should leave Russia in pos-
"session of the same means of aggression would
"only enable her to recommence the war at her
"pleasure."

It was natural that some of the members of the
Government should have qualms. They knew that
Austria (supported for defensive purposes by Prussia)

The
opinion
of the
nation, as
declared
by the
Company,
demands
the de-
struction
of Sebas-
topol.

was at that time on the point of joining her arms to those of the Western Powers; and they could not but know that if the French and English armies were to be withdrawn from the mainland of Europe in order to invade the Crimea, the wholesome union of the Four Powers would of necessity be weakened. The Prime Minister was he who loved peace so fondly that, though peace was no more, he had hardly yet been torn from her cold embrace; and though he lived under a belief that the military strength of the Czar was beyond measure vast, yet of the twelve months which Russia gave him for preparation he had only used three.* Having the heaviness of these thoughts on his mind, he saw it declared aloud, that the country of which he happened to be the Prime Minister could not well do otherwise than invade the Russian dominions. To a prudent man the measure might seem to be rash — to a good man, impressed with horror of war, it might even seem to be very wicked; for it was a violent revival of a war which, unless this new torch were thrown, would expire of its own accord. But the print was clear; like stern Anangke, it pressed upon feeble man's volition, for it was not to be construed away;

* Computing from the time when the Czar's determination to seize the Principalities was known to our Government. If the computations are to be made from the time when the hostile character of Prince Mentschikoff's mission became known, several months more would have to be added. See Lord Aberdeen's evidence before the Sebastopol Committee.

and if an anxious Minister went back and looked
again to see whether by chance he could find some
loop in the wording, and whether possibly he might
be able to fulfil his duty without besieging Sebastopol, he was met by the careful negation which taught
him in four plain words that he could fulfil it "by
"no other means."

Before the seventh day from the manifesto of
the 15th, the country had made loud answer to the
appeal; and on the 22d of June the great newspaper,
informed with the deep will of the people, and taking
little account of the fears of the prudent and the
scruples of the good, laid it down that "Sebastopol
"was the keystone of the arch which spanned the
"Euxine from the mouths of the Danube to the con-
"fines of Mingrelia," and that "a successful enter-
"prise against the place was the essential condition
"of permanent peace." And although this appeal
was founded in part upon a false belief — a belief
that the siege of Silistria had been raised — it seemed
as though all mankind were making haste to adjust
the world to the newspaper; for within twenty hours
from the publication of the 22d of June, truth obeyed
the voice of false rumours, and followed in the wake
of "The Times."*

Of course there were those who saw great obstacles
in the way of the proposed invasion; and they said

* The siege, as we saw above, was raised early in the morning of
the 23d.

that, since Russia was a first-rate military Power, it must be rash to invade her territory and to besiege her proudest fortress, without first gaining some safe knowledge of the enemy's strength. But the narrative, then coming home in fragments from the valley of the Danube, was heating the minds of the people in England.

When first England learnt that the Turks were to be besieged in their fortress of Silistria by a great Russian army under the renowned Paskievitch, few believed that the issue was doubtful, or even that the contest could be long sustained. But as soon as it became known that, day after day, the military strength of the Czar was exerted against the place with a violent energy, and that every attack was fiercely resisted, and always, as yet, with success, our people began to give their heart to the struggle; and their eagerness rose into zeal when they heard that two young English travellers had thrown themselves into the fortress — were heading the Turkish soldiery, and were maintaining the conflict by day and by night.

The English were not of such a mettle as to be able to hear of tidings like these without growing more and more eager for warlike adventure. And in their hearts they liked the fact, that the few young English travellers who helped to save Silistria, and to turn away the war from the Danube, were men who did these things of their own free will and pleasure, without the sanction of the public autho-

rities; for our people are accustomed to think more
highly of their fellow-countrymen individually than
they do of our State machinery; and they can easily
bear to see their Government in default, and can even
smile at its awkwardness, if all the shortcomings of
office are effectually compensated by the vigour of
private enterprise. Nasmyth has passed away from
us. I knew him in the Crimea. He was a man of
quiet and gentle manners, and so free from vanity
— so free from all idea of self-gratulation — that
he always seemed as though he were unconscious of
having stood as he did in the path of the Czar, and
had really omitted to think of the share which he had
had in changing the course of events; but it chanced
that he had gone to the seat of war in the service
of "The Times," and naturally the lustre of his
achievement was in some degree shed upon the keen,
watchful Company which had had the foresight to
send him at the right moment into the midst of
events on which the fate of Russia was hanging; for
whilst the State armies of France and England were
as yet only gathering their strength, "The Times"
was able to say that its own officer had confronted
the enemy upon the very ground he most needed to
win, and helped to drive him back from the Danube
in great discomfiture.

Thus, day after day in that month of June, the
authority of the Newspaper kept gaining and gaining
upon the Queen's Government; and if Lord Aberdeen

had any remaining unwillingness to renew the war
by undertaking an invasion of Russia, his power of
controlling the course of the Government seems to
have come to its end in the interval between the
23d and the 28th of June. He continued to be the
Prime Minister. His personal honour stood so high
that no man attributed his continuance in office to
other than worthy and unselfish motives; but for those
who lay stress upon the principle that office and power
ought not to be put asunder, it was irksome to have
to mark the difference between what the Prime Minister
was believed to desire, and what he was now consenting to do.

No good
stand
made in
Parlia-
ment
against the
invasion.
Parliament was sitting, and it might be imagined
that there was something to say against the plan for
invading a province of Russia at a moment when all
the main causes of the dispute were vanishing; but
the same causes which I have spoken of as para-
lysing all resistance to the beginning of the war now
hindered every attempt to withstand its renewal; for
the orators who were believed to be tainted with the
doctrines of the Peace Party were still lying under
the ban which they had brought upon themselves by
their former excesses of language. So now again in
June, as before at the opening of the session, the
counsels of these eloquent men were lost to the world.
They became as powerless as the Prime Minister;
and the cause which they represented was so utterly
brought to ruin, that the popular demand for an

invasion, which carried with it the virtual renewal of an otherwise expiring war, had the sound of that voice with which a nation speaks when the people are of one mind.

So now, in presenting to his colleagues this his favourite scheme of an enterprise against Sebastopol, the Duke of Newcastle was upheld — nay, was urged and driven forward — by forces so overwhelming, that scruples and objections and fears were carried away as by a flood; and when it was proposed in the Cabinet to go and fetch, as it were, a new war, by undertaking this bold adventure, there was not one Minister present who refused to give his consent.

Forthwith the Duke of Newcastle announced the decision of the Government to the General commanding the English army in Bulgaria. He did this by a private letter written on the 28th of June,* and nearly at the same time he prepared the draft of a Despatch* which was to convey to the English headquarters, in full detail and in official form, the deliberate instructions of the Queen's Government. This paper was to be the instrument for meting out to the General in command the allowance of discretion with which he was to be intrusted. A Despatch recommending the expedition, but leaving to the General in command the duty of determining whether

Prepara-tion of the instruc-tions ad-dressed to Lord Raglan.

---

* The contents of this will be given in another chapter.

Invasion of the Crimea. III. 7

CHAP.
XXXI.

it could be prudently undertaken, would not have
been followed by any invasion of the Crimea; and
that which brought about the event was, not the
decision of the Cabinet already mentioned, but the
peculiar stringency of the language which was to
convey it to the English headquarters.* It therefore seems right to speak of what passed when the
terms of this cogent Despatch were adopted by Lord
Aberdeen's Cabinet.

The Duke of Newcastle so framed the draft as
to make it the means of narrowing very closely the
discretion left to Lord Raglan; and it was to be
expected that the Duke might wish his Despatch to
stand in this shape, because he was eager for the
undertaking, and very willing to bear upon his own
shoulders a large share of the responsibility which it
entailed; but it is difficult to believe that all the
other members of the Government could have intended
to place the English General under that degree of
compulsion which is implied by the tenor of the instructions. It is certain, however, that the paper
was well fitted to elicit at once the objections of
those who might be inclined to disapprove it on
account of its cogency; for it confined the discretion
to be left to the General with a precision scarcely
short of harshness.

---

* The truth of this statement will be shown, as I think, in a future
chapter, and, indeed, it is well enough proved by the tenor of Lord
Raglan's reply to the despatch.

The Duke of Newcastle took the Despatch to
Richmond, for there was to be a meeting of the
members of the Cabinet at Pembroke Lodge, and he
intended to make this the occasion for submitting
the proposed instructions to the judgment of his colleagues. It was evening — a summer evening — and
all the members of the Cabinet were present when
the Duke took out the draft of his proposed despatch
and began to read it.   Then there occurred an incident, very trifling in itself, but yet so momentous
in its consequences, that, if it had happened in old
times, it would have been attributed to the direct
intervention of the immortal gods.   In these days,
perhaps, the physiologist will speak of the condition
into which the human brain is naturally brought
when it rests after anxious labours, and the analytical
chemist may regret that he had not an opportunity
of testing the food of which the Ministers had par-
taken, with a view to detect the presence of some
narcotic poison; but no well-informed person will
look upon the accident as characteristic of the men
whom it befell; for the very faults, no less than the
high qualities of the statesmen composing Lord
Aberdeen's Cabinet, were of such a kind as to secure
them against the imputation of being careless and
torpid.   However, it is very certain that, before the
reading of the paper had long continued, all the
members of the Cabinet, except a small minority,

7*

were overcome with sleep.* For a moment the noise
of a tumbling chair disturbed the repose of the
Government; but presently the Duke of Newcastle
resumed the reading of his draft, and then again the
fated sleep descended upon the eyelids of Ministers.
Later in the evening, and in another room, the
Duke of Newcastle made another and a last effort
to win attention to the contents of the draft, but
again a blissful rest (not this time actual sleep) interposed between Ministers and cares of State; and all,
even those who from the first had remained awake,
were in a quiet, assenting frame of mind. Upon the
whole, the Despatch, though it bristled with sentences
tending to provoke objection, received from the
Cabinet the kind of approval which is often awarded
to an unobjectionable sermon. Not a letter of it
was altered; and it will be seen by-and-by that that
cogency in the wording of the Despatch, which could
hardly have failed to provoke objection from an
awakened Cabinet, was the very cause which governed
events.

Instruc-
tions sent
to the
French
com-
mander. The instructions addressed from Paris to the
French commander did not urge him to propose the
invasion of the Crimea, nor even to lend the weight
of his opinion to the proposed enterprise; but they
forbade him from advancing towards the Danube.
If it should be clear that the English were willing

* See Note in the Appendix.

to undertake the expedition to the Crimea, then the French commander was not to be at liberty to hold back.*

CHAP. XXXI.

* I deduce this conclusion, in an inferential way, from the general tenor of the materials at my command, and not from any one document distinctly warranting the statement.

CHAPTER XXXII.

CHAP.
XXXII.
The Allies
at Varna.
Their
state of
prepara-
tion in the
middle of
July.
 AT the time when the instructions from the Home
Governments reached the camp of the Allies, the
Generals were preparing for an active campaign in
Bulgaria, and Marshal St Arnaud had around him,
in the neighbourhood of Varna or moving thither,
four strong divisions of infantry, with cavalry and
field-artillery. He had no siege-train.

Lord Raglan had around him four divisions of
infantry, the greater part of a division of cavalry,
and of his field-artillery seven batteries. He had
also on board ship off Varna the half of a battering-
train, and the other half of it was nearly ready to
be despatched from England.

The French Marshal was receiving and expecting
constant additions to his force; and Lord Raglan had
been apprised that a reserve division of infantry
under Sir George Cathcart would speedily reach the
Bosphorus.

So long as the French and English forces remained
camped in the neighbourhood of Varna, their command of the sea-communication insured to them the
arrival of the supplies which were sent to them; but

the means of land-transport were not yet within their reach. It was estimated that, in order to move effectively in the interior, the English army alone would require packhorses or mules to the number of 14,000. To obtain these was difficult, but not impossible; and at the time to which we point, about 5000 had been collected. By a continuance of these exertions in Bulgaria, and by due activity in forwarding munitions and stores from England, it is probable that the English force, after a further interval of about six weeks or two months, might have been prepared to move as an army carrying on regular operations; but of course this would only be true upon the supposition that the army should always march through countries yielding sufficient forage.

The preparations of the French were not, perhaps, quite so far advanced as our own; but it is probable that the two armies would have been found ready at about the same time for an active campaign in Bulgaria.

The ships of the Allied Powers were at hand, and their fleets had dominion over all the Euxine home to the Straits of Kertch. They had the command of the Bosphorus, the Dardanelles, the Mediterranean, of the whole ocean; and of all the lesser seas, bays, gulfs, and straits, from the Gut of Gibraltar to within sight of St Petersburg. The Czar's Black Sea fleet existed, but existed in close durance, shut up under the guns of Sebastopol.

CHAP.
XXXII.
Informa-
tion ob-
tained
by the
Foreign
Office as
to the
defences
of the
Crimea.
In the matter of gaining information respecting
the enemy's resources, our Foreign Office had not
been idle; and a great deal of material, bearing upon
this vital business, had been carefully got together
and collated. It resulted from these data, that,
spread over vast space, Russia might nominally have
under arms forces approaching to a million of men;
but that the force in the Crim Chersonese, including
the 17,000 men who formed the crews of the ships,
did not, at the highest estimate, amount to more
than 45,000; and that, although there were a few
battalions which Russia might draw towards Sebastopol
from her army of the Caucasus, she had no more
speedy method of largely reinforcing the Crimea than
by availing herself of the troops then in retreat from
the country of the Danube, and marching them round
to Perekop by the northern shores of the Euxine.

Neither the ambassadors of France and England
at Constantinople, nor any of their generals or
admirals, had succeeded in obtaining for themselves
any trustworthy information upon this vitally momentous business. For their failure in this respect
more blame attaches upon the ambassadors than
upon the military and naval commanders; because
the ambassadors had been in the Levant during a
period of many months, in which (since the war
was impending, but not declared) they might have
bought knowledge from Russian subjects without
involving their informers in the perils of treason.
The duty of gathering knowledge by clandestine

means is one so repulsive to the feelings of an English
gentleman, that there is always a danger of his neglecting it, or performing it ill. Perhaps no two men could be less fit for the business of employing spies than Lord Stratford and Lord Raglan. More diligence might have been expected from the French, but they also had failed. Marshal St Arnaud had heard a rumour that the force of the enemy in the Crimea was 70,000, and Vice-Admiral Dundas had even received a statement that it amounted to 120,000; but these accounts were fables. In point of fact, the information obtained by our Foreign Office approached to near the truth, and the Duke of Newcastle had the firmness — it was a daring thing to do, but it turned out that he was right — he had the firmness to press Lord Raglan to rely upon it. It was natural, however, that a General who was within a few hours' sail of the country which he was to invade, and was yet unable to obtain from it any, even slight, glimmer of knowledge, should distrust information which had travelled round to him (through the aid of the Home Government) along the circumference of a vast circle; and Lord Raglan certainly considered that, in regard to the strength of the enemy in the Crimea and the land defences of Sebastopol, he was simply without knowledge.

Lord Raglan conceived that he was absolutely without any trustworthy information.

CHAPTER XXXIII.

CHAP.
XXXIII.
The In-
structions
for the
invasion
of the
Crimea
reach the
Allied
camp.

On the evening of the 13th of July Marshal St Arnaud received a telegraphic despatch from his Government. The despatch had been forwarded by way of Belgrade, and was in cipher. The message came in an imperfect state. Part of it was intelligible, but the rest was beyond all the power of the decipherer; yet the interpreted symbols showed plainly that the whole message, if only it could be read, would prove to be one of deep import. It forbade Marshal St Arnaud from making any advance towards the Danube, and told him to look to the event of his army being conveyed from Varna by the fleet. This was all that could be deciphered. There were the mystic letters and figures which laid down, as was surmised, the destiny of the Allied armies, and no one could read. At night Colonel Trochu came to Lord Raglan's quarters, and communicated all that could be gathered from the telegraphic despatch. The English General had just received the Duke of Newcastle's letter of the 28th, but had not yet broken the seal of it. Now, however, Lord Raglan opened the letter, and in a few moments he was able to give M. Trochu the means of inferring the matter contained in the illegible part of his despatch. Apparently it was the desire of both the Home Governments that the Allied commanders should prepare to make a descent upon the Crimea and lay siege to Sebastopol.

On the 16th of July the despatch of the 29th of June was received at the English headquarters; and a despatch forwarded from Paris at nearly the same time reached the hands of Marshal St Arnaud.

Since the proposed expedition involved the employment of both land and sea forces, the duty of determining upon the effect to be given to the instructions from home devolved upon those who had the command of the Anglo-French armies and fleets. These were three: Marshal St Arnaud (having Admiral Hamelin under his orders), Lord Raglan, and Vice-Admiral Dundas.

The men who had to determine upon the effect to be give to the instructions

Marshal St Arnaud had not weight proportioned to the magnitude of his command. Reputed at first to be daring even to the verge of rashness, we have seen him so cautioned and schooled into strategic prudence as to have determined to place hundreds of miles of territory, and even the great range of the Balkan, between the French and the Russians; and now, within the last week, he had been almost reproved by his Government for want of enterprise. Colonel Trochu, admitted into consultation upon the most momentous affairs, seemed to wield great authority. At Constantinople and at Varna, no less than in Paris, the Marshal had been made the victim of

Marshal St Arnaud.

unsparing tongues. Indeed at this time two of his
divisional generals openly indulged in merciless invectives against their chief; and soldiers all know
that a general officer thus setting himself against the
commander-in-chief is never without a great following. Perhaps, as had been at first supposed, it may
have been true that boldness and craving for adventure were the true lines of the Marshal's character;
but if that were so, his native ideas had been over-
laid by much counsel, and bent into unwonted shapes.
After a while, as will be seen, his mind, fatigued by
advice, and now and then broken down by bodily
illness, began to lapse into a state which rendered
him almost passive in very critical moments. Naturally,
he had been cowed by the result of his endeavours to
have his own way against Lord Stratford and Lord
Raglan. He was without ascendancy in the camp of
the Allies.

Colonel Trochu was a student of the principles
applicable to formal inland warfare, and it was to be
expected that, the more the obstacles to the proposed
undertaking were canvassed, the more likely it would
be that he would throw the weight of his scientific
advice into the negative scale.

Upon the whole, it resulted, from the composition
of the various forces acting upon the mind of M. St
Arnaud, that, whatever opinion he might lean to, he
was not strong enough to be able to act upon events.
If the English should decide against the project, he
would be well content, and perhaps much relieved.

If, on the other hand, the English should press for its adoption, then the French Marshal would do his best to carry it to a good conclusion. CHAP. XXXIII.

The French fleet was commanded by Admiral Hamelin. It was understood that he disapproved the expedition, but he was under the orders of the chief who commanded the land-forces. *Admiral Hamelin.*

It was not at that time a part of the project to move any very large proportion of the Turkish army to the coast of the Crimea, and therefore the opinion of Omar Pasha would hardly become a governing ingredient in the counsels of the Allies. It was known, however, that he deprecated the proposed invasion. *Omar Pasha.*

The English fleet was commanded by Vice-Admiral Dundas. Most of the Vice-Admiral's latter years had been passed in political and official life, and it was by force of politics that he had now become troubled with the business of war; for his seat at the Admiralty Board, and his subsequent appointment in peace-time to the command of the Mediterranean fleet, were things which stood in the relation of cause and effect. He had not sought to return to scenes of naval strife, but the war overtook him in his marine retirement, converting his expected repose into anxious toil. He was an able, a steadfast, a genial man, and his square Scottish head, and his rough, shrewd, good-humoured eyebrows, had grown grey in the faithful service of a political party. By nature he was so stout-hearted that he could afford to give free, *Admiral Dundas.*

manly counsel without the least dread lest men should
say he was too cautious. His habits as a working
subordinate member of Government, and perhaps,
also, his natural temperament, inclined him to take
a homely view of questions — a view recommended
by what men term "common sense." I am sure,
though I never heard him say so, that he believed
the war to be extremely foolish, and that the less
there was of it the better it would be for the Whigs
and for all the rest of mankind. He spoke and went
straight forward. He thoroughly disapproved the project of invasion, and he said so in plain words. His
opinion sprang, not from dread of peril to the forces
which he himself commanded, but from anxiety —
anxiety in every way honourable to him — for the
safety of the English army. That that anxiety was
altogether vain, or even that it was weakly founded,
few men, speaking with the light of the past, will
be ready to say. Still less will it be thought that the
Vice-Admiral was wrong in giving bold expression
to his views.

Admiral Dundas's command was of course independent of the General in command of the English
army; but the feasibility of the sea-transit was not
at all in question,* and it was plain, therefore, that
the decision would properly rest with those who were
responsible for the direction of the land-forces. So,

---

* Dundas, I think, said fairly and bluntly that he could undertake
to land the army on the coast of the Crimea, but not to supply it, nor to
bring it back.

although he held stoutly to his own opinion, the CHAP.
Vice-Admiral did not fail to give assurance that, if XXXIII.
the decision of the Generals should be in favour of
undertaking the expedition, they might rely upon
the aid of the English fleet.

There remained Lord Raglan; and now it is time Lord
to give the words of the instructions which had been Raglan.
addressed to him, as we have already seen, by the
Secretary of State.

The private letter which was the forerunner of
the detailed despatch ran thus: —

"Since I last wrote to you, events unknown to The in-
"you at the date of these letters have been brought structions
"to us by the telegraph, and the raising the siege the Home
"of Silistria, and the retreat of the Russian army ment.
"across the Danube (preparatory, probably, to a
"retreat across the Pruth), give an entirely new
"aspect to the war, and render it necessary at once
"to consider what shall be our next move.

"The Cabinet is unanimously of opinion that,
"unless you and Marshal St Arnaud feel that you
"are not sufficiently prepared, you should lay siege
"to Sebastopol, as we are more than ever convinced
"that, without the reduction of this fortress and the
"capture of the Russian fleet, it will be impossible
"to conclude an honourable and safe peace. The
"Emperor of the French has expressed his entire
"concurrence in this opinion, and, *I believe*, has
"written privately to the Marshal to that effect.
"I shall submit to the Cabinet a despatch to you on

"this subject, and if it is approved you may expect
"it by the next mail. In the mean time I hope
"you will be turning over in your own mind, and
"considering with your French colleague, what it
"will be safe and advisable to do." *

The promised despatch was in these words: —

"*Secret.*

"War Department, 29th June 1854.

    "MY LORD,

"In my despatch of the 10th April, marked
"'Secret,' I directed your Lordship to make careful
"inquiry into the amount and condition of the Russian
"force in the Crimea, and the strength of the fortress
"of Sebastopol.

"At the same time I pointed out to your Lordship
"that, whilst it was your first duty to prevent, by
"every means in your power, the advance of the
"Russian army on Constantinople, supposing any
"such intention to exist, it might become essential for
"the attainment of the objects of the war to under-
"take operations of an offensive character, and that
"the heaviest blow which could be struck at the
"southern extremities of the Russian empire would
"be the taking or destruction of Sebastopol. The
"events which have recently occurred, and which
"have become known to Her Majesty's Government
"by means of the telegraph from Belgrade, — the
"gallant and successful resistance of the Turkish

    * Private letter from the Duke of Newcastle to Lord Raglan, dated
28th June 1854.

"army — the raising of the siege of Silistria — the
"retreat of the Russian army across the Danube,
"and the anticipated evacuation of the Principali-
"ties, — have given a new character to the war,
"and will render it necessary for you without delay
"to concert measures with Marshal St Arnaud, and
"with Admirals Dundas and Hamelin, suited to the
"circumstances in which these events have placed
"the Allied forces.

"The safety of Constantinople from any invasion
"of the Russian army is now, for a time at least,
"secured; and the advance of the English and French
"armies to Varna and Pravadi has succeeded in its
"object, without their being called upon to meet the
"enemy in action.

"Any further advance of the Allied armies should
"on no account be contemplated. To occupy the
"Dobrutscha would be productive of no beneficial re-
"sults, and would be fatally prejudicial to the health
"of the troops; and even if the Russian army should
"not recross the Pruth, but continue in the occupa-
"tion of the Principalities, it is the decided opinion
"of Her Majesty's Government that, for the present
"at least, no measures should be taken by you to
"dislodge them.

"The circumstances anticipated in my despatch
"before referred to have, therefore, now arrived; and
"I have, on the part of Her Majesty's Government,
"to instruct your Lordship to concert measures for
"the siege of Sebastopol, unless, with the information

"in your possession but at present unknown in this
"country, you should be decidedly of opinion that it
"could not be undertaken with a reasonable prospect
"of success. The confidence with which Her Majesty
"placed under your command the gallant army now
"in Turkey is unabated; and if, upon mature reflec-
"tion, you should consider that the united strength
"of the two armies is insufficient for this undertak-
"ing, you are not to be precluded from the exercise
"of the discretion originally vested in you, though
"Her Majesty's Government will learn with regret
"that an attack, from which such important con-
"sequences are anticipated, must be any longer de-
"layed.

"The difficulties of the siege of Sebastopol appear
"to Her Majesty's Government to be more likely to
"increase than diminish by delay; and as there is
"no prospect of a safe and honourable peace until
"the fortress is reduced and the fleet taken or de-
"stroyed, it is, on all accounts, most important that
"nothing but insuperable impediments — such as
"the want of ample preparations by either army, or
"the possession by Russia of a force in the Crimea
"greatly out-numbering that which can be brought
"against it — should be allowed to prevent the
"early decision to undertake these operations.

"This decision should be taken solely with re-
"ference to the means at your disposal, as compared
"with the difficulties to be overcome.

"It is probable that a large part of the Russian

"army now retreating from the Turkish territory may
"be poured into the Crimea to reinforce Sebastopol.
"If orders to this effect have not already been given,
"it is further probable that such a measure would be
"adopted as soon as it is known that the Allied
"armies are in motion to commence active hostilities.
"As all communications by sea are now in the hands
"of the Allied Powers, it becomes of importance to
"endeavour to cut off all communication by land
"between the Crimea and the other parts of the
"Russian dominions. This would be effectually done
"by the occupation of the Isthmus of Perekop; and I
"would suggest to you that, if a sufficient number of
"the Turkish army can now be spared for this pur-
"pose, it would be highly important that measures
"should be taken without delay for sending an ade-
"quate force to that point, and associating with the
"troops of the Sultan such English and French officers
"as would assist, by their advice, in holding perma-
"nently the position. With the same object, im-
"portant assistance might be rendered by Admiral
"Dundas, if he has yet been able to obtain any
"vessels of a light draught which would prevent the
"passage of Russian troops to the Crimea through
"the Sea of Azov.

"It is unnecessary to express any opinion, at
"this distance from the scene, as to the mode in
"which these operations should be conducted, or the
"place at which a disembarkation should be effected;
"and as the latter will, of course, be decided with

8*

"the advice and assistance of the French and Eng-
"lish Admirals, it is equally unnecessary to impress
"upon your Lordship the importance of selecting
"favourable weather for the purpose, and avoiding
"all risks of being obliged by storms to withdraw
"from the shore the vessels of war and transports
"when only a partial landing of the troops has been
"effected.

"I will not, in this despatch, enter into any con-
"sideration of the operations which it would be de-
"sirable to undertake in Circassia or the coast of
"Abasia. The reduction of the two remaining for-
"tresses of Anapa and Sujak Kaleh would be,
"next to the taking of Sebastopol, of the greatest
"importance, as bearing upon the fortunes of the
"war; but not only is their fall of far less moment
"than that of Sebastopol, but the capture of the
"latter might possibly secure the surrender of the
"Circassian fortresses.

"In the event, however, of delay in undertaking
"these operations being inevitable, and the transports
"being in consequence available for any other ser-
"vice, I wish you to consider, with his Highness
"Omar Pasha and Marshal St Arnaud, whether
"some part of the Turkish army might not be con-
"veyed by steam from Varna, and, by a combined
"movement with the forces of General Guyon and
"Schamyl, so entrap the Russian army in and
"around Tiflis as to compel its surrender to superior
"numbers.

"I have only further to express to you, on the "part of Her Majesty's Government, their entire "reliance in your judgment, zeal, and discretion; "and their conviction that, whilst you will not ex- "pose the army under your command to unnecessary "risk, you will not forget that to the gallantry and "conduct of your troops their countrymen are now "looking to secure, by the blessing of Providence, "the great object of a just war, the vindication of "national rights, and the future security of the peace "of Europe.

> "I have the honour to be,
> "My Lord,
> "Your Lordship's obedient humble servant,
> > "NEWCASTLE."

"General the Lord Raglan, G. C. B.,
     "&c. &c. &c."

In common circumstances, and especially where the whole of the troops to be engaged are under one commander, it cannot be right for any Sovereign or any Minister to address such instructions as these to a General on a distant shore; for the General who is to be intrusted with the sole command of a great expedition must be, of all mankind, the best able to judge of its military prudence, and to give him orders thus cogent is to dispense with his counsel.

But in this war the united forces of France and England were under two commanders; and, besides, since the expedition was dependent upon naval co-operation, the Admirals of the two fleets would

necessarily be taken into council. It is true that
the French Admiral was under the orders of Marshal
St Arnaud, but there was no corresponding arrangement in regard to the English services, and our Admiral's command was independent of the General
commanding the land-forces.

Thus it seemed to the Home Government that
the question, if left to be decided on the shores of
the Black Sea, would have to be weighed, not by
one commander, but by a council of at least four,
and to be actually decided by a council of not less
than three; and it could scarcely be expected that
such a body, deliberating freely, would come to that
vigorous decision which might easily perhaps be
attained by any one of them singly. On the other
hand, the two Governments were perfectly agreed.
Upon the whole, therefore, there was some ground
for resolving to transmit to the camps at Varna the
benefit of that concord which reigned between Paris
and London, and to subject the Generals and Admirals to the overruling judgment of the authorities
at home.

Again, the chief reason which makes it unwise
to fetter the discretion of Generals — namely, the
superior knowledge which they are supposed to have
of the enemy's strength and of the field of operations — was in this instance wanting; for the Generals in the camp at Varna had absolutely no trustworthy information except what came to them from
Paris or London; and in their power of testing the

statements which reached them in this way they were below the Home Governments, for they did not so well know the sources from which the accounts were drawn.

Justice requires that these considerations should have their weight, for they tend in some measure to explain the extreme stringency of the instructions. The Minister who framed them had determined, with a boldness very rare in modern times, to take upon himself an immense weight of responsibility; and, having brought himself to this strong resolve, he rightly and generously did all he could to simplify the task of the General whom he ventured to direct, and to make the path of duty seem clear.

But Lord Raglan had a station in the Allied camp which made it very difficult for the Home Government to take his burthen upon themselves by any mere bold form of words. He commanded the landforces, but he was clothed with a power of older date than the Queen's commission. He had been privy to the business of the wars which England waged in the great days; and if he had seen how Wellington ordered affairs in the field, he had witnessed too his endurance, and helped him in the patient, unapplauded toil by which he prepared the end. Men serving under Lord Raglan were none of them blind to the distance which history herself interposed betwixt their General and themselves. There were none near the chief who would not feel bitter pain if they imagined that words or acts of

The power of deciding for or against the expedition becomes practically vested in Lord Raglan alone.

CHAP.
XXXIII.

theirs had thrown upon his face a shadow. of displeasure. There were no men near him who would not fly with alacrity to execute his slightest wish. The ascendancy of the English General over his own people could not but reach into the French camp. Upon the whole, Lord Raglan had so great an authority in the camp of the Allies, and amongst public men in England, that if he had taken upon himself to resist the pressure of the Secretary of State, he would not have been left without support. On the other hand, if he should determine to follow the will of the Home Government, he would carry the French Marshal with him. So, in effect, the power of deciding for or against the expedition had passed from Paris and from London, and was all concentred in the English General.

Lord
Raglan's
delibera-
tions.

Of the general officers in the English camp there was one whom Lord Raglan had always been anxious to have near at hand: this was Sir George Brown. He was a Scotsman, sixty-six years old, and had served, with a great repute for his daring forwardness, in some of the most bloody scenes of the Peninsular War. He was of an eager, fiery nature, and devoted to the calling of a soldier. After the peace of 1815 he began to hold office in the general staff of the army at the Horse Guards, and in time he became Adjutant-General. He now commanded the Light Division. His zeal, and his lengthened toils in the Adjutant-General's office, had drawn him too far in a narrow path, and he overplied the idea of discipline; but he abounded in energy, and he was in many respects an accomplished soldier. He wrote on military subjects with clearness, with grace, and seemingly with a good deal of ease.

After receiving the Duke of Newcastle's despatch, Lord Raglan sent for Sir George Brown, and expressed to him a wish to have his opinion about it. He handed the paper to Sir George across the table, and then went on with his writing, leaving Sir George to consider its contents at his leisure. When he had read it, Lord Raglan asked him to give him his opinion. Before giving it, Sir George naturally inquired what information Lord Raglan had obtained in regard to the strength of Sebastopol, and what force he expected might be opposed to him in the Crimea.

Lord Raglan's answer was that he had no information whatever; that neither he nor Marshal St Arnaud knew what amount of force the enemy had there; that they believed and hoped there might not be more than 70,000 men in the peninsula; but that in fact, it had not been blockaded, and that no means had been taken to procure information, and that, therefore, they did not in reality know they might not be opposed by 100,000 men, or even more.

Then Sir George Brown said: "You and I are "accustomed, when in any great difficulty, or when "any important question is proposed to us, to ask "ourselves how the Great Duke would have acted "and decided under similar circumstances. Now, I

CHAP.
XXXIII.

"tell your Lordship that, without more certain infor-
"mation than you appear to have obtained in regard
"to this matter, that great man would not have ac-
"cepted the responsibility of undertaking such an
"enterprise as that which is now proposed to you!
"But, notwithstanding that consideration, I am of
"opinion that you had better accede to the proposal
"and come in to the views of the Government, for this
"reason, that it is clear to me, from the tenor of the
"Duke of Newcastle's letter, that they have made up
"their minds to it at home, and that, if you decline
"to accept the responsibility, they will send some
"one else out to command the army who will be
"less scrupulous and more ready to come in to their
"plans."

Lord
Raglan's
determi-
nation.

This suggestion did not at all govern Lord
Raglan's decision. At the time he disclosed no
opinion of his own; but he soon made up his mind.
His decision was governed by views which must be
explained. He believed that the enterprise was one
of a very hazardous kind, and was not warranted
by any safe information concerning the state of the
enemy's forces. Having that conviction, why did he
not feel bound to assert it, notwithstanding the ur-

The
grounds
on which
It rested.

gency of the Home Government? Lord Raglan was,
as might be supposed, deeply imbued with reverence
for the authority of the Duke of Wellington; and,
rightly interpreted, that authority is surely the safest
guide that an English general can follow. But there
is a certain danger in the precepts of the Great Duke,

unless when they are construed down to their right CHAP.
degree of significance by applying to them the splen-XXXIII.
did context of his deeds — for he was accustomed
to use sayings founded on quaint and very literal
readings of our English law; and the loyalty of his
nature rose so high above the reach of all cavil, that
the maxims which he uttered seemed to give a noble
simplicity to the tenor of his public life, though in
reality he rarely or never permitted them to derange
his policy, still less to confuse him in the management of war. Naturally, therefore, men were in
danger of being misled by a too narrow reading of
his precepts. Now, one of the Duke's theories
was, that an officer commanding an army on foreign
service owed obedience to the Secretary of State —
obedience close akin to that which a military subordinate owes to his military chief. If this precept
were to be narrowly construed, a Secretary of State
who conveyed the wishes of the Government to a
general commanding forces abroad would be in
danger of finding that he had shut out from his
counsels the one man in all the world who could best
advise him; and the relations of the Austrian generals
with the old Aulic Council at Vienna would have
to be adopted as a guide, instead of being valued
as a warning. Against this doctrine, understood in
its narrow sense, the Duke of Wellington's whole
military career in Europe was an almost unceasing
rebellion; and it would be hard to find an instance
in which he suffered his designs to be bent awry

by the military opinions of the Home Government.
During the Peninsular War he did not surely pass
his time in obeying the Home Government, but
rather in setting it right, and in educating it, if so
one may speak, for the business of carrying on war.[*]

It is known, however, that Lord Raglan accepted
the Great Duke's precept without much qualification;
and when he applied it to the despatch which had
come to him from the Secretary of State, he saw, as
he believed, where the path of duty lay; for now, in
all its potency, the strange sleep which had come
upon the Cabinet on the 28th of June began to tell
upon events. But for this, or some like physical
cause, it could hardly have chanced that fifteen men,
all gifted with keen intellect, and all alike charged
with a grave, nay, an almost solemn duty, would
have knowingly assented to the draft of a long
and momentous despatch, without seeking to wedge

[*] The fierce, wilful, and contemptuous way in which the Duke of
Wellington dealt with a Secretary of State who ventured to think he
might take him at his word, and make him obey his wish, must be
familiar to every reader of the Despatches; but I may refer to the
specimen which will be found in Sir Arthur Wellesley's letter to Lord
Castlereagh of the 5th of September 1808. I mean the passage beginning, "In respect to your wish that I should go into the Asturias,
"to examine the country and form a judgment of its strength, I have to
"mention to you that I am not a draughtsman." It happened that,
just six days before — namely, on the 30th of August — Sir Arthur had
addressed to the same Secretary of State his customary professions of
obedience: "I shall do whatever the Government may wish;" but he
never thought of suffering himself to be hindered from penning an
angry refusal on the 5th of September merely because he had used a
submissive phrase on the 30th of August.

into it some of those qualifying words which usually
correct the imprudence and derange the grammatical structure of writings framed in Council. A few qualifying words of this sort would have enabled Lord Raglan to act upon his own opinion. But the tranquil mood of the Cabinet on the evening of the 28th of June had prevented the mutilation of the despatch; and it retained so perfectly all that bold singleness of purpose which characterised the mind of the framer, that it virtually directed the English General to undertake the invasion, unless it should happen that he had obtained fresh knowledge of the enemy's strength — fresh knowledge of such a kind as would enable him to controvert the statements sent out to him by the Home Government, and say distinctly that the Russian forces in the Crimea were too numerous to be encountered with common prudence by the Allied armies. Now, Lord Raglan had not succeeded in obtaining any information at all on the subject, and, therefore, the one circumstance which might have relaxed the stringency of the despatch was entirely wanting. In the state of things which actually existed, the Duke of Newcastle's communication was little short of an absolute order from the Secretary of State. The English General determined to obey it.

It was thus that Lord Raglan persuaded himself into the belief that he would be justified in foregoing his own opinion, and acceding to the will of the Home Government; but perhaps, though he knew it

not, he was under the power of a motive more heating than this bare process of the reason.   There
were sentences in the despatch which seemed as
though they were meant for the guidance of one
not sufficiently prone to action.   The writer seemed
to have busied himself in closing the loops by which
a general might seek to escape from the obligation
of having to make the venture.   In reality, as we
have seen, the despatch had been framed with a view
of giving unanimity to a council of generals and
admirals, but it reached its destination at a time
when (for the purpose of this decision) the whole
power of the camp at Varna was centred in the
English General.   Whether meant for the guidance
of a council or not, the despatch was addressed to
one man — and that man was Lord Raglan. Some
may deem it wrong, and may call it a plan of life
too closely deriving from times of chivalry; but it
is still the habit of the English gentleman to think
that his personal honour is no part of the property
of the State, and that even, for what may seem the
public good, he ought not to do a violence to his
self-respect.   He has his code formed in the time
of his boyish conflicts or of his early manhood; and
if there be fire and strength in his nature, he will
not depart from it merely because he has become
responsible and mature in years.   Lord Raglan was
of the bodily nature of those whose blood flushes hot
to the face under the sting of an indignant thought;
and if mortal eyes could have looked upon him when

he resolved the contents of the despatch, they would
have seen him turn crimson in poising the question
whether he ought to resist the pressure of the Queen's
Government, — and to resist because of mere danger.
What the Duke of Newcastle meant was to do all he
reasonably could to enforce the invasion; and, so intending, he did honestly in making his order as peremptory as possible; but if, in any times to come, it
shall be intended that an English general commanding on a foreign service is to exercise his judgment
freely and without passion, the Secretary of State
must not challenge him as Lord Raglan was challenged
by the despatch of the 29th of June.

Lord Raglan's decisions governed the counsels of
the Allied camp; for although the Staff of the French
army* (including, as I believe, M. St Arnaud himself)
were adverse to the undertaking, the Marshal's instructions were so framed that, if the English should be
ready to go forward, he was virtually ordered to
concur in the enterprise;** and we have seen that he
had not such a weight in the French camp as would
have enabled him to oppose any valid resistance to
the wishes of his own Government and the determination of the English General.

In announcing his decision to the Home Govern-

His deci-
sion gov-
erned the
counsels
of the
Allies.

* This will be shown by the narrative in cap. 37, post.
** Lord Raglan had the advantage of knowing (by means of a communication from Lord Cowley) that the "Emperor quite concurred in
"the views of the British Cabinet."

ment, Lord Raglan thus wrote to the Duke of New-castle: —

He an-
nounces
it to the
Home
Govern-
ment.
"It becomes my duty to acquaint you that it was "more in deference to the views of the British "Government as conveyed to me in your Grace's "despatch, and to the known acquiescence of the "Emperor Louis Napoleon in those views, than to "any information in the possession of the naval and "military authorities, either as to the extent of the "enemy's forces, or their state of preparation, that "the decision to make a descent upon the Crimea was "adopted.

"The fact must not be concealed that neither the "English nor the French Admirals have been able to "obtain any intelligence on which they can rely with "respect to the army which the Russians may destine "for operations in the field, or to the number of men "allotted for the defence of Sebastopol; and Marshal "St Arnaud and myself are equally deficient in in-"formation upon these all-important questions, and "there would seem to be no chance of our acquiring "it."[*]

The Duke
of New-
castle's
reply.
The Duke of Newcastle's reply to this despatch was in full consistency with that fearless and un-shrinking assumption of responsibility which had marked his instructions of the 29th of June.

"I wish," he writes,[**] "that circumstances which

[*] 19th July.
[**] Private letter to Lord Raglan, 3d August 1854.

"are engrossing my attention this afternoon per-
"mitted my expressing to you the feelings of intense
"anxiety and interest which your reply of the 19th
"of July to mine of the 29th of June have created in
"my mind. I cannot help seeing, through the calm
"and noble tone of your announcement of the deci-
"sion to attack Sebastopol, that it has been taken in
"order to meet the views and desires of the Govern-
"ment, and not in entire accordance with your own
"opinions. God grant that success may reward you,
"and justify us!

"I wrote to the Queen the moment I received your *The Queen's expression of feeling.*
"despatch, and in answer she said: 'The very impor-
"'tant news which he conveyed to her in it, of the
"'decision of the generals and admirals to attack
"'Sebastopol, have filled the Queen with mixed
"'feelings of satisfaction and anxiety. May the
"'Almighty protect her army and her fleet, and
"'bless this great undertaking with success!'

"Let me add my humble aspirations and prayers
"to those of our good Queen. The cause is a just
"one, if any war is just; and I will not believe that
"in any case British arms can fail. May honour,
"victory, and the thanks of a grateful world attend
"your efforts! God bless you and those who fight
"under you!"

CHAPTER XXXIV.

On the 18th of July a conference took place at Marshal St Arnaud's headquarters. It was attended by the Marshal, by Lord Raglan, and by Admiral Hamelin, by Admiral Bruat (who was the second in command of the French fleet), by Vice-Admiral Dundas, and by Rear-Admiral Sir Edmund Lyons, who was the second in command of the English fleet. It lasted four hours.

Perhaps most of the members of the conference imagined that they were met for the purpose of determining upon the expediency of undertaking the invasion; but Lord Raglan had already made up his mind, not merely to support the wish of his Government in the Allied camp, but to cause its actual adoption; and he was so constituted that he could bring the resources of his mind to bear upon the object in view with as much abundance and strength as if he had himself approved or even devised it. Clearly a discussion upon the expediency of undertaking the enterprise would have been fatal to it; for no member of the conference, except Lyons and (possibly) Bruat, could have conscientiously argued

that the scheme was wise or even moderately prudent.
How was it to be contrived that a council of war,
disapproving the enterprise, should be prevented from
strangling it?

As almost always happened in conferences where
Lord Raglan had the ascendant, the grand question
was quietly passed over, as though it were either
decided or conceded for the purpose of the discussion,
and it was made to seem that the duty which remained to the council was that of determining the
time and the means. The French had studied the
means of disembarking in the face of a powerful
enemy. Sir Ralph Abercromby's descent upon the
coast of Egypt in the face of the French army was
an enterprise too brilliant and too daring to allow
of its being held a safe example, for he had simply
landed his infantry upon the beach in boats, without
attempting, in the first instance, to bring artillery into
action. It seems that hardly any stress of circumstances will induce a French general to bring his
infantry into action upon open ground without providing for it the support of artillery. Naturally,
therefore, the French authorities at Varna were
impressed with the necessity of being able to land
their field-guns in such a way as to admit of their
being brought into action simultaneously with the
landing of their battalions; and, having anticipated
some time before that a disembarkation in the face of
an enemy might be one of the operations of the war,
they had already begun to make the boats required

9*

Lord Rag-
lan's way
of eluding
objec-
tions.

for the purpose. These were flat-bottomed lighters,
somewhat in the form of punts, but of great size,
and so constructed that they would receive the gun-
carriages with the guns upon them, and allow of the
guns being run out straight from the boat to the
beach. It was understood that the building of these
flat lighters would take about ten days; and it was
determined that, in the mean time, a survey of the
coast near Sebastopol should be made from on board
ship, in order to determine the spot best suited for a
descent.

Recon-
naissance
of the
coast.
With a view to cover the reconnaissance and
draw off the enemy's attention, the Allied Admirals
cruised with powerful fleets in front of the harbour
of Sebastopol; and meanwhile the officers chosen for
the service went northward along the coast in the
Fury, seeking out the best place for a landing. The
officers who performed this duty were, on the part of
the French, General Canrobert and Colonel Trochu,
with one engineer and one artillery officer; and on
the part of the English, Sir George Brown, Lieut.-
Colonel Lake, R.H.A., Captain Lovel, R.E., and
Captain Wetherall, of the Quartermaster-General's
department. The Fury was steered by no common
hand.

In the moment when Lord Raglan determined to
treat the instructions of the Government as imperative, and to put them in course for execution, he
came to another determination (a determination which
is not so mere a corollary from the first as men un-

versed in business may think): he resolved to carry
the enterprise through. He knew that, though work
of an accustomed sort can be ably done by official
persons acting under a bare sense of duty, yet that
the engine for conquering obstacles of a kind not
known beforehand, when they are many and big
and unforeseen, must be nothing less than the strong,
passionate will of a man. If every one were to perform his mere duty, there would be no invasion of
the Crimea, for a rank growth of hindrances, springing up in the way of the undertaking, would be
sure to gather fast round it, and bring it in time
to a stop.

Amongst the English Generals there was no one
who had given his mind to the enigma which went
by the name of the "Eastern Question;" but Sir Edmund Lyons had been for many years engaged in
the animating diplomacy of the Levant. In Greece,
the activity of the Czar's agents, or, perhaps, of his
mere admirers, had been so constant, and had generated so strong a spirit of antagonism in the minds
of the few contentious Britons who chanced to ob-
serve it, that the institutions called "The Russian
Party" and "The English Party" had long ago
flourished at Athens; and since Sir Edmund Lyons
had been accredited there for several years as British
Minister, he did not miss being drawn into the game
of combating against what was supposed to be the
ever-impending danger of Russian encroachment. Long
ago, therefore, he had been whetted for this strife;

and now that the "Eastern Question" was to be
brought to the issue of a war in which he had part,
he was inflamed with a passionate zeal. Resuming
at once the uniform and the bearing of his old pro
fession, he cast aside, if ever he had it, all semblance
of diplomatic reserve and composure, and threw himself, with all his seaman's heart, into the business of
the war.

Lord Raglan drew Sir Edmund Lyons into his
intimate counsels. I know not whether this concord
of theirs was ever put into words; but I imagine
that, at the least, I can infer from their actions, and
from the tenor of their intercourse, a silent understanding between them — an understanding that no
lukewarmness of others, no shortcomings, no evasions,
no tardy prudence, no overgrown respect for difficulty or peril, should hinder the landing of the Queen's
troops on the coast of the Crimea. From the time
that Lord Raglan thus joined Lyons to the undertaking he gave it a great momentum. To those
within the grasp of the Rear-Admiral's energy it
seemed that thenceforth, and until the troops should
be landed on the enemy's shore, there could be no
rest for man, no rest for engines. The Agamemnon
was never still. In the painful, consuming passion
with which Lyons toiled, and even, as some imagined, in the anxious, craving expression of his features, there was something which reminded men of
a greater name.

This was the officer who steered the Fury. He

carried her in so close to the shore that the coast could be reconnoitred with great completeness. The officers came to the conclusion (a conclusion afterwards overruled, as we shall see, by Lord Raglan) that the valley of the Katcha was the best spot for a landing.

We saw that the Czar's withdrawal from the Principalities would deprive the German Powers of their main ground of quarrel with Russia, and that our plan of engaging in a great marine expedition against Crim Tartary would cause Austria and Prussia to despair of all effective support from the West, thus driving or tending to drive them into better relations with Nicholas. Before the 28th of July there were signs that this change was beginning to set Russia free from the straits in which she had been placed by the unanimity of the Four Great Powers; and tidings which reached the camp at Varna made it appear (though not with truth) that the Russian commander had not only suspended his retreat, but was commencing a fresh movement in advance. To deliberate upon this supposed change in the character of the war, a conference was held at the French headquarters, and was attended by Marshal St Arnaud, Lord Raglan, General Canrobert, Sir Edmund Lyons, General Martimprey, Sir George Brown, and Colonel Trochu. The French Generals grasped this as an occasion for bringing about the relinquishment of an enterprise which they always had held to be rash. They submitted that the

CHAP. XXXIV.

Rumoured change in the plans of the Czar.

Second conference.

general instructions addressed to both of the Allied
commanders made it their duty to provide, in the
first instance, for the safety of the Ottoman territory, and that, until that object was secured, they
were not warranted in attempting an invasion of a
Russian province far distant from the threatened
frontier of European Turkey; that the order to invade
the coast of the Crimea had been framed by the
Home Governments, and acceded to by the Allied
Generals, upon the assumption that the armed inter-

The
French
urge the
abandon-
ment of
the expe-
dition
against
the
Crimea.
vention of Austria, then believed to be imminent, or,
at the very least, a continuance of her menacing
attitude on the flank of the Russian army, would
preclude any attempt by the Czar to resume his war
on the Danube; that that assumption now unfor-
tunately turned out to be unfounded; and that the
abandonment by Austria of the common cause made
it the bounden duty of the Allied commanders to
return to their defensive measures; because it was
now plain that, if they quitted Bulgaria, Omar Pasha,
without aid from any quarter, would have upon his
hands the whole weight of the Russian army. Now,
then, supposing the premises to be conceded, the
French counsellors had made out good grounds for
abandoning a resolution which, only a week ago,
had been adopted by the Allied commanders.

Lord Rag-
lan's way
of bending
the French
to the
plans of
the Eng.
Lord Raglan, however, was resolved that the
enterprise should go on. From the moment he knew
that the siege of Silistria had been raised, he never
doubted that, for that year at least, the invasion of

European Turkey was at an end. But he knew that
clever men who have taken the pains to build up a
neat logical structure, do not easily allow it to be
treated as unsound merely because it rests upon a
sliding foundation. Without, therefore, combating
the French arguments, he quietly suggested that the
time which must needs elapse before the embarkation might throw new light on the probability of a
renewed attack upon Turkey; and he proposed that,
in the mean time, the preparations for the descent
on the Crimea should be carried on with all speed.
This opinion was adopted by every member of the
conference. The preparations were carried on with
increasing energy; and the theory that it was the
duty of the Allied commanders to abandon the enterprise was never put down by argument, but left to
die away uncontested.

Lord Raglan had been struck with the value of
the French plan for landing artillery on flat lighters,
and Sir Edmund Lyons and Sir George Brown were
despatched to Constantinople, with instructions to do
all they could towards supplying the British army
with means which would answer the same purpose.
They had the good fortune to be aided in their
labours by Lieutenant Roberts, a man of great re-
source and energy, who discovered that a platform
resting upon two boats might be made to serve nearly
as well as one of the French lighters.* How these

---

* Roberts had been a Master in the Navy. See the forcible exposition

men toiled, the world will never know, for History
cannot pause to see them ransacking Constantinople
and the villages of the Bosphorus in their search
after carpenters and planks; but before the appointed
time the whole work was done. This was not all.
Sir Edmund Lyons and Sir George Brown propelled
the arrangements for buying and chartering steamers,
trampling down with firmness, perhaps one might say
with violence, all obstacles which stood in the way.
Of those obstacles one of the most formidable was
what was called in those days the "official fear of
"incurring responsibility." Lyons and Sir George
Brown taught men that, in emergencies of this sort,
they should be pursued with the fear of not doing
enough, rather than with the dread of doing too
much. "I cannot venture," said a cautious official
— "I cannot venture to give the price." "Then I
"can," said Sir George Brown; "I buy it in my own
"name!" It is thus that difficulties are conquered.
When the restless Agamemnon came back into the
Bay of Varna with Lyons and Sir George Brown on
board, Lord Raglan was at the head of a truly British
armament. He had the means, by steam-power, and
at one trip, to descend upon the enemy's coast, with
all his divisions of infantry, with his brigade of light
cavalry, and with the whole of his field-artillery; and
he would be enabled, if he landed in face of an

of his services, and of his cruelly frustrated hopes, in the little work
called "The Service and the Reward," by Mr Cayley.

enemy, to bring his guns into action whilst his in-fantry formed upon the beach.

When the Allied commanders determined to execute the orders addressed to them, they saw the importance of endeavouring to veil their project from the enemy. With this view they tried to induce a belief that Odessa was to be the object of attack; but the measures which they took for this purpose were very slight and weak. To deceive the enemy by the mere spreading of a report, the first step for a general to take would be that of uttering the false word to some of his own people. That would be a difficult service for Lord Raglan to perform; and I do not believe that he ever could or ever did perform it.

Another contrivance for diverting the enemy's attention from the Crimea was that of endeavouring to alarm him for his Bessarabian frontier. Partly to attain this end, and partly, as was surmised, with the more ambitious object of striking a blow at some of the Czar's retiring columns, Marshal St Arnaud moved no less than three divisions into the Dobrudja. But, in truth, all secrecy was forbidden to the Allies. The same power which dictated the expedition precluded its concealment. It was in a council of the whole people that England had resolved upon the enterprise; and what advantage there is in knowledge of an enemy's plans, that she freely gave to Russia. It might seem that for the Emperor of the French, who had shown that he was capable of the darkest

secrecy in his own designs, it must have been trying
to have to act with a Power which propounded her
schemes in print. But, happily, he understood England, and knew something of the conditions under
which she moves into action.

Fire at
Varna.
On the 10th of August a fire broke out in the
British magazines at Varna, and a large quantity of
military stores was consumed.

Cholera.
But another and more dreadful enemy had now
entered' the camp of the Allies. From the period
of its arrival in the Levant, the French army had
been suffering much from sickness. In the British
army, on the contrary, though slight complaints were
not unfrequent, the bodily condition of the men had
been, upon the whole, very good; and so it continued up to the 19th of July. On that day, out of
the whole Light Division, there were only 110 in
hospital. But it seems that one of the omens which
portend the visitation of a great epidemic is a more
than common flush of health. With the French, the
cholera first showed itself on board their troop-ships
whilst passing from Marseilles to the Dardanelles. It
then appeared among the French quartered at Gallipoli, and followed their battalions into Bulgaria.
There its ravages increased, and before the beginning
of the last week in July it reached the British army.
By the 19th of August our regiments in Bulgaria
had lost 532 men. But it was amongst the three
French divisions marched into the Dobrudja, and
especially in General Canrobert's Division, that the

disease raged with the most deadly virulence. In
the day's march, and sometimes within the space of only a few hours, hundreds of men dropped down in the sudden agonies of cholera; and out of one battalion alone it was said that, besides those already dead, no less than 500 sufferers were carried alive in the waggons. On the 8th of August it was computed, by an officer of their Staff, that out of the three French divisions which marched into the Dobrudja, no less than 10,000 lay dead or struck down by sickness.

If the cholera had been confined to the landforces, the Generals would not, perhaps, have allowed it to delay their embarkation; but it now reached the fleets. In a few days the crews were in such a state that all idea of attempting to embark the troops was, for the moment, quite out of the question; and on the 11th and 12th of August the Admirals put out from their anchorage, in the hope of driving away the disease with the pure breezes of the sea. But they had scarcely done this when, on board some of the ships, the mysterious pest began to rage with a violence rare in Europe. The Britannia alone lost 105 men. The number of those stricken, and of those attending upon them, was so great, that it was impracticable to carry on the common duties of the ship in the usual way; and if the disease had continued to rage with undiminished violence for three days more, there would have been the spectacle of a majestic three-decker floating help-

less upon the waves for want of hands to work her.
This time of trial proved the quality of those who
remained unstricken.　There was a waywardness in
the course of the disease, on board British ships, for
which it is difficult to account, — it spared the officers.　On Board British ships of war the seaman is
accustomed to look to those who command him with
a strong affectionate reliance; and now the poor sufferers, in their childlike simplicity, were calling upon
their officers for help and comfort.　An officer thus
appealed to would go and lie down by the side of
the sufferer, and soothe him as though he were an
infant.　And this trust and this devotion were not
always in vain.　Even against malignant cholera
the officer seemed to be not altogether powerless;
for, partly by holding the tortured sufferer in his
kind hands, partly by cheering words, and partly by
wild remedies, invented in despair of all regular medical treatment, he was often enabled to fight the
disease, or to make the men think that he did.

Almost suddenly the pestilence ceased on board
the British ships of war.　The dead were overboard,
and the survivors returned to their accustomed duties
with an alacrity quickened by the delight of looking
forward to active operations against the enemy.　In-
stinctively, or else with wise design, both officers and
men dropped all mention of the tragedy through
which they had passed.*

---

* I was for several days on board the Britannia without once, I

In a few days from the time when the cholera
had been raging with its utmost fury, the crews of the fleet were ready to undertake the great business of embarking the troops and landing them on the coast of the Crimea.

In the camps of the Allied armies, at this time, the cholera had abated, but had not ceased. There were fevers, too, and other complaints. Grievous sickness fell upon that part of our camp which had been pitched in the midst of the beauteous scenery of the lake of Devna, but the whole English army at this time began to show signs of failing health. It appeared that, even of the men out of hospital and actually present under arms, hardly any were in the enjoyment of sound health — hardly any were capable of their usual amount of exertion.

This weakly condition of the men was destined to act, with other causes, in bringing upon the army cruel sufferings; and it may be asked whether, with the soldiers in this condition of body, it was right to undertake an invasion. The answer would be this: the medical authorities thought, and with apparently good reason, that, for troops sickening under the fierce summer heats of Bulgaria, the sea voyage, the descent upon another and more healthy shore, and, above all, the animating presence of the enemy, would work a good effect upon the health of the

think, bearing the least allusion to the pestilence which just four weeks before had slain 105 of the ship's crew.

men; and although these hopes proved vain, they
seemed at the time to rest upon fair grounds.   And,
after all, it is hard to say what other disposition of
the troops would have united the advantages of being better and possible.   To remain in Bulgaria, or
to attempt to operate in the neighbourhood of the
Danube, was to linger in the midst of those very at-
mospheric poisons which had brought the health of
the army to its then state; and, on the other hand,
our people at home would hardly have borne to see
the army sent back to Malta, and forced to recede
from the conflict, for the bare reason that some of
the men were in hospital, and that the rest, without
being ill, were said to be in a weakly condition.

CHAPTER XXXV.

OUR Admiral had at his command the means for conveying the British force to the enemy's shore either in steam-vessels or in sailing-ships towed by steam-power; and, until the eve of the embarkation, the French believed that their resources would enable them to achieve a like result. So, at a conference of the four Admirals held on the 20th of August, it was arranged that the whole of the French and English armament should move from the coast at the same time under steam-power; and the 2d of September was looked forward to as the day when the armament might perhaps go to sea, but the exact time would of course depend upon weather and other circumstances beyond the reach of exact calculation.

On the 24th of August the huge operation of embarking the armies had already begun. The French embarked 24,000 infantry and 70 pieces of field-artillery; but since they were straitened in their means of sea-transport, the number of horses they allotted to each gun was reduced from six to four.

The French embarked no cavalry.* A large portion
of the French troops were put on board ships of war,**
and other portions were distributed among a great
number of sailing vessels. Some of these were very
small craft.

Attached to the French army, and placed under
the orders of Marshal St Arnaud, there was a force
of between 5000 and 6000 Turkish infantry. These
men were embarked mainly or entirely on board
Turkish vessels of war.

Sir Edmund Lyons was charged with the duty
of embarking the English forces; and having first got
on board our 60 pieces of field-artillery, completely
equipped, with the full complement of horses belonging to every gun, he proceeded with the embarkation of the 22,000 infantry and the full thousand of
cavalry which Lord Raglan intended to move from
Bulgaria to the coast of the Crimea. To put on
board ship a body of foot-soldiers is comparatively
a simple process; but the shipping of horses involves
so heavy a cost, so great an exertion of human energy,

* They took with them from 80 to 100 horsemen to perform escort
duty; but of course I do not regard this as an exception to the statement that "no cavalry was embarked."

** Our naval officers are strongly opposed to the practice of putting
troops on board ships of war. They are not the men to set their personal convenience against the exigencies of the public service, but they
cannot endure that the efficiency of a man-of-war should be for one
moment suspended. It is well ascertained, too, that the presence of a
great number of soldiers — men who, for the time of the voyage, are
almost necessarily idlers — is injurious to the discipline of a ship.

that he who undertakes such a task upon anything
like a large scale must needs be a man in earnest. On the other hand, it was clear that, for an invasion of the Crimea, a body of cavalry was strictly needed; therefore a sagacious interpreter of warlike signs, who saw that the English General was embarking a thousand cavalry horses, and that the French were embarking none, would be led to conjecture that the English were resolved to make the descent, and that the French were not. It will be seen, by-and-by, that such a conjecture would have been sound.

The time necessary for embarking a given number of foot-soldiers is small in proportion to that required for getting on board an equal number of troopers with their chargers. Nor is this all. The embarkation of infantry is not necessarily stopped by a moderate swell: the embarkation of cavalry is rendered very slow and difficult by even a slight movement of the sea, and is stopped altogether by a little increase of surf. The business of embarking the British cavalry was checked during some days by a wind from the north-east, and its consequent swell; but afterwards the weather changed, and the whole force was got on board without the loss of a man.*

* The French were not so fortunate, for a painful accident occurred in the course of their embarkation. One of their steam-vessels ran down a boat laden with Zouaves. The men, encumbered by their packs, could do little to save themselves; and more than twenty were drowned.

10*

Lord Raglan could not repress the feeling with which he looked upon the exertions of our naval officers and seamen. "The embarkation," he wrote on the 29th of August — "the embarkation is pro-"ceeding rapidly and successfully, thanks to the able "arrangements of Rear-Admiral Sir Edmund Lyons, "and the unceasing exertions of the officers and men "under his orders. It is impossible for me to express, "in adequate terms, my sense of the value of the "assistance the army under my command derives "from the Royal Navy. The same feeling prevails "from the highest to the lowest — from Vice-Admiral "Dundas to the youngest sailor: an ardent desire to "co-operate, by every possible means, is manifest "throughout; and I am proud of being associated "with men who are animated by such a spirit, and "who are so entirely devoted to the service of their "country."

Failure of
the French
calcula-
tions in
regard to
their com-
mand of
steam-
power.
Of course the French, unencumbered with cavalry, were on board before the English embarkation was complete; but the steam-power at the command of the French fell short, and the necessity of a variation from the plan determined upon by the four Admirals was now announced. On the 4th of September, Admiral Hamelin, and an officer on the staff of the French army, informed Vice-Admiral Dundas that their resources would not, as they had expected, enable them to have their sailing transports towed by steamers.

No explanation was given of the failure which
had thus suddenly crippled the French armament. The result was distressing at the time; for it was seen that the whole flotilla would be clogged by the slowness of the sailing-vessels in which the French troops were embarked, and the fate of the enterprise was rendered more than ever dependent upon the accidents of weather. Marshal St Arnaud grew restless.

CHAPTER XXXVI.

CHAP.
XXXVI.
Excite-
ment and
Impa-
tience of
St Arnaud.
WE have seen that the 2d of September had been
looked forward to as the time for the departure of the
united armaments, and on that day, with military
punctuality, Marshal St Arnaud went to Baljik;
but the wind and the waves are still undisciplined
forces, and the French embarkations were not destined to be completed until the evening of the 4th.
The Marshal, therefore, was kept waiting at Baljik;
and meanwhile sickness began to make havoc with
his troops, for they were densely crowded on board
the transports.

The Marshal was much tortured by the anxiety
which he had had to bear during these three painful
days, and (possibly to calm his mind) Vice-Admiral
Dundas seems to have suggested to him that, his
sailing-vessels not being provided with steam-power
to tow them, he might as well cause them at once to
weigh anchor. By these causes, joined to his irrita-
He is in-
duced to
set sail
without
the Eng-
lish, taking
with him
tion at what he thought the backwardness of the
English embarkations, the Marshal was induced to
determine, not merely that he would act upon
Dundas's suggestion, but that he himself would wait

no longer, and would put to sea on the 5th of September with his sailing fleet; so when on the same morning, Lord Raglan reached Baljik, he was surprised by the intelligence that the Marshal had already sailed out on board the Ville de Paris.

CHAP.
XXXVI.
all his
sailing
fleet and
the troops
on board
them.

On the evening of the 6th the British armament was ready, and the arrangements for the voyage of the whole flotilla complete. The French fleet already at sea consisted of fifteen sail of the line, with ten or twelve war-steamers, and the Turkish fleet of eight sail of the line, with three war-steamers; but the French and the Turkish vessels were doing service as transports, and were so encumbered with troops that they could not have been brought into action with common prudence. It was upon the English fleet, therefore, that the duty of protecting the whole armada really devolved; and, supposing that the enemy were aware of the helpless state of the French and Turkish vessels laden with troops, and of the enormous convoy of transports which had to be protected, he might be expected to judge that it was incumbent upon him to come out of the harbour and assail the vast flotilla of transports; for under the guns of Sebastopol the Russians had fifteen sailing ships of the line,* with some frigates and brigs, and also twelve war-steamers, though of these the Vladimir was the only powerful vessel.** To encounter this

The naval forces of the Allies.

Duty devolving on the English fleet.

* Some say sixteen.
** Unless the Bessarabia be counted as a powerful steamer.

force, and to defend from its enterprises the rest of
the armada, the English had ten sail of the line
(including two screw-steamers), two fiftygun frigates,
and thirteen lesser steamers of war heavily armed.

Arrange-
ments in
regard to
the Eng-
lish con-
voy.
The anxious duty of disposing and guiding the
convoy was intrusted by Admiral Dundas to Sir
Edmund Lyons; and, under Sir Edmund's directions,
Captain Mends of the Agamemnon framed the
programme of the voyage.   On the evening of the
6th the captains of transports were called by signal
on board the Emperor, and there Mends read to
them the instructions which he asked them to obey.
The captains thus addressed were not in the Queen's
service, but they were English seamen, and their
answer was characteristic. They were not flighty
men. They respectfully asked for an assurance that,
in the event of death, their widows would be held
entitled to pensions; and as to the question whether,
of their own free will, they would encounter the
chances of a naval action, they answered it with
three cheers.   It is not by the mere muster-roll
of the army or the navy that England counts her
forces.

The forces
and sup-
plies now
on board.
With his force of horse, foot, and artillery, Lord
Raglan had on board the transports (now all collected
at Baljik)* the full number of ammunition-carts
required for the first reserve of ammunition, the

---

* At the time here spoken of there were two artillery transports
lagging, but they were up in sufficient time

beasts required for drawing them, and sixty other carts, also provided with draught-power. But, in order to move so large a force at one trip, it was found necessary to dispense with the bât-horses of the army, and the force was not provided with means of land-transport either for the tents of the men or for the baggage of the officers. There were also on board large supplies of field-ammunition, of food for the troops, and of barley and hay for the horses. In some of the horse-transports there was an insufficiency of the forage required for the voyage. With that grave exception, all the arrangements seem to have been good. Due means had been taken for insuring, so far as was possible, the simultaneous transit, not only of our ships of war, but of the whole force which Lord Raglan had embarked, together with its vast appendage of warlike stores and provisions; for every sailing-vessel, whether she were a ship of war or a transport, was towed by a sufficiently powerful steamer. None of our ships of war carried troops on board; they were all, therefore, ready for action.

In addition to the forces and the means of land-transport which were actually on board, Lord Raglan had in readiness for embarkation the whole brigade of heavy cavalry, another division of infantry, a siege-train,* and some five or six thousand pack-

---

* The additional division of infantry (the 4th Division) was at Varna; the Scots Greys were on the Bosphorus; and the rest of the

CHAP.
XXXVI.
horses. The sick remained in Bulgaria, and such of the men out of hospital as seemed to be in a very weakly state were left at Varna and omployed in garrison duty.

Vice-Admiral Dundas, commanding the whole British fleet, had his flag on board the Britannia; Lyons, in the Agamemnon, had charge of the convoy. Each vessel had assigned to her the place she was to take when the signal for moving should be given.

Before night the whole of the English flotilla, together with that part of the French and the Turkish flotilla which had the command of steam-power, was assembled in Baljik Bay, and in readiness to sail on the morrow.

Departure of the English Armada and of the French steam-vessels.
Men remember the beauteous morning of the 7th of September. The moonlight was still floating on the waters, when men, looking from numberless decks towards the east, were able to hail the dawn. There was a summer breeze blowing fair from the land. At a quarter before five a gun from the Britannia gave the signal to weigh. The air was obscured by the busy smoke of the engines, and it was hard to see how and whence due order would come; but presently the Agamemnon moved through, and with signals at all her masts — for Lyons was on board her, and was governing and

heavy cavalry in Bulgaria, where also the bât-horses were left. The siege-train was on board off Varna.

ordering the convoy. The French steamers of war
went out with their transports in tow, and their
great vessels formed line. The French went out
more quickly than the English, and in better order.
Many of their transports were vessels of very small
size; and of necessity, therefore, they were a swarm.
Our transports went out in five columns of only
thirty each. Then — guard over all — the English
war-fleet, in single column, moved slowly out of the
bay. *

Here, then, and apart from the bodies of foot and
artillery embarked by the French and the Turks,
there was an armament not unworthy of England.
Without combat, and by the mere stress of its presence, our fleet drove the enemy's flag from the seas
which flowed upon his shores, ** and a small but
superb land-force, complete in all arms, was clothed
with the power of a great army by the ease with
which it could be thrown upon any part of the
enemy's coast. ***

* I did not reach the fleet till some three days afterwards, when it
was anchored at the rendezvous; and my impression of the scene in
the Bay of Baljik is derived partly from some MSS. which have been
furnished to me, but partly also from what struck me as a very good
account of it, which I saw in a printed book, by Mr Wood, a
spectator.

** I am justified in speaking of the English fleet as the force which
kept the enemy's ships in duress, because, as we have seen, the French
men-of-war were doing duty as transports, and were not, therefore, in
a state for going into action.

*** I of course speak here of the inherent power of such an
armament, without reference to the fact that strictly-defined in-

Lord Raglan had not suffered himself to be dis-
concerted by the departure of Monsieur St Arnaud,
and the consequent severance of the Allied forces.
No steamer was sent to re-knit his communications
with the errant French Marshal.

structions had been addressed to Lord Raglan, and that the purport of
these had become known to the enemy. The fixedness of the plan of
campaign, and the publicity which it had obtained, reduced the power
of the force to the level of its actual numbers and its intrinsic
strength.

CHAPTER XXXVII.

We have seen that Marshal St Arnaud, under CHAP.
feelings of some vexation, put to sea on the morning XXXVII.
of the 5th of September. He could not but know
that, by his abrupt separation from the British fleet
and army, he had offended against the English
General. Upon reflection, he could not but grieve
that he had done this. But he had put to sea,
and had since heard no tidings from the shore.
No swift steamer had followed him with entreaties
to stay his course. He was left free to pursue his
voyage; and the voyage was growing more and more
dismal.

"The Black Sea" is a truer name than the
"Euxine." Now, as in old times (if the summer be
hardly past), the voyager leaves a coast smiling
bright beneath skies of blue and glowing with sunny
splendour; yet, perhaps, and in less than an hour,
the heavens above and the waters around him are
dark with the gloom and threatening aspect belonging to the Northern Ocean.* Monsieur St Arnaud

* The contrast between the climate of the Black Sea and that of
the countries which surround it is one of the enigmas to which scienti-

CHAP.
XXXVII.

Marshal
St Arnaud
at sea
without
the Eng-
lish.

His
anxiety.

He sails
back.

encountered this change. The wind blew from its
dark quarter. Every hour was carrying the Marshal
farther and farther into the centre of the inhospitable
sea, farther and farther from the English fleet, farther
and farther from Lord Raglan. If he went on, there
was no junction to look for except at an imaginary
point marked with a pencil on the charts, but having
no existence in the material world; and from the
wind and the angry waves, no less than from his
own fast-cooling thoughts, he began to receive a distressing sense of his isolation. The struggle in his
mind was painful, but it came to an end. "I am
"nearly twenty leagues," writes the Marshal, on the
evening of the 6th, to Lord Raglan — "I am nearly
"twenty leagues north-east of Baljik, separated from
"the English fleet, and from the part of my own
"convoy which was to sail with the convoy of the
"English fleet. Admiral Dundas's last letter being
"worded conditionally, so far as concerns his sailing
"this morning, I am not sure of not seeing increased,
"in great proportions, the distance which separates
"me from you, and then there is reason to fear cir-
"cumstances of wind or sea which would render our
"junction difficult, and might compromise everything
"definitively. In this painful situation I decide to
"invite Admiral Hamelin (on his declaration that he
"cannot wait where he is) to return to meet the fleet

fic men have applied their minds; but whether, as yet, with success,
I cannot say.

and the convoy." So the Marshal sailed back.
Thus, happily, ceased the impulse which had threatened to sunder the fleets.

Lord Raglan's answer was stern. He removed the *Lord Raglan's reproof.*
grounds which the Marshal had assigned for his de-
parture, and then pointed gravely to the true line of
duty for the future. "Thanks be to God," he wrote,
"everything now favours our enterprise. Very soon
"we shall reach the appointed rendezvous, and then
"we shall have an opportunity of showing that our
"manner of acting together remains unaltered, and
"that the sincerity of which you speak will continue,
"as at present, to be our guide and our mutual satis-
"faction." *

Coming from Lord Raglan, this language was a
reproof; but the result tends to show that it was
happily adjusted to the object in view. Thenceforth *Its good effect.*
there was no longer any tendency on the part of
Marshal St Arnaud to break away from his colleague. From the hour of the first conference at
the Tuileries, in the spring of the year, Lord Raglan's *Lord Raglan's increasing ascendancy.*
authority in the Allied councils had been always in-
creasing; and now as we shall presently see, it
gained a complete ascendant.

On the 8th the great flotilla, moving under *The whole Allied Armada comes together at sea.*
steam, came up with the French and the Turkish
sailing fleets which had left Baljik on the 5th of
September. The French fleet was in double column,

---

* Translated from the French, in which the letter was written.

and tacking to eastward across the bows of the steam flotilla; but upon being approached, the French ships backed topsails and lay to. Every one of the French vessels had kept its position beautifully; and the moment the signal to lie-to was given, it was obeyed with a quickness which was honestly admired by our seamen. The Turkish fleet also lay-to, and for a while the whole armada of the Allies was gathered together. But the English fleet, being moved by steam, kept on to windward; and presently the French and the Turks began to sail off on opposite tacks. Between the fleets thus departing, the English flotilla of transports passed through in five columns.

But the fleets are again parted.

The rendezvous was to be at a point forty miles due west of Cape Tarkan, and thither moved the three fleets with all their convoy.

Step taken by French officers with a view to stop the expedition against Sebastopol

There were in the French army several officers holding high command — and being otherwise men of great weight — who had become very thoughtful on the subject of the contemplated descent upon the enemy's coast. Personally, they were men quite as dauntless as those who gave no care to the business in hand; but being versed in the study, if not in the practice, of the great art of war, they had become strongly impressed with the hazardous character of the intended enterprise. It seems probable that, up to this time, they had relied upon the mature judgment and the supposed discreetness of Lord Raglan to prevent what they regarded as a rash attempt. It

might well seem natural to them that two Governments in the West of Europe, attempting to dictate
an invasion of a Russian province at a distance of
3000 miles, would, sooner or later, be checked in
their project by the generals commanding the forces;
and, of course, they would have liked that the dis-
favour which unjustly attaches to military prudence
should fall upon the English General rather than
upon themselves or their own commander. But in
the course of the 7th of September it became known
to them that Lord Raglan was already at sea. They
then knew, or rather they then recognised the fact,
that the whole armada was really gliding on towards
the enemy's coast, and the ferment their minds
underwent now brought them to take a strange step.

Lord Raglan was on board the Caradoc; and on
the 8th of September, whilst the fleets lay near to
one another, this vessel was boarded by Vice-Admiral
Dundas. He came to say that a French steamer had
conveyed to him the desire of the Marshal St Arnaud
to see Lord Raglan and the Vice-Admiral Dundas,
and to see them on board the Ville de Paris, because
the Marshal himself was too ill to be able to move.
It happened that the sea at this time was rough, and
the naval men thought that it would be difficult for
Lord Raglan, with his one arm, to get up the side of
the three-decker in which the Marshal was sailing;
Lord Raglan, therefore, deputed his military secretary,
Colonel Steele, to accompany Vice-Admiral Dundas
on board the Ville de Paris.

CHAP.
XXXVII.
St Arnaud
disabled
by illness.

The Vice-Admiral and Colonel Steele found the Marshal sitting up, but in a state of much suffering, and they were informed that he was very ill. He, however, sat at the conference; and the other persons present were — Admiral Hamelin, Admiral Bruat, Admiral Count Buat Wiliaumez, Colonel Trochu, General Rose, Vice-Admiral Dundas, and Colonel Steele. The Marshal took no part in the discussion which ensued. It seems he could hardly speak.

Unsigned
papers
read to
the con-
ference.

It was stated that the meeting had been summoned in order that a paper might be read to it. The document bore no signature, and Marshal St Arnaud was no party to it; but it was stated that it emanated from General Canrobert, General Martimprey, and the principal officers of the French artillery and engineers; and it was said, too, that General Rose* had furnished some of the materials from which it was composed.

The document took it for granted that there were three places for landing which merited discussion — the Katcha, the Yetsa, and Kaffa; and it then went on to show the advantages and the drawbacks which would attend an attempt to land at each of those three spots. The objections to the

* Now Sir Hugh Rose, the officer spoken of as Colonel Rose in vol. i. He was at this time accredited as British Commissioner at the French headquarters. I have no reason for supposing that he intended to give any sanction to the step taken by the French remonstrants; and I imagine that any materials which he may have put in their hands must have been confined to maps or statements showing the physical character of the country about to be invaded.

landing at the Katcha were stated with so much force as to show that the framers of the document entirely disapproved it; and indeed they urged that any landing north of Sebastopol would be surely followed by disastrous results. The document also raised weighty objections to a descent upon the coast near the Yetsa. The only plan which was made to appear at all justifiable was that of a landing at Kaffa; and although the difficulties attending even that operation were placed in a strong light, it was orally stated that the framers of the document considered that plan to be one nearly free from objection.

Now Kaffa was a seaport in the eastern part of the Crimean peninsula, and divided from Sebastopol by many long marches over mountain-roads. The autumn had already come. The landing at Kaffa implied an abandonment, for that year at least, of all attempts against Sebastopol. It was to attack Sebastopol forthwith, and in the year 1854, that the great flotilla with all its precious freight had been gathered together; and now, whilst the vast armada was moving towards the enemy's coast, there came from the men of weight and science in the French army this singular protest — for that is what it really was — against an enterprise already begun.

Marshal St Arnaud was in a painful strait. Being, St Arnaud leaves all to Lord Raglan. as he knew, without ascendancy in the French army, he apparently thought that the weight attaching to the combined opinion of all the protesting officers

11*

was too great to warrant him in meeting their inter-
position with reproof or inattention; yet, suffering as
he did at the time under bodily anguish, he was ill
able to go into the discussions thus strangely forced
on by the remonstrants. He found a solution. He
desired Colonel Trochu to say that he would concur
in any decision to which Lord Raglan might come.

Confer-
ence ad-
journed
to the
Caradoc. The conference, therefore, was adjourned to the
Caradoc; and Lord Raglan and Sir Edmund Lyons
were then present at it, together with all those who
had met on board the Ville de Paris, except only
Marshal St Arnaud.

Thus, then, the ebullition of prudence which had
broken out amongst the officers of the French army
came under the arbitrament of the English General;
and with him, and with him only, it rested to determine the movements of the whole Allied force.

The business of the conference was opened by
Colonel Trochu. This officer, as we have already
seen, was supposed to be better acquainted than
any one else with the mind of the French Emperor;
and his counsels, no longer bending in the direction
of extreme caution, were now rather in favour of
enterprise. The Colonel had possession of the document. He read it aloud; and, as he went on with
the perusal, he commented upon every point; but
he declared that he was no party to the contents of
the paper, and that he did not share the anxieties *

---

* "Préoccupations."

either of the army or the navy as to the disasters
which might be expected to follow from a landing on
the coast to the north of Sebastopol.

Thereupon Admiral Bruat repudiated the supposition of his being a party to the apprehensions attributed to the Admirals. Lyons also repudiated it.
Neither he nor Vice-Admiral Dundas had known
before the conference that any such step as that of
framing and presenting the remonstrance had been
imagined by the French officers, and, as might be
expected, they were both very sure that nothing of
the kind had sprung from the British navy.

The inference which Lord Raglan drew from the
document was, that it evinced "an indisposition to
"the expedition amongst the officers who are sup-
"posed to be looked up to and to exercise influence
"in the French army;" and, "in fact," said he, "we
"were told as much at the meeting here on Friday."

These, then, were the "timid counsels"* of which
the French Emperor afterwards spoke when he
ascribed the glory of overruling them to Marshal St
Arnaud. If it was right, as most men will think it
was, that these counsels should be overruled, there

---

* "Timides avis." When this letter of the French Emperor first
appeared, it was imagined that the imputation of giving "timid"
counsels was intended to be cast upon some of our Generals or Admirals; but the Duke of Newcastle, with a becoming spirit, determined
instantly that this should not be suffered to pass; and the "Moniteur"
was afterwards made to explain officially that the "timides avis" were
attributed by the Emperor, not to any Englishman, but to some un-
named officers in the French service.

was merit due to St Arnaud; but his merit lay, not
in any personal resistance which he was able to
oppose to his counsellors (for he was helpless, as we
have seen, from bodily illness), but in the sagacity
and good sense which had led him to intrust the
decision to his English colleague.

Lord Rag-
lan's way
of dealing
with the
French
remon-
strants.
Lord Raglan's method of dealing with the protest
of the French authorities was characteristic of himself and of the English nature. He did not much
combat the objections set down in the paper, but he
passed them by, and quietly lowered the debate from
the high region of strategy to a question of humbler
sort — a question as to what four steamers could be
most conveniently employed for a reconnaissance on
the enemy's coast.

So the conference which had been summoned to
judge whether the enterprise against Sebastopol
should not be brought to a stop, now found itself
only deciding that the vessels sent on the reconnaissance should consist of one French steamer, together with the Agamemnon, the Caradoc, and the
Sampson.

But, in truth, the powers of the conference had
silently passed into the hands of one man. Thenceforth the protest was dropped; for if its framers had
risen up against the notion of being drawn on into
His now
complete
ascendant.
what they thought a rash venture by the mere
effect of M. St Arnaud's acquiescence, they were
calmed when they came to know that the whole
force at last had a leader. If still they held to

their opinions, they did so in a spirit of cheerful deference, which prevented them from throwing any further obstacle in the way of the enterprise. The armada moved on.

Again and again it has happened that mighty armaments, including the forces of several States and people of diverse races, have been gathered and drawn into scenes of conflict by the will of one man; but, in general, when such things have been done, the compelling mind has been brought to its resolve by the cogency of satisfied reason or by force of selfish desire. What was new in this enterprise was, that he who inexorably forced it on did not of himself desire it, nor deem it to be wise, nor even in a high degree prudent; and the power which had strength to bend the whole armada to the purpose of the invasion was, not ambition inflamed, nor reason convinced, but the mere loyalty of an English officer refusing to stint the obedience which he owed to the Minister of his Queen.

The use he makes of his power.

On the 9th, the whole of the English fleet with all its convoy was anchored in deep water at the appointed rendezvous, a spot forty miles west of Cape Tarkand.

The English fleet at the point of rendezvous.

Lord Raglan made haste to use the great powers with which he was now invested, and he determined to reconnoitre the coast with his own eyes. At four o'clock on the morning of the 10th, General Canrobert and the other French officers who were to attend the reconnaissance came on board the Caradoc. Lord

Lord Raglan in person undertakes a reconnaissance of the coast.

CHAP.
XXXVII.
Raglan had with him Sir Edmund Lyons, Sir John
Burgoyne, and Sir George Brown. Not long after
daybreak the Caradoc neared Fort Constantine, and
then approached the entrance of the harbour. It
was a fair, bright morning, and the Sunday bells
were ringing in the churches when Lord Raglan first
saw the great forts, and the ships, and the glittering,
cupola'd town. Afterwards, the vessel being steered
round off Cape Chersonesus, he could see two old
Genoese forts, and ridges of hills dividing the great
harbour from the southern coast of the peninsula.
What he looked on was for him fated ground, for
the Genoese forts marked the inlet of Balaclava,
and the ridges he saw were the "heights before
"Sebastopol." But the future lay hidden from his
gaze.

The Caradoc was now steered towards the north,
and the officers on board her surveyed the mouths
of the Belbek, the Katcha, the Alma, and the Bulganak, and the coast stretching thence to Eupatoria.
Of the sites thus reconnoitred, General Canrobert
thought the Katcha the one best fitted for a landing.
Lord Raglan entirely disapproved of the Katcha,
and he did not at all like the ground at the mouths
of the other rivers; but when, moving on in the
Caradoc, he was off the part of the coast which
lies six miles north of the Bulganak, he observed
an extended tract of beach, which seemed to him to
be the ground for which the Allies were seeking.
Without generating a debate upon the subject, he

nevertheless elicited so much of the opinion of those around him as he deemed to be useful. Then he declared his resolve. He said that the Allied armies should land at Old Fort.

There are times when, to anxious, doubting mortals, no boon from Heaven is so welcome as the final resolve which is to govern their actions. It was so now. Debating ceased, and a happy alacrity came in its stead. That day our fleet and the swarming convoy close gathered around had been still lying anchored in deep water at the point of rendezvous. To many those long, peaceful Sabbath hours seemed to token a wanton delay, or worse than delay — some faltering in the great purpose of the Allies: but at night the Caradoc came in; and soon, though few could tell whence came the change, nor what had been passing, there flew from deck to deck a joyful belief — a belief that in some way — in some way not yet understood, the enterprise had gathered new force.

The French and Turkish fleets, less amply provided with steam-power than the English, had fallen to leeward; but on the evening of the 11th they were anchored within thirty miles of the British fleet, and the communication was, of course, kept up by steam-vessels.

During the whole of Tuesday the 12th, the French, Turkish, and English fleets were slowly drawing together and converging upon the enemy's coast. Before sunset the armed navies were all near to-

The whole
Armada
con-
verging on
the coast
of the
Crimea.

gether, and from their decks men could make out
with glasses the low cliff to the north of Eupatoria.
The English fleet anchored for the night. The French
Admiral sent to intimate that he would not anchor,
but go on all night, in the hope of being ready for
the landing the next morning. Vice-Admiral Dundas
saw that that hope was vain, because large portions
of the French convoy were still so distant that there
could be no landing on the following day. The
French, it will be remembered, were without steam-
power for their transports, and the breezes were light.
So, although every hour saw fresh clusters of vessels
slowly closing with the fleet, the sea, towards the
west, was always strewed with distant sails, and,
before the hulls of those hove well in sight, the
horizon got speckled again with sails more distant
still. So the English Admiral anchored his fleet for
the night.

The next morning, the 13th, the Ville de Paris,
under tow of the Napoleon steamer, had come up;
and, although, so late as noon, some of the French
ships of war, and very many of their transports,
were still distant, they were under such breezes as
promised to enable them to close before long with
the fleets. So, virtually, the momentous voyage was
over. The weather — and upon that, in such under-
takings, the hopes of nations must rest — the weather
had favoured the enterprise; but the pest of modern
armies had not relented. The cholera had followed
the men into the transports. Many sickened on

board the troop-ships whilst they were still off
Varna or Baljik, and were carried back to die on
shore. During the Voyage many more fell ill, and
many died.

But Marshal St Arnaud, whose illness scarce three
days before seemed bringing him fast to his end, was
now almost suddenly restored, and on the morning
of the 13th he was like a man in health. During The progress
made by
Lord Rag-
lan during
the
Marshal's
illness. the interval of five days, in which the Marshal's
illness had invested his English colleague with a
supreme control, Lord Raglan had used to the
full the occasion which Fortune thus gave him. In
that time he had repressed the efforts of the French
Generals who strove to bring the enterprise to a
stop; he had committed the Allies to a descent upon
the enemy's shores — on his shores to the north
of Sebastopol; he had reconnoitred the coast; he
had chosen the place for a landing; and meanwhile
he had drawn the fleets on, so that now, when men
looked from the decks, they could see the thin strip
of beach where the soldiery of the Allies were
to land.

CHAPTER XXXVIII.

CHAP.
XXXVIII.
Our ignor-
ance of
the coun-
try and
of the
enemy's
strength.

CONCERNING the country which they were going to invade the Allies were poorly informed. Of Sebastopol, the goal of the enterprise, they knew little, except that it was a great military port and arsenal, and was deemed impregnable towards the sea. Respecting the province generally, it was known, by means of books and maps, that Crim Tartary, or "the Crimea," as people now called it, was a peninsula situate between the Black Sea and the Sea of Azof; and there was a theory — not perfectly coinciding with the truth — that the only dry communication with the mainland was by the isthmus of Perekop. It was understood that the north of the peninsula had the character of an elevated steppe — that towards the south it was rocky and mountainous — — and that the undulating downs which connected the steppe with the mountainous region of the south were seamed with small rivers flowing westward from the summits of the highland district. *   It was

* A great body of most valuable information respecting the Crimea had been imparted to the English public by General (then Colonel) Mackintosh, and the Colonel had also addressed important reports on

believed that the main of the inhabitants were Tartars, men holding to the Moslem faith. Of the enemy's forces in this country, the Allies, in a sense, were ignorant; for although the information which had come round to them by the aid of the Foreign Office was in reality well founded, they did not believe at the time that they could at all rely upon it, and therefore they were nearly as much at fault as if they had had no clue. They knew, however, that the peninsula was a province of Russia — that Russia was a great military power — that, so long as three months ago, the invasion had been counselled in print — and that afterwards the determination to undertake it had been given out aloud to the world. From these rudiments, and from what could be seen from the decks of the ships, they inferred that, either upon their landing, or on some part of the road between the landing-ground and Sebastopol, they would find the enemy in strength.

But beyond this little was known; and the imagination of men was left to range so free that, although they were in the midst of their "19th century," with all its prim facts and statistics, the enterprise took something of the character of adventure belonging to earlier ages. Common, sensible, fanciless men — men wise with the cynic wisdom of London clubs — were now by force turned into

This gives to the expedition the character of an adventure.

the same subject to the military authorities. What I intend to indicate in the text is, not that the means of knowledge were wanting, but that they had not been extensively taken advantage of.

CHAP.
XXXVIII venturers, intent, as Argonauts of old, in gazing
upon the shores of a strange land to which they were
committing their lives. From many a crowded deck
they strained their eyes to pierce the unknown. They
could not see troops. They saw a road along the
shore: now and then there appeared a peasant with
a cart; now and then a horseman riding at full speed.
Neither peasant nor horseman seemed ever to pause
in his duty that he might cast a glance of wonder
at the countless armada which was gathering in upon
his country. At the northern end of the bay there
was a bright little town: maps showed that this was
Eupatoria.

Occupa-   At noon on the 13th the English fleet had drawn
tion of
Eupatoria. near to this port of Eupatoria. There were no Russian forces there except a few convalescent soldiers;
and the place being defenceless, Colonel Trochu and
Colonel Steele, accompanied by Mr Calvert the interpreter, were despatched to summon it. The governor
or head man of the place was an official personage
in a high state of discipline. He had before his eyes
the armed navies of the Allies, with the countless
sails of their convoys; and to all that vast armament
he had nothing to oppose except the forms of office.
But to him the forms of office seemed all-sufficing,
and on these he still calmly relied; so, when the
summons was delivered, he insisted upon fumigating
it according to the health regulations of the little
port. When he understood that the Western Powers
intended to land, he said that decidedly they might

do so; but he explained that it would be necessary
for them to land at the Lazzaretto, and consider themselves in strict quarantine.

On the following day the place was occupied by a small body of English troops. The few Russian inhabitants of the place, being mainly or entirely official personages, had all gone away, but the Tartar inhabitants remained; and although these men did not exhibit, as some might have expected, any eager or zealous affection for the allies of the Caliph, they seemed inclined to be friendly. Thoughtful men cared deeply to know whether between these natives and the Allies the relation of buyer and seller could be established — for it was of vital moment to the success of the expedition that the Allies should be able to obtain supplies of cattle and forage in the invaded country; and it was probable that much would turn upon the success of the first attempt to make purchases from the people of the country. The first experiment which was made in this direction elicited a curious proof of the difficulty which there is in causing mighty nations to act with the fore-thought of a single traveller. It was to be expected that, at the commencement of any attempted inter-course, the willingness of the natives to sell would depend upon their being tempted by the coins to which they were accustomed; because just at first they would not only be ignorant of the value of foreign money, but would also dread the consequence of being found in possession of coin plainly received

from the invaders. Yet the precaution of bringing
Russian money had been forgotten by the public
authorities; and when Mr Hamilton of the Britannia
was preparing to land, with a view of endeavouring
to begin a buying-and-selling intercourse with the
natives, he had nothing to offer except English so-
vereigns. It chanced, however, that there were two
or three English travellers on board the flag-ship,
and that these men (foreseeing the likelihood of their
having to buy horses or make other purchases from
the natives of the invaded country) had supplied
themselves with some of the gold Russian coins called
"half-imperials," which were to be obtained without
difficulty at Constantinople. The travellers — Sir
Edward Colebrooke, I think, was one of them — advanced as many of these as they could spare to the
public authorities; and Mr Hamilton being thus
enabled to land with a small supply of the magic
half-imperials, and being, besides, a good-tempered,
humorous man, with a tendency to make cordial
speeches in English to all his fellow-creatures alike,
whether Russian, or Tartar, or Greek, he was able
to make a merry beginning of that intercourse with
the natives which was destined to become a fruitful
source of strength to the Allied armies. The gains
made by the first sellers soon drew fresh supplies
into the place from the surrounding country; the
commissariat afterwards began its operations in the
town, and in time a good lasting market was opened
to the invaders.

After receiving the surrender of Eupatoria on the afternoon of the 13th, the assembled armada moved down towards the south. All day there were sailing-vessels approaching from a distance, and closing at last with the French fleet; but before night (with the exception, it is believed, of two or three small lagging transports) the three fleets, and the host of vessels which they convoyed, were anchored near Old Fort in Kalamita Bay. The united armada extended in a line parallel with the coast, and in a direction, therefore, not far from north and south. The French and the Turkish fleets were on the south or right-hand side; the British fleet took the north, and formed the left of the Allied line.

CHAP. XXXVIII.
The whole armada gathers towards the chosen landing-place.

CHAPTER XXXIX.

THE ground chosen by Lord Raglan for the landing of all the Allied forces is five or six miles north
of the Bulganak River. It gained its name of "Old
Fort" from an indication appearing on the maps,
rather than from any slight traces of the structure
then remaining. Along this part of the coast the
cliffs rise to a height of from 60 to 100 feet, and for
the most part they impend too closely over the sea
to allow much room for the beach. Near "Old Fort,"
however, the high grounds so recede that at first
sight they appear to embrace a small bay or inlet of
the sea, but upon a nearer approach it is perceived
that the inner part of the seeming bay is a salt-water
lake, and that this lake is divided from the sea by
a low, narrow strip of beach. A little further north
the same disposition of land and water recurs; for
there, also, another salt lake, called the lake of
Kamishlu, is divided from the sea by a low, narrow
strip of beach a mile and a half in length. The
first-mentioned strip of beach — namely, the strip
opposite to Old Fort — was the one which Lord
Raglan had chosen for the landing of all the Allied
armies.

BLATE No 2

The landing places of the Allies.

A.B. The ground chosen for the landing
      place of the allied armies.
C. The spot where the buoy was to be.
D. The spot where during the night the French placed the buoy.
E.F. The ground where the English ...

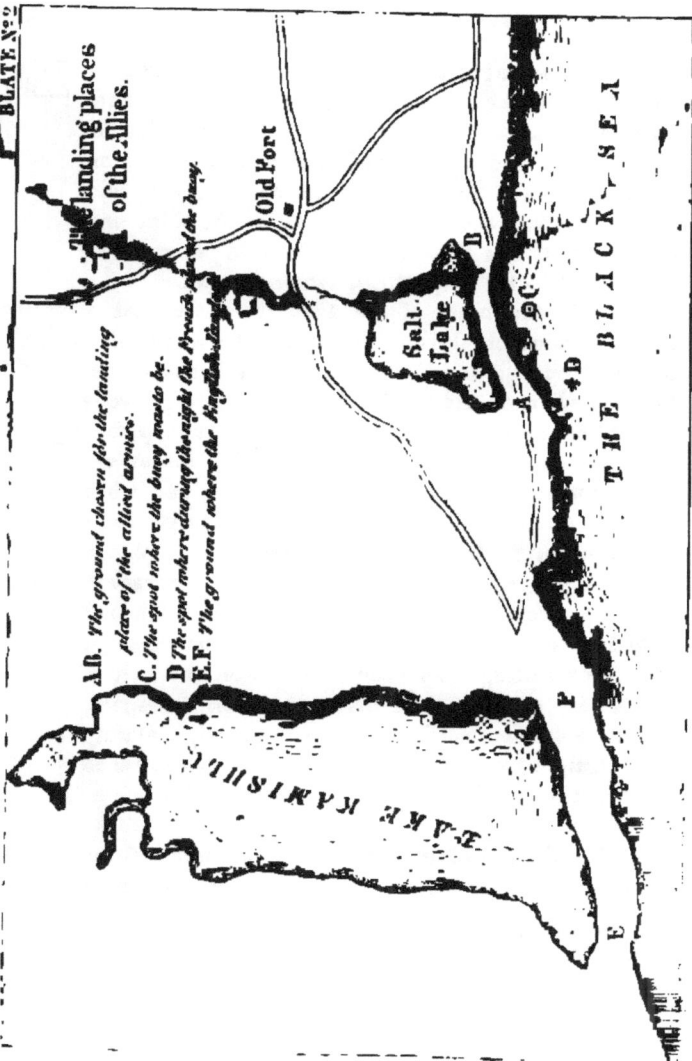

Old Port

Salt Lake

THE BLACK SEA

LAKE KAMISHLI

It was arranged that a buoy should be placed off
the centre of the chosen ground to mark the boundary between the French and the English flotilla.
The French and the Turkish vessels were to be on
the south of the buoy, the British on the north; and
in the evening and night of the 13th the ships and
transports of the three nations drew in as near as
they could to their appointed landing-places.

But in the night of the 13th there occurred a Step taken
by the
French in
the night.
transaction which threatened to ruin the whole plan
for the landing, and even to bring the harmony between the French and the English forces into grievous
jeopardy.   During the darkness, the French placed
the buoy opposite, not to the centre, but to the extreme north of the chosen landing-ground; and when
morning dawned, it appeared that the English ships
and transports, though really in their proper places,
were on the wrong side of the buoy — or rather,
that the buoy was on the wrong side of them.*
Whether the act which created this embarrassment
was one resulting from sheer mistake on the part of
our allies, or from their over-greediness for space,
or from a scheme more profoundly designed, it plainly
went straight towards the end desired by those French
officers who had been labouring to bring the enterprise to a stop.   For what was to be done?   If the This destroys the
whole plan
of the
landing.
English, disregarding the altered position of the
buoy, were to persist in keeping to their assigned

* See Lord Raglan's written account of this transaction in the
Appendix at the end of volume IV. Note No. II.

12*

CHAP.
XXXIX.

landing-ground, their whole flotilla, their boats and their troops, when landed, would be hopelessly mixed up with the French; and what might be expected to follow would be ruinous confusion — nay even, perhaps, angry and violent conflict between the forces of the Allies. To propose to move the buoy, or to get into controversy with the French at such a time, would be to delay and imperil the whole undertaking; and yet the boundary, as it stood, extruded the English from all share in the chosen landing-ground. It might seem that the whole enterprise was again in danger of failure, but again a strong will interposed.

Sir Edmund Lyons.

From the moment when Lord Raglan consented to undertake the invasion, he seems to have acted as though he felt that the belief which he entertained of its hazardousness was a reason why he should be the more steadfast in his determination to force it on. Nor was he without the very counsel that was needed for overcoming this last obstacle. Lyons, commanding the in-shore squadron of the British fleet, was intrusted with the direction of our transports and the whole management of the landing. Moving long before dawn in the sleepless Agamemnon, he saw where the buoy had been placed by the French in the night-time, and gathered in an instant all the perilous import of the change. He was more than a mere performer of duty, for he was a man driving under a passionate force of purpose. Without stopping to indulge his anger, he darted upon the means

His way of dealing with the emergency.

of dealing with the evil. He had observed that about
a mile to the north of "Old Fort" there was that
strip of beach, before spoken of, which divided the
lake of Kamishlu from the sea. There Lord Raglan
and he now determined that the landing of the British
forces should take place. It was true that this plan
would sever the French from the British forces during the operation of landing, but the evil thus encountered was a hundred-fold less grave than the evil
avoided — for, even in the face of an enemy, the
separation of the French from the English would
have been better than dispute or confusion; and,
moreover, the observations of the previous day had
led the Allies to conjecture that the enemy did not
intend to resist the landing. The morning showed
that this conjecture was sound: therefore, great as
was the danger from which the Alliance had been
delivered, it turned out in the result that the immense advantage of having two extended landing-
places instead of one, was not counterbalanced
by any evil resulting from the severance of the two
armies.

In point of security from molestation on the part
of the enemy, both of the two landing-places were
happily chosen. Both of them were on shores which
allowed the near approach of the fleets, and placed
the whole operation under cover of their guns. Also
both landing-places were protected on the inland side
by the salt lakes, which interposed a physical obstacle
in the way of any front attack by the enemy; and

New land-
ing-place
found for
the Eng-
lish at
Kamishlu.

the access to the flanks of the disembarking armies
was by strips of land so narrow that they could be
easily defended against any force of infantry or cavalry.   It is true that the line of disembarkation of
either army could have been enfiladed by artillery
placed on the heights; but then those heights could
be more or less searched by a fire from the ships;
and the enemy had not attempted to prepare for
himself any kind of defence on the high ground.

Position
of the
English
flotilla
adapted
to the
change.

The necessity of having to carry the English flotilla
to a new landing-place occasioned, of course, a painful
dislocation of the arrangements which had already
been acted upon by the commanders of the transports;
but after much less delay and much less confusion
than might have been expected to result from a de-
rangement so great and so sudden, the position of
the English vessels was adapted to the change.

The cause
and the
nature of
the change
kept
secret.

Meanwhile, few of the thousands on board understood the change which had been effected, or even
saw that they were brought to a new landing-ground.
They imagined that it was the better method or
greater quickness of the French which was giving
them the triumph of being the first to land.   Both
Lord Raglan and Lyons were too steadfast in the
maintenance of the alliance to think of accounting
for the seeming tardiness of the English by causing
the truth to be known; and even to this day it is
commonly believed that the English army effected
its landing at Old Fort.

The bend of the coast-line at Kalamita Bay is of

such a character that a spectator on board a vessel close in-shore is bounded in his view of the sea towards the south by the headland near the Alma; but if he stands a little way out to sea, the coast opens, and he then commands an unobstructed view home to the entrance of the Sebastopol harbour. So, whilst the in-shore squadrons approached the beach so closely as to be able to cover the landing, the bulk of the English fleet, commanded by Dundas in person, lay far enough out to be able to command the whole of the vast bay from Eupatoria to Sebastopol, keeping up an unbroken chain of communication from cape to cape, and always held ready to engage the Russian fleet if by chance it should come out and give battle.* Detached vessels reconnoitred the coast, and practised their gunners upon every encampment or gathering of troops which seemed to be within range. As though in the arrogant, yet quiet assertion of an ascendant beyond dispute, one solitary English ship, watching off the Sebastopol harbour, stood sentry over the enemy's fleet. Men had heard of the dominion of the seas — now they saw it.

CHAP. XXXIX. Position of the in-shore squadrons.

Of the main English fleet.

The plan of the English disembarkation was imi- Plan of the landing.

* It has been already explained that the French men-of-war were doing duty as transports, and were not therefore in a condition to engage the enemy. There were people who thoughtlessly blamed Dundas for not taking part with the in-shore squadron in the bustle of the landing. Of course his duty was to hold his off-shore squadron in readiness for an engagement with the Sebastopol fleet; and this he took care to do.

tated from the one adopted by Sir Ralph Abercromby
when he made his famous descent upon the coast of
Egypt; and it was based upon the principle of so
ranging the transports and the boats as that the relative position of each company, whilst it was being
rowed towards the shore, should correspond with that
which it would have to take when formed upon the
beach.*

All the naval arrangements for the landing were
undertaken by Sir Edmund Lyons; but to dispose
the troops on the beach — to gain a lodgment — to
take up a position, and, if necessary, to intrench it
— these were duties which specially devolved upon
the Quartermaster-General. The officer who held this
post was General Airey; and since it was his fate
to take a grave part in the business of the war,
and to share with Lord Raglan his closest counsels,
it seems useful to speak here at once, not of the
quality of his mind (for that will best be judged by
looking to what he did, and what he omitted to do),
but rather to speak of those circumstances of his
life, and those outer signs and marks of his nature,
which any bystander in the camp would be likely to
hear of or see.

A strictly military career in peace-time is a poor
schooling for the business of war; and the rough

General
Airey.

* The plans and the papers of instructions for the landing will
perhaps be given in the Appendix; but I abstain from giving a
detailed account of the operation, because it was not resisted by the
enemy.

change which had once broken in upon Airey's professional life helped to make him more able in war than
men who had passed all their lives in going round
and round with the wheels. Airey was holding one
of the offices at the Horse Guards when he was
suddenly called upon by his relative Colonel Talbot,
the then almost famous recluse of Upper Canada, to
choose whether he and his young wife would accept
a great territorial inheritance, with the condition of
dwelling deep in the forest, far away from all cities
and towns. Airey loved his profession, and what
made it the more difficult for him to quit it was the
favour with which he was looked upon by the Duke
of Wellington. It chanced that he had once been
called upon to lay before the Duke the maps and
statements required for showing the progress of a
campaign then going on against the Caffres; and the
Duke was so delighted with the perfect clearness of
the view which Airey was able to impart to him,
that he instantly formed a high opinion of an officer
who could look with so keen a glance upon a distant
campaign and convey a lucid idea of it to his chief.
Airey communicated to the Duke of Wellington
Colonel Talbot's proposal, and explained the dilemma
in which he was placed. "You must go," said the
Duke; "of course you must go — it is your duty to
"go; but we will manage so that whenever you
"choose you shall be able to come back to us." Airey
went to Canada. It had been no part of Colonel
Talbot's plan to smooth the path of his chosen in-

heritor. He gave him a vast territory — he gave
him no home.

Isolated in the midst of the forest, and with no
better shelter than a log-hut half-built, the staff-
officer, hitherto expert in the prim traditions of the
Horse Guards, now found himself so circumstanced
that the health, nay, the very life of those most dear
to him, was made to depend upon his power to
become a good labourer. He could not have hoped
to keep his English servants a day if he had
begun by sitting still himself and ordering them
to do the rough work to which they were unaccus-
tomed; so he worked with his own hands, in the
faith that his example would make every kind of
hard work seem honourable to his people; and
being endued with an almost violent love of bodily
exertion, he was not only equal to this new life,
but came to delight in it. Clad coarsely during
the day, he was only to be distinguished from the
other workmen by his greater activity and greater
power of endurance. Many English gentlemen have
done the like of this, but commonly they have ended
by becoming altogether just that which they seemed
in their working hours—by becoming, in short, mere
husbandmen. It was not so with Airey. When his
people came to speak to him in the evening, they
always found him transformed. Partly by the subtle
change which they were able to see in his manner,
partly even by so outward a thing as the rigorous
change in his dress, but most of all perhaps by his

natural ascendant, they were prevented from forget-
ting that their fellow-labourer of the morning was
their master — a master to whom they were every day
growing more and more attached, but still their master. He therefore maintained his station. He did
more: he gained great authority over the people
about him; and when he bade farewell to the wilderness, he had become like a chief of old times — a
man working hard with his own hands, yet ruling
others with a firm command.

It was during a period of some years that Airey
had thus wrestled with the hardships of forest life.
At the end of that time Colonel Talbot died; and
Airey, then coming home to England, resumed his
military career. Those who know anything of the
real business of war will easily believe that this
episode in the life of General Airey was more likely
to fit him for the exigencies of a campaign and for
the command of men than thrice the same length of
time consumed in the revolving labours of a military
department; nay, perhaps they will think that, next
to a campaign, this manful struggle with the wilderness was the very work which would be the most
sure to set a mind free from the habits, the bylaws,
and the petty regulations of office.

Before the expedition left England, Lord Raglan
had asked Airey to be his Quartermaster-General.
Airey, preferring field-duty with the divisions, had
begged that some other might be appointed, and
Lord Raglan acceded to his wish; but when, on the

eve of the departure of the expedition from Varna,
Lord De Ros returned to England, the Quartermaster-
Generalship was again pressed upon Airey in terms
which made it unbecoming for him to refuse the
burthen. His loyalty and affectionate devotion to
Lord Raglan were without bounds; and he imagined
that he was always acting with a strict deference to
the wishes of his chief. But then Airey was a man
of great ardour, of a strong will: and having also
a rapid, decisive judgment, he certainly accustomed
himself to put very swift constructions upon Lord
Raglan's words. No one ever used to see him in the
pain of suspense between two opinions. Either he
really knew with minuteness Lord Raglan's views, or
else he was so prone to take a great deal upon himself,
that in his zeal for the public service he might almost
be called unscrupulous. Men who were hesitating
and trying to make out what was the path of their
duty, soon came to know that Airey was the officer
who would thrust away their doubts for them; because, rightly or wrongly, whether with or without
due authority, he used to speak in such a way as to
untie or to cut every knot. He was himself, it would
seem, unconscious of exercising so much power as he
really did; but it is certain enough that those who
complained of his ascendancy were not very wrong
in believing that he held a great sway; for though,
being guileless and single-hearted, he always liked to
receive his first impulsions from the chief, yet, when
once he was thus set moving, his strong will used to

burst into action with all its own proper force, and very much, too, in its own direction.

Notwithstanding this proneness to action, his manner had all the repose which is thought to be a sign of power. He did not, in general, speak at all until he could speak decisively; and he was more accustomed than most other Englishmen are to use that degree of precision and completeness of language which makes men content to act on it. Officers hesitating in the pain of suspense used to long to hear the tramp of his coming — used to long to catch sight of his eager, swooping crest (it was always strained forward and intent) — his keen, salient, sharp-edged features — his firm, steady eye — for they knew that he was the man who would release them from their doubts. He was gifted by nature with the kind of eloquence that it is good for a soldier to have. His oral directions to those in authority under him were models of imperative diction; but when he spoke of what he had seen, the vivid pictures he drew were marked with a sharpness of outline hardly consistent with a perfect freedom from exaggeration — they wanted the true English haze. He was too eager for action to be able to stand still weighing phrases; and I imagine that he did not even know how to try the exact strength and import of words in the way that a lettered man does. Upon the whole, his qualities were of such a kind as to make it impossible for him to be without great weight in the army. His

friends would call him a man plainly fitted for high
command — his adversaries would say that power
in his hands was likely to be used dangerously; but
all would alike agree that, whether for good or
whether for evil, he had from nature the means of
impressing his own will on troops.

The first day's landing. The arrangements of the French were like those
of the English; and at half-past eight o'clock on the
morning of the 14th of September 1854, their first
boat touched the shore.   The English had made
such good haste to retrieve the time spent in moving
to their new landing-place, that very soon afterwards
their disembarkation began.

The morning was fine; the sea nearly smooth.
The troops of the Light Division were in the boats,
and the seamen were at their oars, expecting the
signal.   The signal was given, and instantly, from
along the whole of the first line of transports, an
array of boats freighted with troops — boats ranged
upon a front of more than a mile — darted swiftly
towards the shore.   It was said that the boat commanded by Vesey of the Britannia was the first to
touch the beach.   He was an officer who would do
all man could to be foremost.

As soon as the boats had landed, the soldiers
stepped ashore, and began to form line upon the
beach; but presently afterwards they piled arms.
There were some Tartar peasants passing along the
coast-road with small bullock-waggons.   The wag-
goners showed little or no alarm, and, knowing that

they could not move off quickly with bullocks, they did not attempt to get away. Apparently they were not struck with any sense of unfairness when they saw that the English took possession of the waggons; and yet it could scarcely have been explained to them at that moment (as it afterwards would be) that everything taken by the English from private owners would be paid for at a just price. One of the waggons was laden with small pears, and the soldiers amused themselves with the fruit whilst the natives stood and scanned their invaders.

After a while, many of the battalions which had landed were ordered forward to occupy the hill on our right; and thenceforth, during all the day, the acclivity was sparkling with the bayonets of the columns successively ascending it. But what were those long strings of soldiery now beginning to come down from the hill-side and to wind their way back towards the beach; and what were the long white burthens horizontally carried by the men? Already? already, on this same day? Yes; sickness still clung to the army. Of those who only this morning ascended the hill with seeming alacrity, many now came down thus sadly borne by their comrades. They were carried on ambulance-stretchers, and a blanket was over them. Those whose faces remained uncovered were still alive. Those whose faces had been covered over by their blanket were

dead. Near the foot of the hill the men began to
dig graves.

Zeal and
energy
of the
sailors.
But meanwhile the landing went merrily on. It
might be computed that, if every man in the navy
had only performed his strict duty, the landing
would have taken some weeks. It was the supererogation, the zeal, the abounding zeal, which seemed
to achieve the work. No sailor seemed to work
like a man who was merely obeying — no officer
stood looking on as if he were merely commanding;
and though all was concert and discipline, yet every
man was labouring with the whole strength of his
own separate will. And all this great toil went on
with strange good-humour — nay, even with thoughtful kindness towards the soldiers. The seamen knew
that it concerned the comfort and the health of the
soldiers to be landed dry, so they lifted or handed
the men ashore with an almost tender care: yet not
without mirth — nay, not without laughter far
heard — when, as though they were giant maidens,
the tall Highlanders of the 42d placed their hands
in the hands of the sailor and sprang by his aid to
the shore, their kilts floating out wide while they
leapt.

After mid-day the sea began to lose its calmness,
and before sunset the surf was strong enough to
make the disembarkation difficult, and in some degree hazardous. Yet, by the time the day closed, the
French had landed their 1st, 2d, and 3d divisions of

infantry, together with eighteen guns; and the Eng- CHAP.
lish had got on shore all their infantry divisions, and XXXIX.
some part of their field-artillery.

Some few of the English regiments remained on
the beach, but the rest of them had been marched
up to the high grounds towards the south, and they
there bivouacked. At night there fell heavy rain,
and it lasted many hours. The men were without
their tents.* Lying in wet pools or in mud, their
blankets clinging heavy with water, our young
soldiers began the campaign. The French soldiery
were provided with what they call dog-tents — tents
not a yard high, but easily carried, and yielding
shelter to soldiers creeping into them. It was always
a question in the French army whether these tents
gave the men more health and comfort than they
could find in the open air.

The next morning was fine, but the surf had so
much increased that for several hours the landing was
suspended. After the middle of the day it became
practicable, though still somewhat difficult, to go on
with the work; and great efforts were made to land
the English cavalry and the rest of the artillery, with
the appertaining horses and equipages.

Unless a man has stood in the admiring crowd
which gathers to see the process of landing one horse
upon an open sea-shore; and unless, whilst he carries

* This was because there were no sufficing means of land-transport
for conveying the camp equipage towards Sebastopol. After the
14th the tents were landed, but they were afterwards reshipped.

in his mind the labour and energy brought to bear upon this single object, he can imagine the same toil gone through again and again and yet again, till it has been repeated many hundreds of times, upon a mile and a half of beach, he will hardly know what work must be done before a general can report to his Government that he has landed upon an open coast, with a thousand cavalry and sixty guns ready for the field. By labour never once intermitted (except when darkness or the state of the sea forbade it), and continued from the morning of the 14th until the evening of the 18th, the whole of the English land-force, which had been embarked at Varna (together now with Cathcart's Division), was safely landed upon the enemy's coast.

The result then was, that under circumstances of weather which were, upon the whole, favourable, and with the advantage of encountering no opposition from the enemy, an English force of some 26,000 infantry and artillerymen, with more than a thousand mounted cavalry, and sixty guns, had been landed in the course of five September days; and although the force thus put ashore was without those vast means of land-transport which would be needed for regular operations in the interior, and was obliged to rely upon the attendant fleet for the continuance of its supplies, it was nevertheless so provided as to be able to move along the coast carrying with it its first reserve of ammunition, and food enough for three days.

The operation was conducted with an almost fault-
less skill, and (until a firm lodgment had been gained)
it proceeded in the way that was thought to be the
right one for landing in the face of the enemy.
Though the surf was at times somewhat heavy, not
a man was lost.

With the French, who had no cavalry, and a scanty
supply of artillery horses, the disembarkation was a
comparatively easy task; and if they had so desired
it, the French might have been ready to march long
before the English; but, knowing that their allies,
having cavalry, would necessarily take a good deal
of time, they were without a motive for hurrying;
and during the whole of the five days which the
English took for their disembarkation, a like work
was seen going on at the French landing-place.

The Turks did the work of landing very well; and,
indeed, they quickly showed that they had an advantage over the French and the English in their more
familiar acquaintance with the mode of life proper
to warfare. They landed their camp equipage; for,
with them, the carriage of tents is a very simple business. Two soldiers, one at each end, bear the pole of
a tent between them, and the canvas is carried by
others in turns. So early as the 15th, the first day
after that on which the landing began, the Turks
were comfortably encamped on the ground assigned
to them; and whilst the young troops of France and
England were still sitting wretched and chilled by
the wet of their night's bivouac, the warlike Os-

13*

manlies seemed to be in their natural home. Soli-
man, who commanded them, was able to welcome
and honour the guests who went to visit him in his
tent as hospitably as though he were in the audience-
hall of his own pashalic. He had all his tents well
pitched; and his men, one could see, were still a true
Moslem soldiery — men with arms and accoutrements
bright, yet not forgetful of prayer. He had a supply
of biscuit and of cartridges, and a good stock of horses,
some feeding, some saddled and ready for instant
use. He was not without coffee and tobacco. His
whole camp gave signs of a race which gathers from
a great tradition, going on from father to son, the
duties and the simple arts of a pious and warfaring
life.

CHAPTER XL.

CHAP.
XL.

Deputations from the Tartar villages to the English head-quarters.

WHEN the people of the neighbouring district came to see the strength of the armies descending upon their coast, the head men of villages began to present themselves at the quarters of the Allies. The first of these deputations was received by Lord Raglan in the open air. The men were going up to head-quarters when they passed near a group of officers on foot in blue frock-coats, and they learned that the one whose maimed arm spoke of other wars was the English General. They approached him respectfully, but without submissiveness of an abject kind. Neither in manner, dress, appearance, nor language, would these men seem very strange to a traveller acquainted with Constantinople or any of the other cities of the Levant. They wore the pelisse or long robe, and although their head-gear was of black lamb-skin, it was much of the same shape as the Turkish fez. They spoke with truthfulness and dignity, allowing it to appear that the invasion was not distasteful to them, but abstaining from all affectation of enthusiastic sympathy. They seemed to understand war and its exigencies; for they asked the interpreters to say that such of their possessions as might be wanted by the English army were at Lord Raglan's disposal. Pleased with the demeanour of the men, as well as with the purport of their speech, Lord Raglan told them that he would avail himself of some of their possessions, more especially their waggons and draught animals, but that everything taken for the use of the English army would be paid for at a proper rate. Much to Lord Raglan's surprise (for he was not accustomed to the people of the East), the head man of the village resisted the idea of the people being paid, and anxiously pressed the interpreter to say that their possessions were yielded up as free gifts.

Result of exploring expeditions.
Pure ignorance of the invaded country gave charm to every discovery tending to throw light upon the character and pursuits of the inhabitants; and if our soldiery had found in the villages high altars set up for human sacrifices, they would scarcely have been more surprised than they were when, prying into the mysteries of this obscure Crim Tartary, they came upon traces of modern refinement and cultivated taste. In some of the houses at Kentugan there were pianos; and in one of them a music-book, lying open and spread upon the frame, seemed to show that the owner had been hurried in her flight. But the owners of these dwellings must have been official personages. The mass of the country people were Tartars.

In the villages there was abundance of agricultural wealth. The main want of the country was water; but Airey caused wells to be sunk.

The English system of payment for supplies rapidly began to bear its usual fruit, and the districts from which the people came in to barter with us were every day extending.

In their passage across the Euxine our battalions had not yet been followed by that evil horde who are accustomed to cling to an army, selling strong, noxious drinks to the men. Therefore our army was without crime.* It was with something more than mercy, it was with kindness and gentle courtesy, that the people of the villages were treated by our soldiery; and the interpreters had to strain the resources of the English tongue in order to convey a faint apprehension of the figures of speech in which the women were expressing their gratitude. Their chief favourites, it seems, were the men of the Rifle Brigade. Quartered for a day or two in one of the villages, these soldiers made up for the want of a common tongue by acts of kindness. They helped the women in their household work; and the women, pleased and proud, made signs to the stately "Rifles" to do this and do that, exulting in the obedience which they were able to win from men so grand and

The English army — its absolute freedom from crime.

Kindly intercourse between our soldiery and the villagers.

* This statement, broad as it looks, is meant to be taken literally, and to be regarded as a statement taken from the right official source.

comely. When the interpreter came, and was asked
to construe what the women were saying so fast and
so eagerly, it appeared that they were busy with
similes and metaphors, and that the Rifles were made
out to be heroes more strong than lions, more gentle
than young lambs.

Outrages
perpe-
trated
by the
Zouaves.

A dreadful change came over that village: the
Rifles were withdrawn — the Zouaves marched in.
There followed spoliation, outrage, horrible cruelty.
When those tidings came to Lord Raglan, he was
standing on the shore with several of his people about
him. He turned scarlet with shame and anger. The
yoke of the alliance had wrung him.

The duty
of sweep-
ing the
country
for sup-
plies.

In general, it would fall within the duty of light
horse to sweep the face of the invaded territory and
bring in supplies; but the French were without
cavalry; and although the body of horse which we
had landed was called "the Light Brigade," the
Lancers, the Hussars, and the Light Dragoons of
which it consisted, were not of such a weight and
quality, and were not so practised in foraging, as to
be all at once well fitted for this kind of service.
Besides, it was plain that, in advancing through the
enemy's country, the power of the invaders would
have to be measured by the arm in which they were
weakest, and a material loss in our small, brilliant
force of cavalry might bring ruin upon the whole
expedition. There was the Commissariat. The offi-

cers of that department were gentlemen taken from a branch of the Treasury; and although they could make requisitions on the military authorities with more or less hope of a result, they had no force of their own with which to act. The regimental officers were of course busied with their respective corps. Yet it was certain that the power of operating effectively with the English army would depend upon its obtaining a large addition to its existing means of land-transport. In the result, it was the chief of one of the business departments of our Headquarter Staff who pressed forward into the gap, and succeeded in achieving the work upon which, in a great degree, the fate of the campaign seemed likely to hinge.

From the first General Airey had seen that the mere inert presence of armies in an invaded province is a thing very short of conquest. Conquest, he knew, must generally rest upon the success with which supplies can be drawn from the invaded province; and he never forgot that, unless the country could be made to yield means of land-carriage, the Allies would have to creep timidly along the shore, tethered fast by the short string of carts with which they had come provided; therefore, even within a few minutes from the time when the landing began, he was already striving to gain — not the mere occupation of the soil — not the mere licence for the troops to stand or lie down on the ground — but that hold, that military grasp of the country which

Airey's quick perception of the need to get means of land-transport.

would make it help to sustain the invasion. When
only a few battalions of the Light Division had
landed, and were beginning to form on the beach,
he rode up to the high ground on our right, and
there, at some distance, he caught sight of a long
string of waggons, escorted by a body of Cossacks.
His
seizure of
a convoy.
Instantly he rode back to the beach, got Colonel
Lysons to give him two companies of the 23d Fusiliers, and with these advanced quickly in skirmishing
order. .The Cossacks tried hard to save the convoy
by using the points of their lances against the bullocks, and even against the drivers; but, the Fusiliers advancing and beginning to open fire, the Cossacks at length retreated, leaving Airey in possession
of just that kind of prize which the army most
needed—a prize of some seventy or eighty waggons,
His con-
tinued
exertions.
with their oxen and drivers complete. Never ceasing
to think it was vital to have more and more means
of transport, Airey afterwards despatched the officers
of his department in all directions to bring in supplies. Sending Captain Sankey to Tuzla and Sak,
he thence got 105 waggons. Sending Captain Hamilton to Bujuk Aktash, to Beshi Aktash, to Tenish,
and Sak, he got 67 camels, 253 horses, 45 cartloads
of poultry, barley, and other supplies, with more
than a thousand head of cattle and sheep.* At a

---

* In some but not all of these expeditions Sankey and Hamilton
had cavalry escorts.

later date, and when the army was moving, he took 25 waggons from a village near the line of march. One day, moreover, it happened that Airey sent his aide-de-camp Nolan to explore for water, and, though he was without a cavalry escort, Nolan boldly cut in upon a convoy of 80 government waggons laden with flour, and seized the whole of it. In all some 350 waggons were obtained, with all their teams and with their Tartar drivers.

Their result.

In general, the appropriation of the resources of the country is a business which ranges among mere commissariat annals; but in order to this invasion the seizing of means of land-transport was a business hardly otherwise than vital. Even as it was, the army was brought to hard straits for want of sufficing draught power; and without the cattle and waggons which were seized whilst the troops were landing, the course of events must have been other than what it was.

Those Tartar drivers of whom I have spoken were a wild people, little fit, as it seemed, for the obedience and patient toil exacted from camp-followers; but the descent of the Allies upon the coast was the first military operation that they had witnessed, and before their amazedness ceased, they found themselves unaccountably marshalled and governed, and involuntarily taking their humble part in the enterprise of the Western Powers. Many of them wore the same expression of countenance as

The Tartar drivers.

hares that are taken alive, and they looked as though they were watching after the right moment for escape; but they had fallen, as it were, into a great stream, and all they could do was to wonder, and yield, and flow on. There were few of those captured lads who had strength to withstand the sickness and the hardships of the campaign. For the most part they sank and died.

———

CHAPTER XLI.

THERE were now upon the coast of the Crimea some 37,000 French and Turks,* with sixty-eight pieces of artillery, all under the orders of Marshal St Arnaud; and we saw that 27,000 English, including a full thousand of cavalry, and together with sixty guns, had been landed by Lord Raglan. Altogether, then, the Allies numbered 63,000 men and 128 guns. These forces, partly by means of the draught animals at their command, and partly by the aid of the soldier himself, could carry by land the ammunition necessary for perhaps two battles, and the means of subsistence for three days. Their provisions beyond those limits were to be replenished from the ships. It was intended, therefore, that the fleets should follow the march of the armies; and that the invaders, without attempting to dart upon the inland route which connected the enemy with St Petersburg, should move straight upon the north side of Sebastopol by following the line of the coast.

The whole body of the Allied armies was to operate as a "movable column." **

CHAP.
XLI.
The forces
now on
shore.

The na-
ture of the
operation
by which
the Allies
were to
make good
their ad-
vance to
Sebas-.
topol.

---

* 30,204 Frenchmen and 7000 Turks, according to the French accounts. Lord Raglan, I believe, thought that the French force was less, and put it at 27,000.

** I make this endeavour to elucidate the true character of the

CHAP.
XLI.
Compari-
son be-
tween
regular
operations
and the
system
of the
"movable
"column."

Between an armed body engaged in regular
operations, and that description of force which the
French call a "movable column" the difference is broad;
and there is need to mark it, because the way in which
regular operations are conducted is not even similar to
that in which a "movable column" is wielded. It is,
of course, from the history of Continental wars that
the principle of regular operations in the field is best
deduced. A prince intending to invade his neigh-
bour's territory takes care to have near his own
frontier, or in states already under his control, not
only the army with which he intends to begin the
invasion, but also that sustained gathering of fresh
troops, and that vast accumulation of stores, arms,
and munitions, which will suffice, as he hopes, to
feed the war. The territory on which these resources are spread is called the "base of operations."
When the invading general has set out from this,
his strategic home, to achieve the object he has in
view, the neck of country by which he keeps up his
communications with the base is called the "line of
"operations;" [**] and the maintenance of this line of
operations is the one object which must never be
absent from his mind. The farther he goes, the

operation for the purpose of causing the reader to understand the kind
of hazard which was involved in the march along the coast, and also
in order to lay the ground for explaining (in a future volume) the
causes which afterwards brought upon the army cruel sufferings and
privations.

[**] This is generally, but not invariably, the same line as the one by
which he has advanced.

more he needs to keep up an incessant communication with his "base;" and yet, since the line is lengthening as he advances, it is constantly becoming more and more liable to be cut. Such a disaster as that he looks upon as nearly equal to ruin, and there is hardly anything that he will refuse to sacrifice for the defence of the dusty or mud-deep cart-roads which give him, his means of living and fighting.

On the other hand, the commander of a "movable "column" begins his campaign by wilfully placing himself in those very circumstances which would bring ruin upon an army carrying on regular operations. He does not profess nor attempt to hold fast any "line of operations" connecting him with his resources. He says to his enemy: "Surround me if "you will; gather upon my front; hover round me "on flank and rear. Do not affront me too closely, "unless you want to see something of my cavalry "and my horse-artillery; but, keeping at a courteous "distance, you may freely occupy the whole country "through which I pass. I care nothing for the roads "by which I have come; what I need whilst my task "is doing I carry along with me. I have an enter-"prise in hand; that achieved, I shall march towards "the resources which my countrymen have prepared "for me. Those resources I will reach or else perish." If an army engaged in regular operations were likened to an engine drawing its supplies by means of long pipes from a river, the principle of the "movable column" would be well enough tokened

by that simple skinful of water which, carried on
the back of a camel, is the life of men passing a
desert.

Each of the two systems has its advantages and
its drawbacks. The advantages enjoyed by an army
undertaking regular operations are — the lasting
character of its power, and its comparative security
against great disasters. The general conducting an
army in regular operations is constantly replenishing
his strength by drawing from his "base" fresh troops
and supplies to compensate the havoc which time
and the enemy, or even time alone, will always be
working in his army; and if he meets with a check,
he retires upon a line already occupied by portions
of his force, already strewed with his magazines.
He retires, in short, upon a road prepared for his
reception, and the farther he retreats, the nearer he
is to his great resources. The drawbacks attending
this system are — the great quantity of means of
land-transport required for keeping up the communication, and the eternal necessity of having to be
ready with a sufficient force to defend every mile of
the "line of operations" against the enterprises of
the enemy.

The advantages of the "movable column" are:
that its means of land-transport may be comparatively
small — may, in fact, be proportioned to the limited
duration of the service which it undertakes; and that,
not being clogged with the duty of maintaining a
"line of operations," it has, in truth, nothing to

defend except itself. But grave drawbacks limit the
power of a "movable column." In the first place,
it is an instrument fitted only for temporary use;
because, during the service in which it is engaged, it
has no resources to rely upon except what it carries
along with it. Another drawback is the hazard it
incurs — not of mere defeat, but of total extermina-
tion; for it is a force which has left no dominion in
its wake, and if it falls back, it falls into the midst
of enemies having hold of the country around, and
emboldened by seeing it retreat.

Then, also, a movable column, even though it be
never defeated in any pitched battle, is liable to be
brought to ruin by being well harassed; and very
inferior troops, or even armed peasants, if they have
spirit and enterprise, may put it in peril; for, having
the command of the country all round it, they can
easily prepare their measures for vexing the column
by day and by night. Again, the "movable column"
cannot send its sick and wounded to the rear. It
must either abandon the sufferers, or else find means
of carrying them wherever it marches, and this, of
course, is a task which is rendered more and more
difficult by every succeeding combat. Again, if the
"movable column" is brought to frequent halts by
the necessity of self-defence, there is danger that the
operation in which it is engaged will last to a time
beyond the narrow limit of the supplies which it is
able to carry along with it.

In Algeria the French had brought the system of

using small "movable columns" to a high state of perfection; and there one might see a force, complete in all arms, carrying with it the bread and the cartridges, and driving betwixt its battalions the little herd of cattle which would enable it to live and to fight; one might see it bidding farewell for perhaps several weeks to all its communications, and boldly venturing into the midst of a wilderness alive with angry foes. But the Arabs and Kabyles, though not without some of the warlike virtues, were, upon the whole, too unintelligent and too feeble to be able to put the system of the "movable column" to a test sufficing to prove that the contrivance would hold good in Europe.

Upon the whole, it may be acknowledged that, for operating in a country where the enemy is looked upon as at all formidable, the employment of a "movable column" is a measure which will be likely to win more favour from those who love an adventure, than from those who are acquainted with the art of war.

But whichever of the two methods be chosen, it is of great moment to choose decisively, taking care that the operations are carried on in a way consistent with the principle of the system on which they proceed. A general conducting regular operations must be wary, circumspect, and resolutely patient. The leader of a "movable column" must be swift, and even, for very safety's sake, he may have to be venturesome; for what would be rashness in another

may in him be rigid prudence. The two systems
are so opposite, that to confuse the two, or to import
into the practice of one of them the practice applicable
to the other, is to run into grave troubles and dangers.
Yet this is what the Allies did. When the English
Government committed to this enterprise a large proportion of their small, brilliant army, and appointed
to the command of it a general mature in years, and
schooled by his long subordination to Wellington,
they acted as though they meant that the army
should engage with all due prudence in regular
operations. When they ordered that this force
should make a descent upon the Crimea without
intending to prepare for it a base of operations
at the landing-place, they caused it to act as a
"movable column." It will be seen hereafter that,
from this ambiguity of purpose, or rather from this
dimness of sight, the events of the campaign took
their shape.

Again, it is right to see how far it be possible
to change with the same force from one of the two
systems to the other. Upon this, it can be said that
an army engaged in regular operations may well
enough be able to furnish forth a "movable column;"
but to hope that a "movable column" will be able to
gather to itself all at once the lasting strength of an
army prepared for regular operations, is to hope for
what cannot be. It is true, as we shall see hereafter,
that by dint of great effort and the full command of
the sea, the two mighty nations of the West were able

14*

CHAP.
XLI.
in time to convert the remains of their "movable "column" into an army fitted for regular operations; but we shall have to remember that, before the one system could be effectually replaced by the other, the soldiery underwent cruel sufferings.

The Allies were to operate as a "movable column."
The 63,000 invaders now preparing to march towards the south were the largest, and by far the best appointed, force that the Powers of modern Europe had ever dared to engage in what (as distinguishing it from regular operations) may rightly be called an adventure. Their plan was to advance towards the north of Sebastopol, suffering the enemy to close round their rear, and intending to march every day to a new point of contact with the fleet. It was only at the mouths of the rivers that the cliffs between Old Fort and Sebastopol left room for anything like a landing-place; and (except so far as concerned the mere interchange of signals) the land-forces, whilst marching from the banks of one river to the banks of another, could not expect to be in communication with the fleets. Moreover, the Allied Generals were still in ignorance of the numerical strength of the enemy whom they were thus to defy. All they knew was that, so far as concerned his numbers of brave, steady, highly-drilled troops, the Czar was reported to be the foremost potentate of the world; and that the publicity of the Allied counsels had given him a good deal of time for reinforcing the garrisons of the invaded province.

It may be said that, since the Allied armies were

to be attended along the coast by their fleets, they
were not in the strictest sense a "movable column."
Each night, no doubt, they expected to be in communication with their ships; but, during each of the
marches they were about to undertake, their dangers
were to be in all respects the same as those which
attend upon any other "movable column;" for every
morning they were to cast loose from the ties which
connected them with their resources, as well as with
their means of retreat, and were to ground their
hopes of recovering their communications upon their
power to force their way through a country held by
the enemy. In short, the Allied armies were a
"movable column;" but a movable column which
could hope to find means of succour, and, if necessary,
of retreat, by fighting its way to a point of contact
with the attendant fleets, and covering its withdrawal
by a victory. There is the more need for showing
this by dint of words, since it happened that the true
nature of the expedition was obscured by the course
of events. It passed for a measure more prudent
than it really was, because Prince Mentschikoff, being
wilful and unskilled, did not take the right means
for exposing its rashness.

The march now about to be undertaken by the
invaders was of such a kind that an enterprising
enemy who understood his calling might bring them
to a halt whenever he chose; and, forcing them to
try to convert their flank into a front, might compel

CHAP. XLI.

Perilous character of the march from Old Fort.

them to fight a battle with their back to the sea-cliff — to fight, in short, upon ground where defeat would be ruin. When, therefore, on the 19th of September 1854, the Allied armies broke up from their bivouacs and marched towards the south, they were engaging in a venturesome enterprise.

It seems that, although by human contrivance a whole people may be shut out from the knowledge of momentous events in which its armies are taking a part, there is yet a subtle essence of truth which will permeate into the mind of a nation thus kept in ignorance. To a degree which freemen can hardly imagine to be possible, the first Napoleon had succeeded in hiding the achievements of the English army from the sight of the French people; and since the French in after years were little tempted to gather up by aid of history the events which they had been hindered from learning in the form of "news," there was — not merely in the French army, but even in all France — a very scant knowledge of the way in which the two mighty nations of the West had encountered one another in the great war. Yet, now that the time had come for testing the faith which one army had in the prowess of the other, it suddenly appeared that a belief in the quality of the English soldier was seated as deep in the mind of the French army as though it were a belief founded upon historic knowledge. This will be understood by observing the relative place which the French commander was content to take in the order of march, and by looking at it in connection with what then promised to be the character of the impending campaign.

When once the invaders had landed and seized the coast-road, the one line of communication which the Russians could trust to for linking the garrison of Sebastopol to the mainland was by the great road which passes through Bakshi Serāi and Simpheropol. It was vital to the Russian commander to be able to hold this road, for by that his reinforcements were to come. On the other hand, he had to try to cover Sebastopol; but such was the direction in which the Allies were preparing to march upon the place that, by manœuvring with his back towards the great road passing through Simpheropol, he could cling to his line of communication, and yet be able to come down upon the flank of the invading armies whilst they were marching across his front. In this way he would cover Sebastopol much more effectively than by risking his communications in order to place his army like a mere inert block between the invaders and their prey. Moreover, he was known to be relatively strong in cavalry, and the country was of such a kind that the Allies, advancing from Old Fort to the Belbec, would have upon their left a fair, undulating steppe, such as horsemen exult to look upon. It was, therefore, to be expected that the whole stress of the task undertaken by the invaders would be thrown, in the first instance, upon that

portion of the Allied force which might be chosen to
form their left wing.

The
French
take the
right.
In the armies of Europe the right is the side of
precedence, and from the time that the Western
Powers had begun to act together in Turkey, the
French had always claimed, or rather had always
taken, the right.   Now, it happened that, both in
Turkey and in the Crimea, the side of precedence
was the side nearest to the sea, whilst the left was
the side nearest to the enemy. Lord Raglan had
observed all this, but he had observed in silence;
and finding the right always seized by our Allies,
he had quietly put up with the left. Yet he was
not without humour: and now, when he saw that, in
this hazardous movement along the coast, the French
were still taking the right, there was something like
archness in his way of remarking that, although the
French were bent upon taking precedence of him,
their courtesy still gave him the post of danger. This
he well might say; for, so far as concerned the duty
of covering the venturesome march which was about
to be undertaken, the whole stress of the enterprise
was thrown upon the English army. The French
force was covered on its right flank by the sea, on
its front and rear by the fire from the steamers, and
on its left by the English army. On the other hand,
the English army, though covered on its right flank
by the French, was exposed in front, and in rear,
and on its whole left flank, to the full brunt of the

enemy's attacks. If the Russian General should act
in anything like conformity to the principles of the
art of war, the whole weight of his attacks would
have to be met, in the first instance, by the English
alone; and although the French would have an
opportunity of acting as a reserve, they would do so
under circumstances rendering it very difficult for
them to retrieve any check sustained by their Allies.
In short, the French could not but know that, if the Their
enemy should direct his enterprises against the open ness and
left flank of the invaders, the least weakness on the good
part of the English might enable him to roll up the sense.
whole Allied force, involving French and English
alike in one common disaster. Yet so steadfast was
the trust which the French reposed in the English,
so unshaken the courage and good sense with which
they committed themselves to the prowess of their
ancient foe, that they never for an instant sought to
meddle with the duty of covering the march from
an attack on the left flank. They planned that the
English should be there.

On the morning of the 19th of September the The ad-
Allied armies began their advance towards the south. begun.
On the right, and nearest the sea, the French army
marched in a formation adopted by Marshal Bugeaud
at the battle of Isly. The outline of the ground
covered by their troops took the shape of a lozenge
— a lozenge, whereof the foremost apex was formed The order
by the 1st Division, the angles on either flank by of march.

the 2d and 3d, and the rearmost point by the 4th Division. Within the mascle or hollow lozenge thus formed, there marched the Turkish battalions and those portions of the artillery and the convoy which were not specially attached to one or other of the divisions. Each French division* marched in two columns, consisting each of one brigade, and the artillery and encumbrances belonging to each division marched between the two brigades. Each brigade was in regimental column at sectional distance. The Allied fleets, slowly gliding along the coast, covered the French army on its right flank, and carefully reconnoitred every seam and hollow of the ground in front which could be reached by the eyes of men looking from the ships.

Since the English army was to advance in a way which left it open to the enemy in front, in rear, and on its left flank, Lord Raglan of course deemed it likely that he would be attacked in his march; and that, upon smooth, open ground, his army would be called upon to defend both itself and its trailing convoy against the assaults of an enemy who was strong in the cavalry arm. But this task was

---

* It was intended and ordered that the 1st and 4th French Divisions should affect a losenge formation analogous to that which characterised the general order of march, but the direction was not practically attended to. No one knows better than an African General the art of enfolding the helpless portions of a column in battalions of infantry; but the French force being covered on all sides in the way already described, no elaborate precautions were needed.

rendered less hard than it would otherwise be by
the quality of the English soldier, and the peculiar
order of battle in which he loves to fight. He fights
in line; and therefore, with his moderate force of
infantry and artillery, Lord Raglan was able to
resolve that, from whatever quarter the onset might
come, he would be ready to meet it with a front of
bayonets and field-artillery, extending along nearly
two miles of ground.

In order to be able, at a few minutes' notice, to
show a front of this extent either towards the south,
the east, or the north, Lord Raglan kept each of his
infantry divisions massed in close column, and he
disposed his 1st, 2d, 3d, and Light Divisions in
such a way that the whole body had both a front
and a depth of two divisions. A body which moves
in columns of this kind is said to be marching "in
"grand divisions."* The distances between the
divisions were so arranged that, without dislocation,
they could form line either in front or towards the
flank. The artillery attached to each division marched
on the right or seaward flank of the force to which
it belonged.

The advance-guard consisted of the 11th Hussars
and the 13th Light Dragoons under Lord Cardigan.

* There are four or five different terms which have been used by
experienced generals in describing this disposition of troops, but the
authority on which I place the most reliance sanctions the term used
in the text.

In rear of the small infantry advance-guard, which
followed the horsemen, there marched a detachment
of the Rifles in extended order. Then, on the right,
came the 2d Division; and, on the left, the Light
Division. The 3d Division marched in rear of the
2d, and the Light Division was followed by the 1st
Division. Of the 4th Division, the 63d Regiment
and two companies of the 46th had been left (with
a squadron of the 4th Light Dragoons) to clear the
beach at Kamishlu; but the remainder of the division,
under Sir George Cathcart, marched in rear of the
1st Division. Along the left flank of the advancing
columns, and at a distance from them of some 200
yards, were riflemen in skirmishing order, and a line
of skirmishers from the same force closed the rear
of the infantry. On the left flank, and nearly in
the same alignment as the leading infantry divisions,
was the 8th Hussars; and on the same flank, but in
an alignment less advanced than the rear-most of the
infantry columns, there was the 17th Lancers. The
cattle and the baggage marched in rear of the 3d
Division, and so as to be covered towards the left
by the 4th Division. Then followed the rear-guard,
and then a line of Rifles disposed at intervals in
extended order. Last of all came the 4th Light
Dragoons, under Lord George Paget.

The
march.
Thus marched the strength of the Western Powers.
The sun shone hotly, as on a summer's day in England; but breezes springing fresh from the sea floated

briskly along the hills. The ground was an undulating steppe alluring to cavalry. It was rankly covered with a herb like southernwood; and when the stems were crushed under foot by the advancing columns, the whole air became laden with bitter fragrance. The aroma was new to some. To men of the western counties of England it was so familiar that it carried them back to childhood and the village church; they remembered the nosegay of "boy's love" that used to be set by the Prayer-Book of the Sunday maiden too demure for the vanity of flowers.

In each of the close-massed columns which were formed by our four complete divisions there were more than 5000 foot-soldiers. The colours were flying; the bands at first were playing; and once more the time had come round when in all this armed pride there was nothing of false majesty; for already videttes could been seen on the hillocks, and (except at the spots where our horsemen were marching) there was nothing but air and sunshine, and at intervals the dark form of a single rifleman, to divide our columns from the enemy. But more warlike than trumpet and drum was the grave quiet which followed the ceasing of the bands. The pain of weariness had begun: Few spoke — all toiled. Waves break upon the shore; and though they are many, still distance will gather their numberless cadences into one. So, also, it was with one ceaseless hissing sound that a wilderness of tall crisping herb-

age bent under the tramp of the coming thousands.
As each mighty column marched on, one hardly
remembered at first the weary frames, the aching
limbs which composed it; for — instinct with its own
proper soul and purpose, absorbing the volitions of
thousands of men, and bearing no likeness to the
mere sum of the human beings out of whom it was
made — the column itself was the living thing —
the slow, monstrous unit of strength which walks the
modern earth where empire is brought into question.
But a little while and then the sickness which had
clung to the army began to make it seen that the
columns in all their pride were things built with the
bodies of suffering mortals.

Sickness
and falling
strength
of many
of the
soldiers.
We saw that, before the embarkation, our troops
had fallen into a weak state of health, and that, even
of those who were free from serious illness, there
were hardly any who had been able to keep their
accustomed strength. It had been hoped that the
voyage would bring back health and strength, but
the hope proved vain; and Lord Raglan, knowing
the weakly state of the men, had ordered that they
should be allowed to enfold the few things they most
needed in their blankets, and to land and march
without their knapsacks. Yet now, before the first
hour of march was over, the men began to fall out
from the ranks. Some of these were in the agonies
of cholera. Their faces had a dark, choked look;
they threw themselves on the ground and writhed,

but often without speaking and without a cry. Many
more dropped out from mere weakness. These the
officers tried to inspirit, and sometimes they succeeded; but more often the sufferer was left upon
the ground. It was vain to tell him, though so it
was believed at the time, that he would fall into the
hands of the Cossacks. The tall stately men of the
Guards dropped from their ranks in great numbers.
It was believed at the time that the men who fell
out would be taken by the enemy; but the number
of stragglers at length became very great, and in the
evening a force was sent back to bring them in.

During the march the foot-soldiers of the Allied
armies suffered thirst; but early in the afternoon the
troops in advance reached the long-desired stream
of the Bulganak; and as soon as a division came in
sight of the water, the men broke from their ranks,
and ran forward that they might plunge their lips
deep in the cool, turbid, grateful stream. In one
brigade a stronger governance was maintained. Sir
Colin Campbell would not allow that even the rage
of thirst should loosen the discipline of his grand
Highland regiments. He halted them a little before
they reached the stream, and so ordered it that, by
being saved from the confusion that would have
been wrought by their own wild haste, they gained
in comfort, and knew that they were gainers. When
men toil in organised masses, they owe what well-
being they have to wise and firm commanders.

It was on the banks of this stream of the Bulganak that the Allied armies were to bivouac for the
night.

CHAPTER XLII.

EARLY in the afternoon, Lord Raglan, riding in advance of the infantry divisions, had reached the banks of the river, and observing a group of Cossacks on the brow of the hill towards the south, he ordered the squadrons which Lord Cardigan had with him* to move forward and reconnoitre the ground. Lord Lucan was present with this portion of his cavalry force.

Where the post-road from Eupatoria to Sebastopol crosses the Bulganak, the ground on the south side of the river rises gradually for some hundreds of yards from the banks of the stream, then dips a little, then rises again, then dips rather deeply, and then again rises up to the summit of the ridge which bounds the view of an observer in the valley of the Bulganak.

Our reconnoitring squadrons went forward a great way into the lower dip, and when they were there, it was perceived that, confronting them from the hill above, there was a body of cavalry 2000 strong.

---

* The 11th Hussars and 13th Light Dragoons.

Our four squadrons halted and formed line. The
Russian cavalry came forward a little, then halted,
and, throwing out skirmishers, attempted some long
fruitless shots with their carbines. Our squadrons
also threw out skirmishers.

But Lord Raglan, who had remained with his
Staff on the northern side of the hollow, had now
discerned the formidable body of cavalry which was
confronting our four squadrons; and Airey, being
gifted with a keen, far-reaching sight, was able to
make out that the glitter which could be seen between the second crest and the summit was the play
of the sun upon the points of bayonets, and that in
the upper hollow there were several battalions. It
was soon made plain that, within a few hundred
yards of our four squadrons, the enemy was present
with all three arms, and in some force. He had
there, as we now know, about 6000 men of his 17th
Division, two batteries of artillery, a brigade of regular cavalry, and nine sotnias of Cossacks.

Lord Raglan, whose army was still on its march,
saw that he must take care to avoid provoking an
action; but also he had to provide for the retreat of
the four squadrons, which stood rooted in the centre
of the lower hollow, so near to an overwhelming
enemy's force of all arms, and so far from their supports, that they were in some danger. The problem
was to extricate them, and to do this, if possible,
without getting into that sort of conflict which would
be likely to bring about a serious engagement.

Lord Raglan saw that what made the Russians hesitate was the steadiness and the exact ceremonious formation of the little cavalry force of four squadrons which tranquilly confronted them; and that, if he were to withdraw it before he had made arrangements for covering its retreat, it would be pursued and roughly handled by overwhelming numbers. He was anxious — for, small as was this little body of horse, it was a large proportion of his whole strength in the cavalry arm; but he saw that its safety would be best provided for by bringing up troops to its support, and allowing it in the mean time to remain where it was, confusing the enemy by its obstinate presence and its careful array. He ordered up in all haste the Light and the 2d Divisions, the 8th Hussars, and 17th Lancers, and afterwards the nine-pounder batteries attached to the Light Division. When our infantry divisions came up they were formed in line, and the cavalry supports took a position in left rear of the advanced squadrons. All these operations the enemy suffered to take place without resistance, and when they were completed his opportunity was gone.

So, all being now in readiness, Lord Raglan wished that the four squadrons should forthwith retire; and the more so as he was apprehensive lest these horsemen, in their evident longing for a combat, should be tempted to charge the body of cavalry in their immediate front. Still, he was unwilling to embarrass Lord Lucan (close as he then was to the

15*

enemy) by an order too precise or imperative. In
these circumstances Airey·galloped forward to give
effect to Lord Raglan's wishes.

When Airey came up, he found that by communi-
cating Lord Raglan's wishes without delivering a
positive order, he was supplying materials for a debate between Lord Lucan and his brigadier. Yet
for a wordy debate the time and the place were ill-
fitted, for the four squadrons, as we have seen, were
within but a little distance of overwhelming forces.
There is some obscurity as to the exact way in
which Airey brought his will to bear; but he saw
what was wanted, and he said the force must retire
immediately, and by alternate squadrons. Though
he spoke in terms which might have meant that he
was only giving his own opinion, yet perhaps the
decisiveness of his speech and manner led to the
impression that he was delivering Lord Raglan's
orders. Be this as it may, the result was quickly
attained. Lord Lucan understood that he had to go
forthwith to Lord Raglan. Lord Cardigan understood that the force was to retire immediately, and
by alternate lines. The operation instantly commenced, and was conducted with excellent precision,
for during the whole retreat there were always two
squadrons out of the four which were showing a
smooth front to the enemy.

The moment the withdrawal of our little cavalry
force began, the enemy's artillery-teams, unseen before, came bounding up from the hollow, and his

guns, being quickly unlimbered, were soon in battery upon the ridge. With these he opened fire upon our retreating squadrons; but he saw that these horsemen, no longer isolated, were retiring upon ample supports of all arms; he did not, therefore, venture to pursue with his cavalry. Two men in our cavalry force were wounded, and four or five horses killed. The six-pounder guns attached to our cavalry replied to the enemy's artillery without good effect; but when our nine-pounder guns were brought into action, they caused the enemy's artillery to limber up and retire. They also, it seems, inflicted some loss upon the enemy's cavalry, for it was said that as many as thirty-five of his troopers were killed or wounded. The Russians were soon out of sight.

The slight combat thus occurring on the Bulganak was the first approach to a passage of arms between Russia and the Western Powers. The pith of what had happened was this: — The Russians had been making a reconnaissance in force at a time when Lord Raglan was making a reconnaissance with only four squadrons; and as the nature of the ground concealed the enemy's strength, our lesser force was exposed for some minutes to a good deal of danger; but the enemy, being slow to take advantage of fortune, had given the English General full time to extricate his squadrons by the use of the three arms. Lord Raglan was so well pleased with the success of this last operation, and with the

CHAP.
XLII.

steadiness shown by our cavalry, that, even on the night of the Alma (when it might have been supposed that the impressions produced by the battle would have superseded the recollection of the previous day), he spoke with complacency of this affair on the Bulganak.

CHAPTER XLIII.

WHEN this affair was concluded, Lord Raglan began to prepare for a contingency of graver import. The enemy, as it now appeared, had a force of all arms in the immediate neighbourhood, and it was known that he had his whole field-army within a few hours' march of the Bulganak. On the other hand, Lord Raglan was exposed to attack in front, left flank, and rear; and even on his right flank he was without immediate support, for the course of the day's march had thrown an interval of a mile between the French and the English armies. It was to be apprehended that the enemy, issuing during the night from his intrenched position on the Alma, would place himself in such a position as to be able to fall upon our army in front and flank at dawn of day. Lord Raglan, therefore, determined that the troops should bivouac in order of battle, and so as to be rapidly able to show a deployed front to the enemy either in front or flank. He placed the troops himself, fixing their exact position with minute care.

The first brigades of the 2d and Light Divisions

CHAP.
XLIII.

Apparently dangerous situation of the English army.

Lord Raglan causes it to bivouac in order of battle.

were drawn up in line parallel with the river, and some hundreds of yards in advance of it. The first brigades of the 1st and 3d Divisions were placed in an oblique line receding from the left of the Light Division, and going back to the river's bank. The troops thus deployed formed, with the river, a kind of three-sided enclosure, in which the principal part of the cavalry and the encumbrances of the army were enfolded. The second brigade of each of the divisions already named was formed in column in rear of the first or deployed brigade. The 4th Division and the 4th Light Dragoons were placed in observation on the northern side of the river. Finally, Colonel Lagondie, one of the French Commissioners at our headquarters, was requested to suggest to Prince Napoleon the expediency of his drawing his division somewhat more near to the English right. *

Our troops piled arms, and bivouacked in order of battle. ** There was a post-house at the point where the road crossed the river, and there Lord Raglan passed the night.

The situation of our army seemed to be critical; but when morning dawned it appeared that the enemy, attempting nothing, had drawn off to his intrenched position on the Alma.

---

* Colonel Lagondie fulfilled his mission; but on his return, being a near-sighted man, he rode into the midst of a Cossack picket, and was taken prisoner.

** See the Plan.

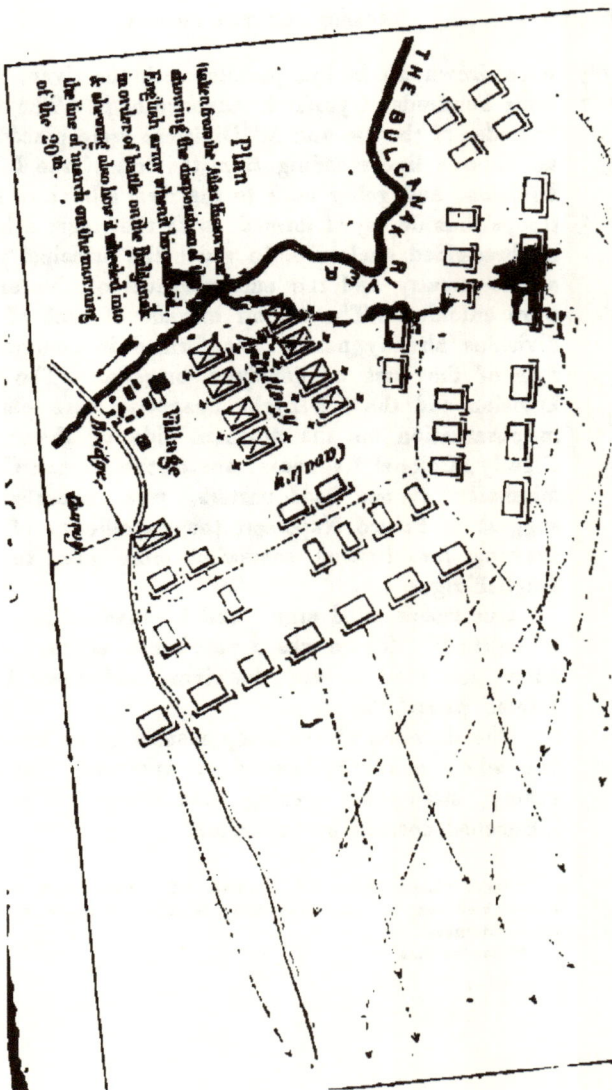

THE BULGANAK RIVER

Plan

(taken from the 'Atlas Historique')
shewing the disposition of the
English army when it became
in order of battle on the Bulganak
& shewing also how it wheeled into
the line of march on the morning
of the 20th.

Infantry

Cavalry

Village

Bridge

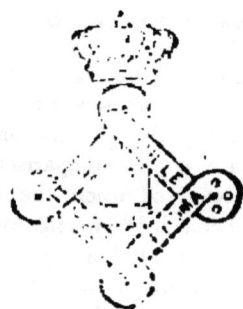

So the peril which the Allies had been encounter-
ing for the last twenty-four hours was now at an end; and the duty of carrying the position on the Alma might be regarded as easy, in comparison with that which would have devolved upon the invaders if our left flank had been briskly attacked on their march. It is common to attribute great results to careful design; but the truth is, that the Allies owed their prosperous landing and their tranquil march to the forbearance of the Russian commander.

CHAPTER XLIV.

I.

FOR an army undertaking to withstand the march of invaders who come along the shore from the north, the position on the left bank of the Alma is happily formed by nature, and is capable of being made strong. The river springs from the mountain-range in the south-east of the peninsula, and its tortuous channel, resulting at last in a westerly course, brings it down to the sea near the headland called Cape Loukool. In that region the right or northern bank of the stream inclines with a very gentle slope to the water's edge; but on the south or left bank the river presses close against a great range of hills, and the rocky ground which forms their base, being scarped by the action of the river in its swollen state, gives a measure of the loud, red torrent thrown down in flood-times from the sides of the Tchatir Dagh. Yet, so long as it flows in its summer bed, the pure grey stream of the Alma, though strong and rapid even then, can be crossed in most places by a full-grown man without losing foot. There are, however, some deeps which would force a man to swim a few

strokes; and, on the other hand, the river is passed
in several places by easy and frequented fords. Near the village of Bourliouk, at the time of the action, there was a good timber bridge.

Along the course of the stream, on the north or right bank, there is a broad belt of gardens and vineyards, enclosed by low stone walls, and reaching down to the water; but on the left or south side there are few enclosures, for in most places the rock formation, which marks the left bank of the river, has its base so close down to the water's edge as to leave but little soil deep enough for culture.

The smooth slopes by which the invader from the north approaches the Alma are contrasted by the aspect of the country on the opposite bank of the river; for there the field is so broken up into hills and valleys — into steep acclivities and narrow ravines — into jutting knolls and winding gullies — that with the labour of a Russian army, and the resources of Sebastopol at his command, a skilled engineer would have found it hard to exhaust his contrivances for the defence of a ground having all this strength of feature.

It is the high land nearest to the shore which falls most abruptly: for when a man turns his back to the sea, and rides up along the river's bank, the summits of the hills on his right recede from him more and more — recede so far that, although they are higher than the hills near the shore, they are connected

CHAP.
XLIV.
with the banks of the stream by slopes more gently
inclining.

The main features of the ground are these: first
and nearest to the sea-shore there is what may be
called the "West Cliff" — for the ground there rises
to a height of some 350 feet, and not only presents,
looking west, a bluff buttress of rock to the sea,
but also on its northern side hangs over the river so
steep that a man going up along the bank of the
stream has at first an almost sheer precipice on his
right hand; and it is only when he all but reaches
the village of Almatamack that he finds the cliff
losing its severity. At that point the ground becomes so sloping and so broken as to be no longer
difficult of ascent for a man on foot, nor even for
country waggons. In rear — Russian rear — of the
cliff there are the villages of Hadji-Boulat, Ulukul
Tiouets, and Ulukul Akles.

Higher up the river, but joined on to the West
Cliff, there is a height, which was crowned at the
time of the war by an unfinished turret intended
for a telegraph. This is the Telegraph Height. At
top, the West Cliff and the Telegraph Height form
one connected plateau or table-land; but the sides
of the Telegraph Height have not the abrupt character which marks the West Cliff. They are steep,
but both towards the river and towards the east
they are much broken up into knolls, ridges, hollows,
and gullies. At all points they can be ascended by
a man on foot, and at some by waggons. These

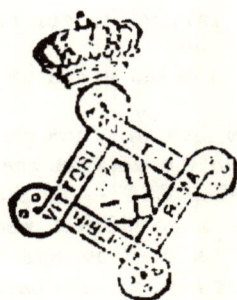

Plan indicating in a general way, the form of the opening called "The Pass" through which the Post Road after crossing the Alma, bends up over the hills.

steep sides of the Telegraph Height are divided from
the river by a low and almost flat ledge with a vary-
ing breadth of from two to six hundred yards. The
ledge was a good deal wooded at the time of the
war, and on some parts of it there were vineyards
or orchards.

To the east of the Telegraph Height the trending
away of the hills leaves a hollow or recess, so formed
and so placed that its surface might be likened to a
huge vine-leaf — a vine-leaf placed on a gentle incline,
with its lower edge on the river, its stem at the
bridge, and its main fibre following the course of the
great road which bends up over the hill towards
Sebastopol. This opening in the hills is the main
Pass; and through it (as might be gathered from
what has just been said) the Causeway or great post-
road goes up from the bridge.* Across the mouth
of the Pass, at a distance of a few yards from the
bridge, there are small natural mounds or risings of
ground, having their tops at a height of about sixty
feet above the level of the river. These are so ranged
as to form, one with the other, a low and uneven
but almost continuous embankment, running from
east to west, and parallel with the river. The natural
rampart thus formed controls the entrance to the

---

* In speaking of this opening as a "Pass," I have followed the
example of one whom I regard as a great master of the diction applicable to military subjects; but it is not, of course, meant that there
is anything at all Alpine in the character of this range of low hills —
hills less than 400 feet high.

CHAP.
XLIV.

Pass from the north; for it not only overlooks the bridge, but also commands the ground far and wide on both sides of the river, and on both sides of the great road. Behind, the ground falls and then rises again, till it mingles with the slopes and the many knolls and hillocks which connect it with the receding flanks of the Telegraph Height on the one side, and the Kourgané Hill on the other.

Still higher up the river, but receding from it in a south-easterly direction, the ground rises gradually to a commanding height, and terminates in a peak. This hill is the key of the position. It is called the Kourgané Hill. Around its slopes, at a distance of about three hundred yards from the river, the ground so swells out as to form a strong rib — a rib which bends round the front and the flanks of the bastion there built by nature, giving a command towards the south-west, the west, the north-west, and the north-east. Towards the west this terrace, if so it may be called, is all but joined to those mounds which we spoke of as barring the mouth of the Pass. Behind all these natural ramparts there are hollows and dips in the ground, which give ample means for concealing and sheltering troops; but from the jutting rib down to the bank of the river, the slope is gentle and smooth like the glacis of a fortress. It was on this Kourgané Hill that Prince Mentschikoff established his headquarters.

The immediate approach to the river from its right bank is everywhere gentle, but the ground on its south side is a good deal scarped by the action of the water; and all along that part of the river which flows opposite to the Kourganè Hill and the main Pass, the left bank rises almost vertically from the water's edge to a height of from eight to fifteen feet.

On the north bank of the river, and at a distance of about a mile from its mouth, there is the village of Almatamack. On the same bank, but more than a mile and a quarter higher up the stream, there stood at the time of the war a large white homestead. Yet a mile higher up the river on the same bank, and nearly facing the mouth of the Pass, there stands the large straggling village of Bourliouk. The cottages and farm-buildings which skirt this village on its eastern side extend far up the river. From Bourliouk to the easternmost part of the position the distance is two miles.

To ascend the position from the north there are several frequented ways: —

1. Close to the sea, and to the mouth of the river, there is a singular fissure in the rock, and through this a narrow way leads round, and up to the top of the cliff. This road was not traversed by artillery on the day of the battle, but it is believed that this was because the guns could not be brought across the river at the point where it flows into the sea.

2. From the ford at the village of Almatamack

there is a waggon-road which leads up to the top of
the plateau.   It was practicable for artillery.

3.   From the white homestead there is a road
which crosses the river and goes up to the plateau;
but, either because of the badness of the ford, or
else the too rugged ascent beyond it, this road could
not be used for artillery.   The want of a road for
their guns in this part of the field was the main
cause which hampered the French army.

4.   On the western side of the village of Bourliouk there is a frequented ford across the river,
and from that spot two waggon-roads, forking off at
no great distance from one another, lead up to the
Telegraph and the villages in its rear.   The westernmost of these roads was found to be practicable for
artillery.

5.   Opposite to Bourliouk two almost parallel
waggon-roads lead up from the bank of the river to
the top of the plateau.

6.   The Great Causeway, or post-road leading
from Eupatoria, goes through the eastern skirts of
Bourliouk, crosses the bridge, enters the Pass, and
ascends by a gentle incline towards the low chain
of mounds running across its mouth.   After piercing
that natural rampart, it bends into the southerly
course which leads it to Sebastopol.

7.   To the east of the main Pass there are other
roads; but they are not further spoken of here, because all the hill-side in that part of the field is more
or less accessible to artillery.

Except at the West Cliff, every part of the position can be reached by men on foot.

In the rear — Russian rear — of the hills which form this position, the ground falls, and it rises again at a distance of two miles.

Down to the edge of the vineyards, the whole of the field on the north or right bank of the river is ground tempting to cavalry; and although the south side of the stream is marked, as we saw, by stronger features, still the summits of the heights spread out broad, like English "Downs." Except the sheer sides of the cliff, and the steeps of the Telegraph Height, there is little on the higher ground to obstruct the manœuvres of horsemen.

From the sea-shore to the easternmost spot occupied by Russian troops, the distance for a man going straight was nearly five miles and a half; but if he were to go all the way on the Russian bank of the river he would have to pass over more ground; for the Alma here makes a strong bend, and leaves open the chord of the arc to invaders who come from the north.*

---

*'I am aware that in distances, and in other material points, this description of the position differs widely from the result of the hasty surveys which were made, soon after the battle, by English officers. The French Government plans bear such strong marks of having been made with great care and labour, that, in general, I have ventured to take them for my guide in preference to those of my own country-men.

II.

Against any plan for occupying the whole of this range of hills by the forces of the Czar there were two cogent reasons: one was, that the summits of the West Cliff, and even of part of the Telegraph Height, were exposed to fire from the ships; the other, that the position was too wide for the numbers which were brought to defend it.

Mentschi-
koff's plan
for avail-
ing him-
self of the
position.

But the whole of the naval and military resources of the Crimea had been intrusted to the direction of Prince Mentschikoff. With him it rested to make head against the invasion; and it seems he had been so forcibly struck with the great apparent steepness of the West Cliff and the heights connected with it, that he thought it must be wholly inaccessible to troops. He conceived, therefore, that he might safely omit to occupy it, and might be content to take up a narrow position, beginning on the eastern slopes of the Kourgané Hill, and terminating on the west of the Telegraph Height at a distance of more than two miles from the sea.* By this course, as he thought, he would elude both of the obstacles which interfered with his hold of the position; for his extreme left would be comparatively distant from the shipping, and the whole ground occupied would be

---

* The Russian accounts estimate the distance at only two versts, but I adhere, as before stated, to the French plans.

so far contracted that the troops which he had at his
command might suffice to hold it. Upon this plan he acted. So, although the position of the Alma, as formed by nature, had an extent of more than five miles, the troops which stood charged to hold it had a front of only one league. Prince Mentschikoff rested upon the assumption that the whole of the ground which he proposed to leave unoccupied was inaccessible to troops; but if he had walked his horse into the road, which was within half a mile of his extreme left, he would have found that it led down to a ford opposite to the village of Almatamack, and was perfectly practicable for artillery. His army had been on the ground for several days, yet, with a strange carelessness, he not only omitted to break up or to guard this road from Almatamack, but made all his dispositions exactly as though no such road existed.

The forces brought forward to defend this position His forces. for the Czar were 3400 cavalry, 33,000 infantry, and 2600 artillerymen, making altogether 39,000 men,* with 106 guns.

Prince Mentschikoff commanded in person. He His personal position. was a wayward, presumptuous man, and his bearing towards the generals under his command was of such a kind that he did not or could not strengthen himself by the counsels of men abler than himself.** In times

* 39,017. See post, p. 346 et seq., where the details of the force are fully given.

** I infer this from the fact that, the day before the action, General

16*

CHAP.
XLIV.

past he had been mutilated by a round-shot from a Turkish gun. He bore hatred against the Ottoman race; he bore hatred against their faith. He had opened his mission at the Porte with insult; he had closed it with threats. And now — a sequence rare in the lives of modern statesmen — he was out on a hill-side, with horse and foot, having warrant — full warrant this time — to adduce "the last reason of kings."

His plan
of cam-
paign.

So far as regards the general scheme of the campaign, his conception, it seems, was this: he would suffer the Allies to land without molestation, because he desired that the defeat which he was preparing for them should be, not a mere repulse, but a crushing and signal disaster. He would not attack them on their line of march, because he liked better to husband his strength for the great position on the Alma. It seemed to him that there he could hold his ground against the invaders for three weeks; and his imagination was that, baffled for many days by the strength of his position, drawing their supplies from the ships with pain and uncertainty, and encumbered more and more every day with wounded men, the Allies would fall into evil days. In the mean time the troops long since despatched from Bessarabia would begin to reach him by way of Perekop and Simpheropol; and thus reinforced, he would in due season take the .

Kiriakoff, an officer of high reputation, was attempting indirect methods of calling Prince Mentschikoff's attention to the defectiveness of his arrangements. — *Kiriakoff's Statement.*

offensive, inflicting upon the Western Powers a chas-
tisement commensurate with their rashness.

Prince Mentschikoff rested this structure of hope   His reli-
upon the assumption that he could hold the position   ance on the natural
on the Alma for at the least many days together, and   strength of the
against repeated assaults.   Yet he took little pains   position.
to prepare the ground for a great defence.*   On the
jutting rib which goes round the front of the Kourgané Hill, at a distance of about 300 yards from
the river, he threw up a breastwork — a work of a   The means
very slight kind, presenting no physical obstacle to   he took for strength-
the advance of troops, but sufficiently extended to be   ening it.
capable of receiving the fourteen heavy guns with
which he armed it.**   This work was called the
"Great Redoubt."***   Prince Mentschikoff was delighted with this earthwork.   "Is not this a grand
thing?" said he to General Kiriakoff the day before
the action; "see, it will do mischief both ways."
And he then pointed out how, whilst the face of the
redoubt commanded the smooth slope beneath it, the
guns at the shoulder of the work would throw their
fire across the great road on either side of the bridge.

* I say this in the teeth of the English despatches, and, I fear, of
many written and oral statements from officers; but I am sure that
every engineer who saw the ground will support my assertion.

** Twelve only, according to Prince Gortschakoff. The pieces
were 32-pounders and 24-pound howitzers.

*** The work was formed by cutting a shallow trench and throwing
up the earth in front of it. I follow the military authorities in calling
these works "redoubts," because our people at home came to know of
them under this description; but the term is not accurate, for they were
open towards the rear.

CHAP.
XLIV.

On the same hill, but higher up and more to his right, the Prince threw up another slight breastwork, which he armed with a battery of field-guns. This was the Lesser Redoubt.

The vineyards at some points were marked and cleared so as to give full effect to the action of the artillery; but except the two redoubts, no field-works were constructed by the Russian General. Wilful and confident, he was content to rest mainly upon the natural strength of the ground, the valour of his troops, and the faith that he had in his own prowess as a commander. He even omitted, as we have seen, to break up or to guard the waggon-road which led up from Almatamack to the left of his position. The Prince did not attempt to occupy the West Cliff; but some days before the action a battalion* and half a battery had been placed overlooking the sea in the village of Ulukul Akles, in order, as was said, to "catch marauders," or to prevent a descent from the sea in the rear of the Russian army; and the detachment remained in that part of the field until the time when the battle began.

Disposition of his troops.

On the ledge which divided the river from the steep broken side of the Telegraph Height Prince Mentschikoff placed four Militia** battalions, and

---

* The No. 2 battalion of Minsk.

** I adopt this inaccurate term as the best I can find to describe these semi-regular troops, because to call them, as the Russians do, "reserve battalions," would tend to confuse, by suggesting the idea of "reserves" in the ordinary sense. I thought at one time I might have

supported them by three battalions of regular infantry,* placed only a hundred and fifty yards in
their rear, and by a fourth battalion** drawn up in
a neighbouring ravine.*** Further still in rear, he
held in hand, as a reserve for his left wing, the four
battalions of the "Moscow" corps which had joined
him that morning.† These, with two batteries of
artillery,†† were all the forces occupying that part
of the position which was about to be assailed by
the French.††† Including the battalion and the half-
battery at Ulukul Akles, they consisted of thirteen
battalions of infantry with twenty guns, and numbered altogether rather more than 10,000 men. §

Forces
originally
posted in
the part
of the
position
assailed
by the
French

---

called them "depôt battalions," but upon the whole it seemed to me
that the term "militia" would be less likely to convey a wrong notion
than the term "depôt." They are troops regarded as very inferior in
quality to troops of the line. The four battalions which I call "militia"
were the "reserve" battalions of the 19th Division. — *Anitchkoff,
Chodasiewicz.*

 * Nos. 2, 3, and 4 of the Taroutine corps. — *Anitchkoff, Chodasiewicz.*

 ** The No. 1 battalion of the same corps. — *Ib.*

 *** Chodasiewicz.

 † The battalions of the Moscow corps. — *Anitchkoff, Chodasiewicz.*

 †† Viz., the Nos. 3 and 5 batteries of the 17th brigade of artillery.

 ††† The four batteries of the Minsk corps, with several guns, were
afterwards moved into this part of the ground, as will be seen by-
and-by.

Thirteen battalions of 750 each,	. .	9,750
One battery of position, 263 men,	. .	263
One light battery, ...	. .	210
Half of another light battery,	. . .	105
		10,328

Anitchkoff and Chodasiewicz, writing with opposite feelings, and

They formed the left wing of the Russian army, and were commanded by General Kiriakoff. The battalions were placed at intervals, checkerwise, and each battalion was massed in column of companies. A line of skirmishers was thrown out in front; but for want, as was said, of better ground to act upon, these skirmishers were kept within ten yards of the "Militia" battalions. The two batteries of artillery were not at first so placed as to be of any use. No part of this force on the Telegraph Height was covered by intrenchments, or by any kind of field-work.

Forces originally posted in the part of the position assailed by the English.
In the main Pass, facing the bridge, and destined to confront the 2d Division of the English army, Prince Mentschikoff placed four battalions of light infantry,* with one battalion of rifles;** and three out of those five battalions had orders to advance and skirmish in the vineyards. The other two battalions were kept massed in column. Near the bridge was posted a battalion of sappers and miners.*** Astride the great road, and disposed along the chain of hillocks which runs across the Pass looking down on the bridge, the Prince placed two batteries of

differing in many things, are strictly in accord as to the number of battalions posted in this part of the field.

   * The four battalions of the Borodino corps. — *Anitchkoff, Chodasiewics.*

   ** The sixth battalion of Riflemen. — *Anitchkoff, Chodasiewics.*

   *** Anitchkoff.

field-artillery.* These two batteries, acting together, and comprising sixteen guns,** are here termed "the "Causeway batteries." The force in this part of the field formed the centre of the line, and was under the command of Prince Gortschakoff.***

The right wing of the Russian army was the force destined to confront, first our Light Division, and then the Guards and the Highlanders. It was posted on the slopes of the Kourganè Hill. Here was the Great Redoubt, armed with its fourteen heavy guns;† and Prince Mentschikoff was so keen to defend this part of the ground, that he gathered round the work, on the slopes of the hill, a force of no less than sixteen battalions of regular infantry,††

* Light batteries, Nos. 1 and 2 of the 16th Artillery brigade. — Anitchkoff, Chodasiewics.

** Prince Gortschakoff says that these guns were eighteen in number.

*** The Borodino corps formed part of General Kiriakoff's command; but the nature of the ground and the course which the action took prevented him from having it in his actual control; and Gortschakoff, in the absence of the General commanding in chief, was the General to whom the corps would have to look for guidance.

† Prince Gortschakoff puts the numbers of these guns at twelve. Chodasiewicz supposed that the redoubt was armed with the guns of the No. 2 battery of the 16th Artillery brigade; but the calibre of the gun and the howitzer now at Woolwich prove that the ordnance which armed the redoubt were not a part of the regular field-artillery, but were brought from Sebastopol.

†† The four battalions of the Kazan, or Prince Michael's corps, the four battalions of the Vladimir corps, the four battalions of the Sousdal corps, and the four battalions of the Uglitz corps. — Anitchkoff, Chodasiewics.

besides the two battalions of sailors,* and four
batteries of field-artillery.** The right of the forces
on the Kourganè Hill rested on a slope to the east
of the Lesser Redoubt,*** and the left on the great
road.   Twelve of the battalions of regular infantry
were disposed into battalion-columns posted at intervals and checkerwise on the flanks of the Great
Redoubt; the other four battalions, drawn up in
one massive column, were held as a reserve for the
right wing on the higher slope of the hill.   Of the
four field-batteries, one armed the Lesser Redoubt,
another was on the high ground commanding and
supporting the Great Redoubt, and the remaining
two were held in reserve.†   General Kvetzinski

* Chodasiewics.   Anitchkoff calls this force a half battalion only;
but Chodasiewicz saw the two battalions in march with their four
guns, and I accept his statement. Anitchkoff says that these men were
thrown forward as skirmishers in the vineyards.

** The No. 2 heavy battery of the 16th Artillery brigade, the No. 3
battery of position of the 17th brigade of Artillery, and the No. 3 battery of position, half of the No. 3 light battery of the 14th Artillery
brigade, and the half battery belonging to the sailors. — Anitchkoff, or
Chodasiewicz. The latter supposes that some of these batteries were
posted more towards the centre with the reserve battalions.

*** It fired five guns only at the time when the Highlanders advanced; but it is believed that the three additional guns requisite to
complete the battery were in the work at the beginning of the action.
It was probably the No. 2 battery of the 16th Artillery brigade referred
to in the former note.

† Although I gather the numbers and descriptions of these forces
from Russian authorities, I draw much of my knowledge of the way in
which they were disposed from the observation of our officers; and it
should be observed that the above statement applies to the state of the
field at the time when the battle was going on, and not to the dispositions which Prince Mentschikoff may have made in the earlier part
of the day.

commanded the troops in this part of the field. On his extreme right, and posted at intervals along a curve drawn from his right front to his centre rear, Prince Mentschikoff placed his cavalry, — a force comprising 3400* lances, with three batteries of horse-artillery.**

Each of these bodies of horse, when brought within sight of the Allies, was always massed in column.

Thus, then, it was to bar the Pass and the great road, to defend the Kourgané Hill and to cover his right flank, that the Russian General gathered his main strength; and this was the part of the field destined to be assailed by our troops. That portion of the Russian force which directly confronted the English army, consisted of 3400 cavalry, twenty-four battalions of infantry, and seven batteries of field-artillery, besides the fourteen heavy guns in the Great Redoubt, making together 23,400 men*** and eighty-six guns.

* The Russian official authorities confess to but 3000. The force consisted of the brigade of Hussars, 6th division of cavalry, and two regiments of Cossacks of the Don. — *Chodasiewicz.*

** The No. 12 Light-Horse battery, 6th brigade of Horse-Artillery (*Chodasiewicz*), and two batteries of the Cossacks of the Don. — *Anitchkoff.*

*** Twenty-four battalions at 750 each, ... 18,000
Three heavy batteries at 263 each, ... 789
Six light batteries at 210 artillerymen each, . . . 1,260
Cavalry, ... 3,400
Men, . 23,449
Nine batteries at 8 guns each, ... 72
Heavy guns from Sebastopol in the Great Redoubt, 14
Guns, . 86

But besides this force, Prince Mentschikoff, at the commencement of the action, had posted across the great road leading down to the bridge a force of seven battalions of infantry,* with two batteries** of artillery. These troops he called his "Great Re-"serve;" and they were, in fact, his last. Yet he held them so closely in rear of the battalions facing the bridge, that they might be regarded as forces actually operating in support. Plainly this disposition of his troops was governed by a keen anxiety to defend the great road and the Kourganè Hill—for it was so ordered that, to sustain the struggle there, it would cost him but a few moments to bring his last reserves into action; and, in truth, he committed himself so deeply to this, his favourite part of the battle-field, that, when he afterwards endeavoured to shift a portion of his reserves towards his left, he was unable to make their strength tell.

The numbers actually opposed to the French and the English respectively.

It will be seen, however, that in the course of the action the Prince took off to his left, to use against the French, three of the battalions belonging to his great reserve, and also moved in the same direction two light batteries, together with a few squadrons of Hussars, which formed, as it seems, his personal escort. So, omitting only from the calcula-

---

* The four battalions of the Volhynia corps, and three battalions, Nos. 1, 3, 4, of the Minsk corps. — *Anitchkoff, Chodasiewicz.*

** The No. 4 and No. 5 light batteries of the 17th brigade of Artillery; Chodasiewicz and Anitchkoff differ.

tion the change effected by moving those horsemen,[*] it would follow that the whole force which, sooner or later, confronted the French, was a force of 13,000 men[**] and thirty-six guns; and that the force which confronted the English was a force of 26,000 men[***] with eighty-six guns.

The forces with which the Allied commanders prepared to assail this position were thus composed: There were some 30,000 French infantry and artillerymen,[†] with sixty-eight guns; and, added to this force, under the command of the Marshal St Arnaud, was the division of 7000 Turkish infantry.[††] With Lord Raglan, and present under arms, there was a force of fully 1000 cavalry, 25,000[†††] infantry and

---

[*] I omit these horsemen from the calculation because I do not know their number. Anitchkoff calls the body "a portion of the Hussar "brigade." The French official account says the force was one of eight squadrons. I imagine that an estimate putting it at 400 would not be far from the truth.

[**] Strictly 12,998. This figure is attained by adding to the 10,308 before given, the three battalions taken from the Great Reserve (at 750 each) and the 420 artillerymen of the two light batteries which were moved during the action.

[***] Strictly 26,079. This figure is attained by adding to the 23,449 before detailed the four battalions of the Great Reserve which were dealt with by English alone, and by subtracting the 420 artillerymen referred to in the preceding note.

[†] Précis Historique, p. 101-102, which gives 50,204 as the total, but that is a computation of the force embarked; and, since cholera was prevailing, the deductions from strength between the 7th and the 20th of the month must have brought the numbers below 30,000.

[††] Ibid.

[†††] Or, speaking more closely, 24,400. The "morning state" which I have before me is of the 18th September, and it gives as present under arms (without including the cavalry, of which there was no "state") a

CHAP.
XLIV.

artillerymen, and sixty pieces of field-artillery.* In all, the Allied armies advancing upon the Alma comprised near 63,000 men and 128 guns.

St Arnaud, with 37,000 men and sixty-eight guns, and effectually supported by the fire of nine war-steamers,** was destined to confront a Russian force of 13,000 men and thirty-six guns. The English, with 26,000 men*** and sixty guns, had to deal with a Russian force comprising, so to speak, the same number of men,† but having with it eighty-six guns. Therefore the French had to do with somewhat more than one-third of the Russian force; and the other two-thirds of it — two-thirds of it, speaking roughly—were left to the care of the English. St Arnaud was to his adversaries in a proportion not very far short of three to one;†† Lord Raglan was, so to speak, equal in numbers to his

total of 26,004 officers and men, and deducting the 1600 men detached under Colonel Torrens, there remained 24,404 infantry and artillery-men.

* The official "state" prepared for Lord Raglan gives two troops of horse-artillery, and only seven batteries, but it omits the battery attached to the 4th Division.

** Official despatch of Admiral Hamelin.

*** Or, speaking more closely, 25,404.

† Speaking more strictly, the English were 25,400, and the Russians they dealt with 26,000. In that calculation, as in those preceding it, the change effected by moving the horsemen of the escort is left unnoticed; but if that change be taken into account, by subtracting 400 (the estimated number of the horsemen who were moved) the numbers of the English would be only 200 less than those of the Russians with whom they had to deal.

** Or, more strictly, 37 to 13.

adversaries, and was inferior to them in point of artillery by a difference of twenty-six guns.

That part of the position which was attacked by the French presented some physical obstacles to the advance of the assailants, but was not very strong in a military sense, and was defended by no field-works. The ground attacked by the English did not oppose great physical obstacles to the advance of the assailants, but it was intrenched, and, besides, was so formed by nature as to give great destructive power, and, by consequence, great strength, to an enemy defending it with the resources of modern warfare. The French were covered and supported on their right by the sea and the ships — on their left by the English army.* The English had the French on their right, but they marched with their left flank quite bare; the French advanced upon heights well surveyed from the sea. Except in an imperfect way from maps, the English knew nothing of the ground before them. No spies or deserters had come in.

CHAP. XLIV.

The tasks undertaken by the French and the English respectively.

---

* This sentence, perhaps, may help to elucidate the one which goes before it, by showing what is meant when soldiers speak of "the strength of a position." In these days mere inert physical obstacles are commonly overcome or eluded; and the security of the defender depends not in general upon those geographical features which would make access difficult for travellers, but rather upon such a conformation of ground as will give him the means of doing harm to his assailants.

III.

Late in the evening on the 19th, Marshal St
Arnaud, attended by Colonel Trochu, rode up to the
little post-house on the Bulganak in which Lord
Raglan had established his quarters. He came to
concert a plan of attack for the following day.

Confer-
ence the
night be-
fore the
battle be-
tween St
Arnaud
and Lord
Raglan.

From on board their ships the French had long
been busily engaged in surveying the enemy's position, and by this time they had gathered a good deal
of knowledge of that part of the ground which lies
near the sea-shore. They had ascertained, or found
means of inferring, that the stream was fordable at
its mouth, and they moreover assured themselves
that, at the time of their last observations, the West
Cliff was not occupied in strength by the enemy.

The
French
plan.

Upon these important discoveries Marshal St Arnaud
based his plan of attack. He proposed that the
war-steamers, closing in as nearly as was practicable,
should move parallel with the land-forces, and a
little in advance; that, under cover of their fire,
a portion of the French force should advance along
the shore and seize the West Cliff; and that this
movement should be followed up by a resolute,
vigorous, and unremitting attack upon the enemy's
left flank and left front.* M. St Arnaud was at this

---

* The plan was like that of the great Frederick at Leuthen, but with
the difference that the force advancing to turn the enemy's left was to
be covered and supported by fire from the shipping.

time free from pain; and, knowing that now, at last, he had an enemy in his front, and that a great conflict was near at hand, he seemed to be fired with a more than healthy energy.   Sometimes in English, sometimes in the rapid words of his own tongue, and always with vehement gesture, he laboured to show how sure it was that the attack from his right centre would be fierce, unrelenting, decisive. Lord Raglan, cast in another mould, sat quiet, with governed features, restraining—or only, perhaps, postponing—his smiles, listening graciously, assenting, or not dissenting, putting forward no plan of his own, and, in short, eluding discussion.   This method, perhaps, was instinctive with him; but, in his intercourse with the French, he followed it deliberately and upon system.   He never forgot that to keep good our relations with the French was his great duty; and studying how best to avert the danger of misunderstandings, he had already made it his maxim that there was hardly any danger so great as the danger of controversy.   Whether in any even small degree the English General had been brought to share the opinion entertained of M. St Arnaud in the French capital and in the French army the world will never know. Of a certainty, Lord Raglan dealt as though he held it to be a clear gain to be able to avoid intrusting the Marshal with a knowledge of what our army would be likely to undertake; but my belief is that this, his seemingly guarded method, was not so much based upon anything which may have come

The part taken by Lord Raglan at the conference.

to his ears from Paris or from the French camp, but
rather upon his desire to ward off controversy, and
upon his true native English dislike of all premature
planning. He was so sure of his troops, and so conscious of his own power to act swiftly when the occasion might come, that, although he was now within
half a march of the enemy's assembled forces, he
did not at all long to ruffle his mind with projects — with projects for the attack of a position not
hitherto reconnoitred.

M. St Arnaud's plan of turning the enemy's left
was to be executed by the French army, with the
aid of the shipping; and the part which the English land-forces should take in the action was a matter distinct. But for this, also, the French commander and his military counsellors had carefully taken
thought.

French
plan for
the opera-
tions of the
English
army.
To illustrate the operations which he proposed,
M. St Arnaud produced a rough map, — a map
slightly and rapidly drawn, yet traced with that
spirit and significance which are characteristic of
French military sketches. In this sketch Bosquet's
Division and the Turkish troops were represented as
effecting the turning movement on the enemy's left;
and the 1st and 3d French Divisions were shown
to be so deployed, and so placed, that, in the order
of attack assigned to them by the sketch, they
would confront almost the whole face of the enemy's
position, leaving only one or two battalions to be

dealt with in front by the English troops.* So, to find some occupation for the English, the sketch represented our army as filing away obliquely, in order to turn the enemy's right flank. Of course this plan rested entirely upon the assumption that the enemy's front would be fully occupied (as represented in the sketch) by the French attack.

Lord Raglan's experience or instinct told him that no such plan as this could go for much until the assailing forces should come to measure their line with that of the enemy. So, without either combating or accepting the suggestion addressed to him, he simply assured the Marshal that he might rely upon the vigorous co-operation of the British army. The French plan seems to have made little impression on Lord Raglan's mind. He foresaw, perhaps, that the ingenuity of the evening would be brought to nothingness by the teachings of the morrow.

Whilst the French Marshal was striving, in his vehement way, to convey an idea of the vigour with which he would conduct the attack, his appointed adviser, Colonel Trochu, whose mission it was to moderate the fire of his chief, thought it right to interpose with a question of a practical kind — a question as to the time and place for relieving the French soldiers of their packs. Instantly, if so one may speak, St Arnaud reared, for Trochu had

* See the facsimile of this plan, taken from the "Pièces Officielles," published by the French Government.

CHAP. XLIV.

St Arnaud's demeanour.

17*

touched him with the curb, and in the presence, too, of Lord Raglan. He angrily suppressed the question of the packs as one of mere detail. Yet, on the afternoon of the morrow, that question of the packs was destined to recur, and to govern the movements of the whole French army.

Before the Marshal and Lord Raglan parted, it was agreed that Bosquet with his Division should advance at five o'clock in the morning, and that, two hours later, the rest of the Allied forces should begin their march upon the enemy's position.

Result of
the con-
ference. This determination as to the time for marching was almost the only fruit which St Arnaud drew from the interview. He had thought to engage his colleague in the plan contrived for the guidance of the English at the French headquarters; but when he came to be in the presence of the English General, he unconsciously yielded, as other men commonly did, to the spell of his personal ascendancy; and although he showed the sketch, and may have uttered, perhaps, a few hurried words to explain its meaning, he did not effectually bring himself to proffer advice to Lord Raglan. Either he altogether omitted the intended counsel, or else he so slurred it over as not to win for it any grave notice from even the most careful of listeners.

When the conference ended Lord Raglan came out with his guests to the door of the hut. M. St Arnaud mounted his horse, and was elate; but he was elate, not with the knowledge of having achieved a purpose, but rather, it would seem, from the sense of that singular comfort which anxious men always derived from the mere power of Lord Raglan's presence. Perhaps, when the Marshal reached his quarters, he began to see that, after all, there was a gulf between him and the English General, and that, notwithstanding his energy and boldness, he had been unaccountably hindered from passing it.

IV.

It had been determined that the troops should March of the Allies. get under arms without bugle or drum.

Silently, therefore, on the morning of the 20th of September 1854, the men of the Allied armies rose from their bivouac, and made ready for the march which was to bring them into the presence of the enemy. It was so early as half-past five that Bosquet, with the 2d French Division and the Turkish Battalions, began his march along the coast; and at seven o'clock the main body of the French army was under arms and ready to march. But the position taken up by the English for the defence of the Allied armies on the Bulganak had imposed Causes delaying the march of the English army. upon Lord Raglan the necessity of showing a front towards the east; and for the Divisions so employed a long and toilsome evolution was needed in order

to bring them into the general order of march.* At
that time, too, there was a broad interval between
our extreme right and Prince Napoleon's Division.
Moreover, the line of the coast which the armies
were to follow trended away towards the south-west,
forming an obtuse angle with the course of the
stream (the Bulganak) on which the Allies had
bivouacked; and in the movement requisite for
adjusting the front of the Allied forces to the direction of the shore, the English, marching upon the
exterior arc, had to undergo more labour than those
who moved near the pivot on which the variation of
front was effected.**

This was not all. The baggage-train accompany-
ing our forces, though small in comparison with the
encumbrances usually attending an army in the field,
was large as compared with that of the French; and
Lord Raglan (whose favourite anxiety was concerning his reserve ammunition) refused to allow the
convoy to be stripped of protection. The oblique
movement of the troops towards their right was
tending to leave the convoy uncovered; and in order
that it should be again enfolded, as in the previous
day's order of march, it was necessary to move it far

* Those divisions had been posted nearly at right angles to the
front line, and the segment in which the troops would have to wheel
in order to get into the line of march would be nearly 90 degrees.

** Several military reports and documents explain this, but the plan
prepared by the French Government shows with admirable clearness
the nature of the evolution which the English army had to perform.
See the Plan.

towards our right. Lord Raglan insisted that this should be done; so on the morning of the long-expected battle, and with the enemy in front, St Arnaud and the whole French army, and the English army too, chafed bitterly at the delay they had to endure whilst strings of bullock-carts were slowly dragged westward into the true line of march. Besides, the enemy's cavalry gave the English no leave to examine the ground towards which they were marching; and whilst the French, being next to the sea, could make straight for the cliff already reconnoitred from the ships, the English army advanced without knowledge of that part of the position which it was to confront, and was twice compelled to make laborious changes in the direction of its march. Therefore, for much of the delay which occurred there were good reasons; but not for all. Sir George Brown had been directed on the night of the 19th to advance on the morrow at seven o'clock, and he imagined — it is strange if he, of all men, with his great knowledge of such things, was wrong upon a point of military usage — he imagined that the order would be repeated in the morning, and he waited accordingly. Also the English troops moved slowly. Time was growing to be of high worth, and from causes which justified a good deal, though not quite all, of their delay, the English at this time were behindhand.

In order that the operations of the day might be adjusted to the time which the English army re-

quired, orders were sent forward suspending for a
while the advance of Bosquet's column; and at nine
o'clock the main body of the French army came
to a halt, and cooked their coffee. Whilst they
rested, our troops, by moving obliquely towards their
right, were slowly overcoming the distance which
divided them from the French left, and were at the
same time working their way through the angle
which measured their divergence from the line of
march.

Of those composing an armed force there are few
who understand the hindrances which block its progress; and naturally the French were vexed by the
delay which seemed to be caused by the slowness of
the English army. They, however, conformed with
great care to the tardiness of our advance, and even
allowed our army to gain upon them; for when the
Allies reached the ground which sloped down towards
the Alma, the heads of our leading columns were
abreast of the French skirmishers.[*]

Meanwhile the Allied steamers had been seeking
opportunities for bringing their guns to bear, and at
twenty minutes past ten they opened fire.[**] One or two

---

[*] Lord Raglan was amongst those who observed this fact, and he
stated it in a letter which is before me.

[**] Private MS. by Mr Romaine, the Judge-Advocate. I may here
say generally, to avoid repeated notes, that, whenever I speak of an
event as happening at a time stated with exactness, I do so on the
authority of Romaine. He was a man so gifted with long sight, as well
as with power of estimating numbers, and, though a civilian, was so
thoroughly apt for military business, that Lord Raglan used at a later

of their missiles, though at a very long range, reached
some of those Russian battalions which stood posted
in rear of the Telegraph.

At half-past eleven o'clock the English right had
got into direct contact with the French left, and our
Light and 2d Divisions were marching in the same
alignment as the 1st and 3d Divisions of our French
Allies.

V.

Twice again there were protracted halts. The
last of these took place at a distance of about a mile
and a half from the banks of the Alma. From the
spot where the forces were halted the ground sloped
gently down to the river's side; and though some
men lay prostrate under the burning sun, with little
thought except of fatigue, there were others who
keenly scanned the ground before them, well knowing that now at last the long-expected conflict would
begin. They could make out the course of the river
from the dark belt of gardens and vineyards which

time to call him "the eye of the army." During the action he rode an
old hunter, steady enough to allow him to write without quitting his
saddle; so, whenever he observed a change in the progress of the
action, he took out his watch and pocket-book and made at the minute
the memoranda on which I rely. I am, therefore, very certain that the
spaces of time intervening between any two events spoken of in this
precise way were exactly those which I give; but I have reason to
think that the watches of men in the different camps had been dif-
ferently set

marked its banks; and men with good eyes could descry a slight seam running across a rising-ground beyond the river, and could see, too, some dark squares or oblongs, encroaching like small patches of culture upon the broad downs. The seam was the Great Redoubt; the square-looking marks that stained the green sides of the hills were an army in order of battle.

That 20th of September on the Alma was like some remembered day of June in England, for the sun was unclouded, and the soft breeze of the morning had lulled to a breath at noontide, and was creeping faintly along the hills. It was then that in the Allied armies there occurred a singular pause of sound — a pause so general as to have been observed and remembered by many in remote parts of the ground, and so marked that its interruption by the mere neighing of an angry horse seized the attention of thousands; and although this strange silence was the mere result of weariness and chance, it seemed to carry a meaning; for it was now that, after near forty years of peace, the great nations of Europe were once more meeting for battle.

Even after the sailing of the expedition, the troops had been followed by reports that the war, after all, would be stayed; and the long frequent halts, and the quiet of the armies on the sunny slope, seemed to harmonise with the idea of disbelief in the coming of the long-promised fight. But in the midst of this repose Sir Colin Campbell said to one of his officers,

"This will be a good time for the men to get loose CHAP.
XLIV.
"half their cartridges;"* and when the command
travelled on along the ranks of the Highlanders, it
lit up the faces of the men one after another, assuring
them that now at length, and after long expectance,
they indeed would go into action. They began obeying the order, and with beaming joy, for they came
of a warlike race; yet not without emotion of a graver
kind — they were young soldiers, new to battle.

VI.

Lord Raglan now crossed the front of Prince Meeting
between
M. St
Arnaud
and Lord
Raglan.
Napoleon's Division in order to meet Marshal St.
Arnaud, whose guidon was seen coming towards our
lines.** The two commanders rode forward together,
inclining towards their left. No one was with them.
They rode on till they came to one of those mounds
or tumuli, of which there were many on the steppe.
From that spot they scrutinised the enemy's position
with their field-glasses.

At this interview no change was made in that
portion of the plan which determined that the French

---

* The cartridges are delivered to each man in a packet, and, to
avoid loss of time in presence of the enemy, a sufficient number should
be "shaken loose" before the troops are brought into action.

** They had met before at about half-past nine, but the Russian
cavalry had not then quitted the heights, and they were obliged to postpone their reconnaissance.

should turn the enemy's left; but the part to be
taken by the English was still in question, and
St. Arnaud threw out or revived the idea of a flank
movement by the English on the enemy's right.*
Lord Raglan, however, now gazed upon the real
ground which the French counsellors of the night
before had striven to scan in their imaginations, and,
having an eye for country, he must have begun to
see the truth. He must have begun to see that the
French, hugging the sea-shore, and pouring two fifths
of their whole force against the undefended part of
the opposite heights, would not only fail to confront
the whole Russian army in the way promised by the
sketch, but would in reality confront only a small
portion of it, leaving to the English the duty of
facing the enemy along two-thirds of their whole
front. Of a certainty he did not entertain for a
moment the idea of making a flank attack, but it
was not according to his nature to explain to men
their errors, and it seems he spoke so little that St.
Arnaud did not yet know what the English General
would do;** but presently a general officer rode up
and joined the two chiefs. Then the Marshal, closing
his telescope, turned to Lord Raglan and asked him
"whether he would turn the position or attack it in
"front?" Lord Raglan's answer was to the effect,
that, "with such a body of cavalry as the enemy

* Inferred from what follows.
** Inferred from what follows.

bad in the plain, he would not attempt to turn the position." *

Whilst the chiefs were still side by side, it being now one o'clock, the advance sounded along the lines, and the French and the English armies moved forward close abreast. The Marshal then rode off towards his centre.

VII.

The orders for the advance were sent forward to Bosquet; and, as soon as they reached him, he threw out skirmishers and moved forward in two columns. His right column was the brigade commanded by General Bouat; the left column was Autemarre's brigade. Each brigade, massed in column,** was followed by its share of the artillery belonging to the Division; and Bouat's brigade was followed by the whole of the Turkish Division except two battalions. Towards Bosquet's left, but far in his rear, there moved forward the 1st Division under Canrobert, and the 3d Division under Prince Napoleon. These two divisions advanced in the same alignment. The 4th Division, under General Forey, marched in rear of the 1st and 3d Divisions, and two Turkish battalions escorted the baggage.***

Bosquet's advance.

He divides his force.

* This disposes of the notion which seems to have been really entertained by many of the French—the notion that Lord Raglan stood engaged to turn the enemy's right.

** Regiments in column at section distance.

*** Précis Historique mainly.

CHAP.
XLIV.
Disposi-
tion of the
main body
of the
French
army.

Of the
English
army.

The formation of Canrobert's and Prince Napoleon's Divisions was upon two lines.   The first
brigade of each division was in front and deployed,*
and the second brigade of each division followed the
first brigade, and was massed in column.**

The 4th French Division marched in the same
order as the 1st and 3d Divisions, except that its
leading brigade was not deployed. The artillery of
each division was enfolded between its two brigades.

On the immediate left of Prince Napoleon, Sir
De Lacy Evans marched, with the troops of his Division massed in battalion columns,*** and was followed by the 3d Division in column.   The batteries
belonging to each of these divisions marched on its
right or inner flank.

Immediately on Sir De Lacy's left the Light
Division moved forward under Sir George Brown.
The division was massed in column.† It was sup-
ported by the 1st Division under the Duke of Cam-
bridge, and that in turn was followed by the 4th
Division †† under Sir George Cathcart.   Sir George

* Not deployed into "line," according to the English plan, but
merely brought into a formation, which, leaving each battalion massed
places them all in the same alignment.
** Regiments in column at section distance.
*** In contiguous battalion columns right in front at battalion
distance. Sir De Lacy's touched Prince Napoleon's Division, and it
was thought right to assimilate its order of march to that adopted by
the Prince.
† In double column of companies from the centre.
†† Minus the 63d and two companies of the 46th, left under the command of General Torrens at the place of disembarkation. The force

Cathcart, however, in accordance with a suggestion
made by himself, was authorised to take ground to
his left, and place his force in échelon to the 1st
Division.*

The three great infantry columns thus composing
the left wing of our army were covered in front, left
flank, and rear, by riflemen in extended order, and
by the cavalry. The battery belonging to each division marched on its right or inner flank.

But soon Colonel Lawrence with his riflemen got
on so far in advance as to provoke a fire from the
Russian skirmishers, then swarming in the vineyards
below, and some rifle-balls shot from that quarter
came dropping into the ground near the column
formed by the Light Division. Almost at the same
moment the artillery-men on the Russian heights began to try their range; and although the air was so
clear that our men could see and watch the flight of
the cannon-balls thrown at so long a range, it seemed
prudent for our leading divisions to go into line.
Those divisions, therefore, were halted, and their deployment immediately began.

In deploying, Sir De Lacy Evans, being pressed *The leading divi-*
upon by Prince Napoleon's Division on his right, *sions of*
the Eng-
was compelled to take ground to his left, and to *lish army*
deploy
into line.

actually with Sir George during the action consisted of the 20th, 21st,
and 68th Regiments, the 1st battalion of Rifles, and Townsend's
battery.

* Sir George Cathcart marched with the head of his column (at
quarter distance right in front) in line with the rear companies of the
1st Division.

CHAP.
XLIV.

The Light
Division
not on its
right
ground.

encroach upon a part of the space which Sir George
Brown had expected to occupy with his division.

The deployment of the Light Division was effected by each regiment with beautiful precision,*
but, unhappily, the division was not on its right
ground.

Sir George Brown was near-sighted, and had not
accustomed himself to repair the defect, as some commanders have done, by a constant and well-practised
use of glasses; and, on the other hand, the very fire
and energy of his nature, and his almost violent
sense of duty, prevented him from getting into the
habit of trusting to the eyes of other men. For
hours in the early morning the division had been
wearied by having to incline towards its right. At
half-past eleven the effort was reversed, and the division then laboured to take ground to its left; but
in that last direction it had not taken ground enough.
Lord Raglan, with his quick eye, had seen the fault,
and sent an order** to have it corrected. Not content with this, he soon after rode up to the Division,
and, failing to see Sir George Brown at the moment,
told Codrington that the Division must take more
ground to the left. Then, unhappily, when he had
uttered the very words which would have thrown the

* The deployment was upon the two centre companies of the division. Whilst the movement was proceeding, one man, a sergeant,
was killed by a rifle-ball. This was probably the first death in our
lines.

** Colonel Lysons, I think, carried it.

British army into its true array, and averted much evil, Lord Raglan was checked by his ruling foible. He had already sent the order to the divisional general, and he could not bear to pain or embarrass him by pressing the execution of it upon one of his brigadiers; so he recalled his wholesome words.[*] The Division failed to take ground enough to the left; and when the deployment was complete, Sir George Brown had the grief of seeing his right regiment (the 7th Fusiliers) overlapped by the left — nay, even by the centre — of Pennefather's brigade.[**] The fault was not retrieved: it was fruitful of confusion.

The artillery attached to our two leading divisions was now also drawn up in line, and Sir George Brown reckoned that he alone showed a front extending to nearly a mile.

At the same time the Duke of Cambridge, at Sir George Brown's request, altered the formation of his Division by distributing it into a line of columns.[***]

These changes having been completed, the English army resumed its march; and the leading divisions coming more closely within range, and being a little galled by the enemy's fire, Sir George Brown *The march continued.*

---

[*] I derive my knowledge from an officer who heard Lord Raglan's words.

[**] When the deployment took place the 7th Fusiliers was in rear of the 95th Regiment; and it afterwards, as will be seen, marched through it.

[***] "A line of contiguous quarter-distance columns."

Invasion of the Crimea. III.   18

halted, and tried the experiment of wheeling into open column. Afterwards, however, he returned to his line-formation, and in that order marched forward.*

VIII.

So now the whole Allied armies, hiding nothing of their splendour and their strength, descended slowly into the valley; and the ground on the right bank of the river is so even and so gentle in its slope, and on the left bank so commanding, that every man of the invaders could be seen from the opposite heights.

Spectacle presented to the Russians by the advance of the Allies.

The Russian officers had been accustomed all their days to military inspections and vast reviews, but they now saw before them that very thing for the confronting of which their lives had been one long rehearsal. They saw a European army coming down in order of battle — an army arrayed in no spirit of mimicry, and not at all meant to aid their endless study of tactics, but honestly marching against them, with a mind to carry their heights and take their lives. And gazing with keen and critical eyes upon this array of strangers, whose homes were in lands far away, they looked upon a phenomenon

* My knowledge respecting the movements and evolutions of our infantry divisions is derived mainly from original MSS. in my possession, written by Sir George Brown, the Duke of Cambridge, Sir De Lacy Evans, and Sir George Cathcart.

which raised their curiosity and their wonder, and
which promised, too, to throw some new light on a
notion they had lately been forming.

The whole anxiety of Prince Mentschikoff had
been for his right. If he could hold the Main Pass,
and scare the Allies from all endeavour to turn his
right flank, he believed himself safe; and it had been
clear long ago that his conflict in this part of the
field would be with the English. It was therefore
the more useful to try to spread amongst the Russian
troops an idea that the English, all-powerful at sea,
were thoroughly worthless as soldiers.

The working of this little cheat had been hitherto
aided by circumstance. With the force under Mentschikoff there were two battalions of Russian seamen; and these men, partly from their clumsiness in
manœuvring, partly from their sailor-like whims, and
partly, no doubt, from the mere fact of their being
a small and peculiar minority, had become a subject
of merriment to the soldiery of the regular land-
forces. The Russian soldiery, therefore, were prepared to receive the impression that the red-coats
now discernible in the distance were battalions of
sailors, men of no more use in a land engagement
than their own derided seamen. This idea had fastened
so well upon the mind of the Russian army, that before the battle began it was shared by some of the
more illiterate of the officers, and even, it was said,
in one instance by a general of division.

But the sight now watched with keen eyes from

Notion which the Russian soldiers had been taught to entertain of the English army.

CHAP.
XLIV.
Surprise at
the sight
of the
English
array.
the enemy's heights was one which seemed to have
some bearing upon the rumour that the English were
powerless in a land engagement.   The French and
the Turks were in the deep, crowded masses which
every soldier of the Czar had been accustomed to
look upon as the formations needed for battle; but,
to the astonishment of the Russian officers, the leading
divisions of the men in red were massed in no sort
of column, and were clearly seen coming on in a
slender line — a line only two deep, yet extending
far from east to west.   They could not believe that
with so fine a thread as that the English General was
really intending to confront their massive columns.*
Yet the English troops had no idea that their formation was so singular as to be strange in the eyes of
military Europe.   Wars long past had taught them
that they were gifted with the power of fighting in
this order, and it was a matter of course that, upon
coming within range, they had gone at once into
line.

Meanwhile the war-steamers — eight French and
one English — had pushed forward along the shore
in single file, moving somewhat in advance of the
land-forces; and now, at twenty-five minutes past one
o'clock, the leading vessels opened fire against the
four guns at the village of Ulukul Akles, and again
tried the skill of their gunners upon the distant masses
of infantry which occupied the Telegraph Height and

* Chodasiewics.

the low flat ledge at its base. Convinced that his CHAP. XLIV. chief had been guilty of a grievous error in placing Movement made the Taroutine and the militia battalions on this low without narrow ledge, General Kiriakoff, who commanded in orders by the Tarou- this part of the field, had tried by indirect means to tine and procure a change of plan, but had not ventured to the "Mili-"tia" bat- say anything on the subject to Prince Mentschikoff talions. himself. It is plain, however, that Kiriakoff's opinion, getting abroad, was adopted by the officers of these two corps; for first the militia battalions, and then the battalions of the Taroutine corps, without orders, and without having been assailed or touched (except perhaps by a chance shot or two at very long range from the shipping), began a retrograde movement, and slowly ascended the steep hill till they gained a more commanding position at no great distance from the Telegraph. No effort was made to check this seemingly spontaneous movement.*

IX.

At half-past one o'clock a round-shot from the Half-past opposite heights came ripping the ground near Lord one o'clock. Raglan, and it marked the opening of the battle Cannon-ade di- between the contending land-forces; for in the next rected against the Eng-lish line.

---

* General Kiriakoff's statement, confirmed by Romaine, who observed and noted the movement. The General thought the change of
position requisite; but he admits that a retrograde movement of this
kind, just before the commencement of the battle, was a grave evil.

instant the enemy began to direct a steady cannonade against the English line. At first no one fell; but presently an artilleryman riding in front of his gun bent forward his head, handled the reins with a convulsive grasp, and then, uttering a loud inarticulate sound, fell dead. The peace of Europe had been so long, that to many men the sight was a new one; and of the young soldiers who stood near, some imagined that their comrade had fallen down in a sudden fit; for they hardly yet knew that for the most part, in modern warfare, death comes as though sent by blind chance, no one knows from whence or from whom.

Men of our leading divisions ordered to lie down.

The First Division deployed into line.

Since the enemy's artillery fire had now become brisk, our leading infantry divisions were halted, and the men ordered to lie down. Soon afterwards it was found that the 1st Division had also come within range, and it was then forthwith thrown into line. In preparing for this manœuvre, the Duke of Cambridge took care that ground should not be wanting. Both on his right and on his left he took more ground than had been occupied by the division which marched in his front. Whilst the Light Division in his front was jammed in and entangled with the 2d Division, the Duke had the happiness of seeing his Guards and Highlanders well extended, and competent to act along the whole length of that superb line. The effect of this deployment was, that the extreme right of the Duke's line became a force operating in support of the 2d Division, and that a part of his Highland

Brigade, reaching much further eastward than the
extreme left of the Light Division, became in that
part of the field the true front of the British line.
When this manœuvre was completed, the men of the
1st Division lay down.

Observing the extent of ground occupied by the
1st Division, Lord Raglan at once saw that the 3d
Division would not have room to manœuvre in the
same alignment with the Duke of Cambridge. He
therefore ordered Sir Richard England to support
the Guards. It was this, or some other order sent
nearly at the same time, which, for some reason,
good or fanciful, Lord Raglan chose to have carried
quietly. The directions had been given, and the aide-
de-camp was whirling round his charger, in order to
take a swift flight with the message, when Lord
Raglan stopped him, and said, "Go quietly; don't
"gallop." He seemed to like that whenever the
enemy pointed a field-glass towards the English
headquarters he should look upon a scene of tran-
quillity and leisure.

Sir
Richard
England
ordered
to sup-
port the
Guards.

Our batteries tried their range, but without
effect, and they ceased to fire, reserving their
strength for the time when they would come to
close quarters.

The batteries on the Telegraph Height did not
yet open fire upon the French columns.

Lord Raglan conceived that the operation determined upon by the French ought to take full
effect before he engaged the English army in an

assault upon the enemy's heights; and perhaps, if the whole body of the Allies had been one people, under the command of one general, their advance would have been effected in échelon, and the left would have been kept out of fire whilst the effort on the right was in progress; but the pride of nations must sometimes be suffered to deflect the course of armies; and although there was no military value in any of the ground north of the vineyards, Lord Raglan, it seems, did not like to withhold his infantry whilst the French were executing their forward movement. Since our soldiers lay facing downwards upon the smooth slope which looked against the enemy's batteries, they were seen, every man of them, from head to foot, by the Russian artillery-men, and they drew upon themselves a studious fire from thirty guns.

Fire un-
dergone
by our men
whilst ly-
ing down.
Thus the first trial our men underwent in the action was a trial of passive, enduring courage. They had to lie down, with no duty to perform, except the duty of being motionless; and they made it their pastime to watch the play of the engines worked for their destruction — to watch the jet of smoke — the flash — the short, momentous interval — and then, happily and most often, the twang through the air above, and the welcome sound of the shot at length imbedded in earth. But sometimes, without knowing whence it came, a man would suddenly know the feel of a rushing blast, and a mighty shock, and would find himself bespattered with the brains of the com-

rade who had just been speaking to him. When this happened, two of the comrades of the man killed would get up and gently lift the quivering body, carry it a few paces in rear of the line, then quietly return to their ranks, and again lie down.* This sort of trial is well borne by our troops. They are so framed by nature that, if only they know clearly what they have to do, or to leave undone, they are pleased and animated, nay, even soothed, by a little danger. For, besides that they love strife, they love the arbitrament of chance; and a game where death is the forfeit has a strange, gloomy charm for them. Among the guns ranged on the opposite heights to take his life a man would single out his favourite, and make it feminine for the sake of endearment. There was hardly perhaps a gun in the Great Redoubt which failed to be called by some corrupt variation of "Mary" or "Elizabeth." It was plain that our infantry could be in a kindly humour whilst lying down under fire. They did not perhaps like the duty so well as an animating charge with the bayonet; but if they were to be judged from their demeanour, they preferred it to a church parade. They were in their most gracious temper. Often, when an officer rode past them, they would give him the fruit of their steady and protracted view, and advise him to move a little on one side or the other to avoid a

---

* Casualties of this sort were going on here and there along our line, but the exact incident described in the text was observed in the 30th Regiment.

coming shot. And this the men would do, though
they themselves, however well their quickened sight
might warn them of the coming shot, lay riveted to
the earth by duty.

X.

The level posture of our infantry threw into strong
prominence the figure of every mounted man who
rode along their lines; but the group of horsemen
composing or following the Headquarter Staff was so
marked by the white, flowing plumes of the officers,
that at a distance of a mile and a half it was a
conspicuous object to the naked eye; and a Russian
artilleryman at the Causeway batteries could make
out, with a common field-glass, that of the two or
three officers generally riding abreast at the head of
the plumed cavalcade, there was one, in a dark blue
frock, whose right arm hung ending in an empty

Cannon-
ade di-
rected
against
Lord
Raglan
and his
staff.
sleeve. In truth, Lord Raglan, at this time, was so
often standing still, or else was riding along the line
of our prostrate infantry at so leisurely a pace, that
he and the group about him could not fail to become
a mark for the Russian artillery. The enemy did not,
as it seemed, begin this effort malignantly; and at
first, perhaps, he had no further thought than that of
subjecting the English Headquarters to an ordinary
cannonade, and forcing them to choose a more retired
ground for their surveys.

Still, as might be expected, the Russian artillery-men could not easily brook the conclusion that, whilst the English General chose to remain under their eyes and within range, it was beyond the power of their skill to bend him from his path, or even, as it seemed, to break the thread of his conversation; so, at length growing earnest, they opened fire upon the group from a great number of guns — but in vain, for none of the Staff at this time were struck. Failing with round-shot, the enemy tried shells — shells with the fuses so cut as to burst them in the air a little above the white plumes. This method was tried so industriously and with so much skill, that a few feet over the heads of Lord Raglan and those around him there was kept up for a long time an almost constant bursting of shells. Sometimes the missiles came singly, and sometimes in so thick a flight that several would be exploding nearly at the same moment, or briskly one after the other, right and left, and all around. The fragments of the shells, when they burst, tore their shrill way down from above, harshly sawing the air; and when the novice heard the rush of the shattered missile along his right ear, and then along his left, and imagined that he felt the wind of another fragment of shell come rasping the cloth on his shoulders almost at the same moment, it seemed to him hardly possible that the iron shower would leave one man of the group untouched. But the truth is, that a fragment of shell rending the air with its jagged edges may sound much nearer than it is. None of the Staff were wounded at this time.

Some of the suite were half vexed and half angry; for they knew the value of their chief's life, and they conceived that he was affronting great risk without due motive, and from mere inattention to danger. The storm of missiles generally fell most thickly when Lord Raglan happened to be riding near the great road; for the enemy, having got the range at that point, always laboured to make the bursting of his shells coincide with the moment when our Headquarters were passing. This soon came to be understood, and thenceforth, when the Headquarter group were going to cross the Causeway, they rode at it briskly as at a leap, and spanned it with one or two strides, thus leaving the prepared storm of shells to burst a little behind them. This effort of the Russian artillery against Lord Raglan and the group surrounding him lasted a long time, and was carried on upon a scale better proportioned to the destruction of a whole division than to the mere object of warning off a score of horsemen. If the fire thus expended had been brought to bear on Pennefather's brigade, it might have maimed the English line in a vital part of the field.

XI.

The time was now come when the Allies could measure their front with the enemy's position. It will be remembered that the plan* proposed to Lord Raglan the night before by Marshal St Arnaud rested upon the assumption that the whole of the enemy's forces except two or three battalions would be confronted by the French army, and that, therefore, the only opportunity for important service which the English army could find would be that of making a great flank-movement against the enemy's right; but it had long become plain that only a portion of the Russian army would be met by the French, and that, in providing a front to show against the main body of the Russian army, there remained to the English an ample field of duty; and now that the invading armies had come within cannon-shot range, it began to be seen that the entire front presented by the 1st and 3d French Divisions, and by our 2d and Light Divisions, would be only just commensurate with the length of the position which the Russian commander was occupying.

Russian   Army.

English Army.   French   Army.

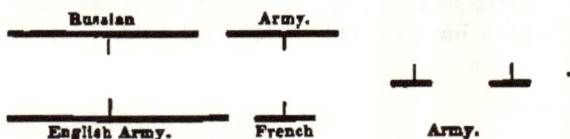

* See the *facsimile*.

CHAP.
XLIV.
Of course, therefore, if Lord Raglan had not al-
ready rejected the French plan of a flank attack by
our forces, it would have now fallen to the ground.
It had never made any impression on his mind.*

The
ground
which
each of the
leading
divisions
had to
assail.
The Allies were now so close to the enemy's position that the General of each of the five leading
divisions could form a judgment as to the particular
sphere of action which awaited him. To Bosquet
the advance against the West Cliff had long ago been
assigned. Canrobert faced towards the White Homestead and those spurs of the Telegraph Height which
lie towards the west. Prince Napoleon confronted
the centre and the eastern steeps of the Telegraph
Height. Sir De Lacy Evans with the 2d Division
faced the village of Bourliouk; and it seemed at this
time that his left would not reach further up the
river's bank than the bridge, for Sir George Brown
had been reckoning that his first or right brigade
would be charged with the duty of attacking the

---

* I infer this from the fact that those with whom Lord Raglan was
thoroughly confidential in such matters never heard him speak of it.
Lord Raglan, as we saw, distinctly and finally rejected the plan at the
close of his interview with St Arnaud. It became a plan simply pre-
posterous as soon as it was apparent that St Arnaud would not confront
any part of the Russian army except their left wing; for to make two
flank movements, one against the enemy's left and the other against his
right, and to do this without having any force wherewith to confront
the enemy's centre, would have been a plan requiring no comment to
show its absurdity. The French accounts, whether official or quasi-
official, have always persisted in saying that Lord Raglan had engaged,
and afterwards failed to make, a movement on the enemy's right flank.
This is the only reason why the matter requires anything like careful
elucidation.

enemy's position across the great road, and that it would be his left, or Buller's brigade, which would assail the Great Redoubt.

The Generals of the five leading Divisions were thus directing their forces, and already the swarms of skirmishers thrown forward by the French, and the thinner chains of riflemen in advance of our divisions, were drawing close to the vineyards, and beginning their combats with the enemy's sharp-shooters; but then, and with a suddenness so strange as to suggest the idea of some pyrotechnic contrivance, the whole village of Bourliouk, except the straggling houses which skirted it towards the east, became wrapped in tall flames.* No man could live in that conflagration; and the result was, that in one minute a third of the ground on which the English army had meant to operate was, as it were, blotted out of the field. If this firing of the village took place under the orders of the Russian commander, it was the most sagacious of all the steps he took that day; for his gravest source of care was the want of troops sufficing for the whole extent of the position at which he grasped, and therefore an operation which took away a large part of the battle-field was of great advantage to him. Our infantry were imme-diately thrown into trouble. The Light Division,

The village of Bourliouk set on fire by the enemy.

The effect which this measure

---

* The great number of haystacks, and the peculiar nature of the hay, were the causes which made the conflagration so instantaneously complete. The hay of that country is full of stiff prickly stems, which resist compression, and so make ample room for air.

CHAP.
XLIV.

had in
cramping
the Eng-
lish line.

as we saw, did not take ground enough on the left,
and the firing of the village now cut short our front
on the right. Sir De Lacy Evans, thus robbed of
space, was obliged to keep his second brigade in rear
of the first, and even then he continued to overlap
the right of the Light Division.

The smoke from the burning village was depressed
and gently turned towards the bridge by the faint
breeze which came from the sea. There, for hours,
in a long fallen pillar of cloud, it lay singularly firm
and compact, obscuring the view of those who were
near it, but not at all staining the air in any other
part of the field.

XII.

General
Bosquet.

The operations of the great column intrusted to
General Bosquet now began to take effect. Bosquet
was a man in the prime of life. Ten years of
struggle and frequent enterprise in Algeria had
carried him from the rank of a lieutenant to the
rank of a general officer;* and he was charged on
this day, not only with the command of his own —
the 2d— Division, but with the command of the
troops which formed the Turkish Contingent. The
whole column under his orders numbered about

* A brigadier; and now, at the time of the Crimean war, he was a
general of division.

14,000 men. The Arabs and Kabyles of Algeria,
though men of a fierce and brave nature, and prone to petty strife, are so wanting in the power of making war with effect, that, as far as concerns the art of fighting, they can scarcely be said to have given much schooling to the bold and skilful soldiery of France; but the deserts, the broad solitudes, and the great mountain-ranges of Northern Africa, have inured the French army to some of those military toils which are next in worth to the business of the actual combat; and for Bosquet, the hero of many a struggle in the passes of the Middle and the Lesser Atlas, it was no new problem to have to cross a stream and carry a body of troops to the summit of a hill with a steep-looking face.

In the morning he had ridden forward, escorted by a few Spahis, to reconnoitre the ground with his own eyes; and thus, and by the aid of the careful surveys effected by the naval men, he was able to assure himself, not only that the river could be passed at its bar, but that troops there crossing it would be likely to find the means of getting round and ascending to the summit of the cliff from the south-west. Examining also the face of the cliff further inland, he saw that the broken ground opposite to the village of Almatamack could be easily ascended by foot-soldiers; and he also, no doubt, perceived that the road leading up from the village (unless it should prove to have been effectually cut or guarded by the

His plan
of opera-
tions.

enemy) would give him a passage for his artillery. Upon these observations Bosquet based his plan. He resolved to march in person with Autemarre's brigade upon the village of Almatamack, there to cross the river, and afterwards endeavour to ascend the plateau at the point where the road from Alma-tamack goes up between the West Cliff and the Telegraph Height; but he ordered General Bouat, with his brigade and with the Turkish Contingent, to incline far away towards his right, to try to pass the river at its bar, and then to find the best means he could for getting his troops up the cliff.

Advance
of Aute-
marre
under
Bosquet
in person.

The two bodies of troops under Bosquet's command began their diverging movement at the same time; and before two o'clock the swarms of skirmishers which covered the front of the columns were pushing their way through the village of Almatamack, and the vineyards on either side of it. A few moments more and they were firing with a briskness and vivacity which warmed the blood of the many thousands of hearers then new to war. One of our officers, kindling a little with the excitement thus roused, and impatient, perhaps, that the French should be in action before our people, could not help drawing Lord Raglan's attention to the firing on our right. But the stir of French skirmishers through thick ground was no new music to Lord Fitzroy Somerset; rather, perhaps, it recalled him for a moment to old times in Estramadura and Castile, when, at the side of the great Wellesley, he learned the brisk ways of Napoleon's infantry. So, when the young officer said, "The French, my Lord, are "warmly engaged," Lord Raglan answered, "Are "they? I cannot catch any return-fire." His practised ear had told him what we now know to be the truth. No troops were opposed to the advance of Bosquet's columns in this part of the field; but it is the custom of French skirmishers, when they get into thick ground near an enemy, to be continually firing. They do this partly to show the chiefs behind them what progress they are making, and partly, it would seem, in order to give life and spirit to the scene.

When General Bouat reached the bank of the *Advance of the detached force under Bouat.* river, he found that the bar of sand at its mouth made it possible for his men to keep good their footing against the waves flowing in from the sea; and in process of time, with all his infantry, including the Turkish battalions, he succeeded in gaining the left bank of the river. He could not, however, carry across his artillery, and he therefore sent it back, with orders to follow the march of Autemarre's brigade.

When he reached the left bank of the river, Bouat found an opening in the cliff before him, which promised to give him means of ascent. Into this opening he threw some skirmishers, and these, encountering no enemy, were followed by the main

19*

body of the brigade, and by the Turkish battalions.
Pursuing the course thus opened to him, Bouat
slowly crept forward with his column, and wound
his way up and round towards the summit of the
cliff. But it was only by marching with a very
narrow front that he was able to effect this movement; and it was not until a late period of the
action that he was able to show himself in force
upon the plateau. Even then he was without artillery. The troops under his command had not an
opportunity of engaging in any combat with the
enemy, because they marched upon that part of
the heights which the Russian General had determined to leave unoccupied.

Meanwhile Bosquet, marching in person with
Autemarre's brigade, traversed the village of Almatamack, forded the river at ten minutes past two
o'clock, and immediately began to ascend the road
leading up to the plateau. The road, he found,
was uninjured, and guarded by no troops. His
artillery began the ascent; and meanwhile the keen
and active Zouaves, impatient of the winding road,
climbed the heights by shorter and steeper paths,
and so swiftly, that our sailors, looking from the
ships (men accustomed to perpendicular racing),
were loud in their praise of the briskness with
which the Frenchmen rushed up and "manned" the
cliff. As yet, however, Bosquet had encountered no
enemy.

It has been seen that the position taken up by *CHAP. XLIV.* Prince Mentschikoff fell short of the sea-shore by a distance of more than two miles, and that he was not in military occupation of the cliff, now ascended by Bosquet with Autemarre's brigade; but also it will be remembered that, at the village in rear of the cliff, called Ulukul Akles, there had been posted some days before one of the "Minsk" battalions of infantry, with four pieces of light artillery, and that the detachment had there remained. These four guns were now brought out of the village, and after a time were placed in battery at a spot near the village of Ulukul Tiouets, and within range of the point where the Zouaves were beginning to crown the summit of the cliff. The "Minsk" battalion was not brought into sight; but at some distance, on the cliff overlooking the beach, there could be seen some squadrons of horse.

Guns brought out against him from Ulukul Akles.

As soon as a whole battalion of Zouaves had gained the summit, they were drawn up and formed on the plateau. No shot was as yet fired by the enemy; and General Bosquet, with his Staff, ascended a tumulus or mound on the top of the cliff, in order to reconnoitre the ground.

Bosquet, after a momentary check, establishes himself on the cliff.

Meanwhile his artillery was coming up, and the first two of his guns had just reached the summit when one of the carriages broke down. This accident embarrassed the rest of the column, and whilst the hindrance lasted the enemy opened fire from his

four guns.* The fire and the breaking-down of the
gun-carriage produced for the moment an ill effect
upon the head of the French column, and one of its
battalions fell back under the shelter of the acclivity.
But this check did not last. The road blocked by
the broken-down gun-carriage was quickly cleared,
the guns were moved up rapidly, and swarms of
skirmishers pressed up in all directions. Then the
troops which were already on the summit moved
forward, and lodged themselves upon a part of the
plateau a little in advance of the steep by which
they had ascended.**

Measures
taken by
Kiriakoff
upon ob-
serving
Bosquet's
turning
move-
ment.
As soon as he began to hear guns in the direction of the West Cliff, Kiriakoff took from his reserves two of his "Moscow" battalions, and posted
them, the one low down and the other higher up,
on that part of the hill which looked down upon the
White Homestead. He also drew from his reserve
eight light pieces of artillery, and placed them in
battery facing towards the sea, so as to command,
though at a long range, the part of the plateau
which Bosquet crossed by the Hadji road. Kiriakoff
did not take upon himself to make any other dispositions for dealing with the turning movement
which threatened his left.

* Half of the No. 4 battery of the 17th brigade of the Russian
artillery.

** Sir Edward Colebrooke saw this operation from the deck of one
of our ships of war, and describes it very well in his memorial. He was
a skilful and very accurate observer of military movements.

Amongst the French who were gaining the summit of the plateau, no one seems to have divined the reason why a little body of Russian horsemen should have made its appearance on the cliff overlooking the sea, nor why, without attempting hostile action, it had tenaciously clung to the ground. Those troopers were the attendants of a man in great trouble. They were the escort of Prince Mentschikoff.

XIII.

The enemy's survey of the Allied armies had been so carelessly made, and had been so little directed towards the sea-shore, that Bosquet, it seems, had already got near to the river before his movement was perceived. Prince Mentschikoff, with Gortschakoff and Kvetzinski at his side, had been standing on the Kourganè Hill, watching the advance of the English army, and giving bold orders for its reception; but presently he was told that a French division was advancing towards the unoccupied cliff on his extreme left. At first he was so shocked by the dislocation which his ideas would have to undergo if his left flank were indeed to be turned, that he had no refuge for his confusion except in mere disbelief, and he angrily refused to

The effect
of Bos-
quet's
turning
movement
upon the
mind of
Prince
Mentschi-
koff.

give faith to the unwelcome tidings.* For days he
had been on the ground which he himself had
chosen for the great struggle; but he was so certain
that he had effectually learnt its character by
glancing at its general features, that he had not, it
seems, had the industry to ride over it, nor even to
find out the roads by which the villagers were accustomed to ascend the heights with their waggons.

He seems to have imagined it to be impossible
that ground so steep as the cliff had appeared to be
could be ascended by troops at any point westward
of the Telegraph Height; but when at length he was
compelled to know that the French and the Turks
were marching in force towards the mouth of the
river, his mind underwent so great a revulsion, that
having hitherto taken no thought for his left, he now
seemed to have no care for any other part of the
position. In his place, a general, calm, skilful, and
conscious of knowing the ground, might have seen
the turning movement of the French and the Turks
with unspeakable joy; but instead of tranquilly re-
garding the whole field of battle under the new
aspect which was given to it by this manœuvre, he
only laboured to see how best he could imitate the
mistake of his adversary — how best he could shift
his strength to the distant unoccupied cliff which
was threatened by Bosquet's advance. The nature

---

* Chodasiewicz.

of the ground enabled him to make lateral movements in his line without much fear of disturbance
from the Allies; and as soon as he saw that the
French were detaching two-fifths of their army in
order to turn his flank, he wildly determined to
engage a portion of his scanty force in a march from
his right hand to his left — in a march which would
take him far to the westward of his chosen ground.
For this purpose he snatched two light batteries
from his centre and his right, gave orders that he
was to be followed by the four "Moscow" battalions
which were the reserve of his left wing, and by the
three "Minsk" battalions which formed part of his
"Great Reserves," and then with some squadrons of
hussars rode off towards the sea.

It was certain that a long time would elapse
before the troops engaged in this vain journey could
be expected to get into action with Bosquet; and,
meanwhile, the power of the whole force engaged in
the flank movement was neutralised. But that was
not all. Prince Mentschikoff's mind was so strangely
subverted by the sensation of having his left turned,
that, although it must needs be a long time before
he could be in force on the West Cliff, he could not
endure to be personally absent from the ground to
which he now fastened his thoughts. So when, with
his Staff and the horsemen of his escort, he had got
to the ground overlooking the sea, near the village
of Ulukul Tiouets, and had seen the first groups of

the Zouaves pouring up on the crest of the hill, he
still remained where he was. Whilst he sat in his
saddle, the appearance of his escort drew fire from
the shipping, and four of his suite were struck down;
but the Prince would not move. It is likely that
the fire assuaged the pain of his thoughts.

His bat-
teries at
length
coming
up, there
begins a
cannonade
between
his and
Bosquet's
artillery.
At this time, it would seem, he gave either no
orders, or none of a kind supplying real guidance
for his generals. Lingering upon the ground without
troops at hand, he impotently watched the progress
of Autemarre's brigade. His light batteries soon came
up; but neither these nor the squadrons of hussars
which formed his escort were the best of implements
for pushing back General Bosquet into the steep
mountain-road by which he had ascended; and in
the hands of Prince Mentschikoff they were simply
powerless. However, his guns, when they came up,
were placed in battery, and Bosquet's guns being
now on the plateau, there began a cannonade at
long range between the twelve guns of the French
and the whole of the light artillery which Prince
Mentschikoff had hurried into this part of the field.
At the same time the French artillery drew some
shots from the distant guns which Kiriakoff had
placed looking seaward on the Telegraph Height;

Bosquet
maintains
himself.
and the annals of the French artillery record with
pride that the twelve pieces which Bosquet brought
up with him engaged and overpowered no less than
forty of the enemy's guns. Nor is this statement

altogether without something like a basis of truth,
for the Russians had now thirty-six pieces of artillery on the West Cliff, or the Telegraph Height; and though most of them at this time were so placed that their gunners could attempt some shots at a more or less long range against Bosquet's guns, the French artillerymen not only held their ground without having a gun disabled, but soon pushed forward their batteries to a more commanding part of the plateau.

By this time the seven battalions of infantry which Prince Mentschikoff had been moving flank-wise were very near to the spot where their General had been eagerly awaiting them; but just as he was about to have these troops in hand, the Prince seems to have come to the conclusion that, after all, he could do nothing in the part of the field to which he had dragged them. He was brought, perhaps, to this belief by seeing that the French and the Turks, who had been crossing the river at its mouth, were now beginning to show their strength towards the westernmost part of the cliff; for he may not have known that this force, being without artillery, could be easily prevented from advancing against his batteries on the open plateau. At all events, Prince Mentschikoff now thought it necessary to reverse his flank movement, and to travel back towards his centre with all the forces which he had brought from thence to his left.

Mentschi-
koff coun-
ter-march-
ing.

But when the Prince began this last counter-movement, he was already beginning to fall under the dominion of events in another part of the field.

Position of
Bosquet
on the
cliff.
Bosquet now stood undisturbed on the part of the plateau which he had reached. But he was not without grounds for deep anxiety. It did not fall to his lot on that day to be engaged in any conflict except with the enemy's artillery; but, from the moment when he began to establish himself on the plateau until towards the close of the action, he was in a dangerously isolated position, for he had no troops around him except Autemarre's brigade; and, until the action was near its end, he got no effective support either from Bouat on his right or from Canrobert on his left.

www.ingramcontent.com/pod-product-compliance
Lightning Source LLC
Chambersburg PA
CBHW021214270326
41929CB00010B/1131